Management Reforms in China

This book is dedicated to my son, Raphael, who may one day stand on the Great Wall.

Management Reforms in China

edited by
Malcolm Warner

St. Martin's Press, New York

First published in the United States of America in 1987

Printed in Great Britain

ISBN 0-312-00849-X

Library of Congress Cataloging-in-Publication Data
Management reforms in China.
   Bibliography: p.
   Includes index.
   1. Industrial management—China.   I. Warner,
Malcolm.
HD70.C5M34   1987   658'.00951   87-4772
ISBN 0-312-00849-X

Contents

Contributors

John Bank is Lecturer in Human Resources Management at Cranfield Institute of Management.

Max H. Boisot is Dean and Director of the Joint China/EEC MBA Programme in Beijing.

Nigel Campbell is Lecturer in Strategic Management at the Manchester Business School.

John Child is Professor of Organization Behaviour and Dean of the Aston University Management Centre.

John S. Henley is Senior Lecturer in the Department of Business Studies at the University of Edinburgh.

Russell D. Lansbury is Professor of Industrial Relations at the University of Sydney.

Liu Guoguang is Professor of Economics and Vice-President of The Chinese Academy of Social Sciences, Beijing.

James M. Livingstone is Professor of Management and Director of the School of Management and Finance at Queen's University, Belfast.

Martin Lockett is Research Fellow at Templeton College, Oxford.

Ng Sek Hong is Lecturer in Management Studies at the University of Hong Kong.

Nyaw Mee-Kau is Senior Lecturer in Management Studies at The Chinese University of Hong Kong, Kowloon.

Leslie Sklair is Senior Lecturer in Sociology at the London School of Economics.

Denis F. Simon is Assistant Professor of Management at the Sloan School, Massachusetts Institute of Technology.

Malcolm Warner is Professor and Research Co-ordinator at Henley, The Management College and Brunel, The University of West London.

Gordon White is Research Fellow at the Institute of Development Studies, The University of Sussex, Brighton.

Preface

This edited collection attempts to describe and assess China's industrial management reforms since 1978 on an *inter-disciplinary* basis. The authors of the respective chapters hail from a variety of countries, although most work in British universities and for schools of management, including the editor. All of the contributors have either carried out empirical research in China, taught on management courses there, or both. Some have Chinese as their mother-tongue, but most have worked through interpreters or with a colleague in the former category. A number of the authors have been involved in the European/Chinese collaborative MBA programme in Beijing.

Most of the contributors are teachers of management, whether their original training was in economics, sociology, industrial relations or related areas of study. They share a common fascination with China as an emergent force in the world economy, and the role of the economic reformers as agents of change in this process internally as well as externally.

The task of compiling this edited volume was facilitated by the informal network, or 'invisible college' to which we belonged and which already existed either owing to personal contacts made while on site in China, or made subsequently to share knowledge and experience of the field. An increasing flow of visitors to Britain from the PRC has helped the flow of communication about management reforms in China, as well as growing media interest. Several *Financial Times* supplements, for example, have been useful in providing up-to-date background information, let alone the more scholarly sources such as the *China Quarterly* with their special issue on the economic reforms (issue No. 100). Reflecting the official Chinese view, the *Beijing Review* arrives by air mail weekly, often focusing on management innovations, and the English-language *China Daily* is now printed in London.

A group of Chinese management teachers have spent a term at the Manchester Business School; and the first Chinese MBA students at British schools of management, although still only a handful, represent a straw in the wind for further collaboration.

As we shall try to show in this volume, the scope of the management reforms has been considerable, first on a pilot basis but now on a wider scale. The particular treatments chapter-by-chapter only partially cover the wave of industrial change and have excluded the agricultural sector. It is too early to see the full effects of the reforms. Nor do we set out to provide microscopic case studies. Most of the chapters are essentially broad-brush in scope, comparing the present trends with past experience since 1949. A number do attempt to present empirical, statistical data, collected by the authors themselves, a relative rarity in the study of 'socialist' economies, unthinkable before 1976 and unlikely in Eastern Europe or the Soviet Union. The very wide range of firms Western scholars in the field have been able to visit, inspect and even use as field-sites, cannot fail to make a startling contrast to experiences elsewhere!

Co-operation from Chinese academic colleagues and students has also been most gratifying, with a genuine interest in learning from the foreign expert, often with expectations set too high. Problems of collaboration should not be ignored. Teaching, researching, even physically getting around China has not been easy on many occasions. Many young Chinese people are learning English, but many older scholars may be able to read it but cannot communicate orally. The older generation often studied in the Soviet Union before 1960 and speak Russian. Not a few papers referred to in this volume recount the painful lessons learnt especially by American management academics in coping in the Chinese classroom, or dealing with indigenous managers generally.

Let us hope that both the more general and the more detailed chapters will be instructive for academic as well as practitioner readers, for management teachers and students, or for those who are simply curious!

Malcolm Warner

Acknowledgements

The editing of this collection of essays was made possible by the support given by my own academic institution and the initial encouragement given to me by the Institute of Industrial Economics, the Chinese Academy of Social Sciences, Beijing (Peking), as part of the British Academy/ESRC Collaborative Exchange scheme, whose support must be acknowledged as far as the development of my own research was concerned, and its further extension into the completion of this edited collection. I am grateful to Professor Jiang Yiwei and his colleagues for their assistance, especially Ms Ding Yi for her help with interpreting and translation. I should also like to express my appreciation to Ms Jill Ford and Ms Penny Clarey for their secretarial and administrative back-up, as well as to Ms Dale Bowman for her help with the art-work. I should also like to thank the *Journal of General Management*, the *European Management Journal*, and Basil Blackwell Ltd for permission to quote paragraphs and quotations from previously published work by the authors in Chapters 5 and 14 respectively.

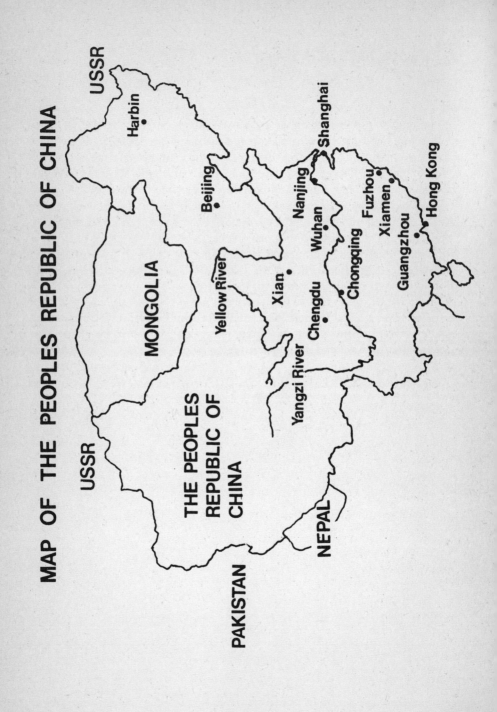

MAP OF THE PEOPLES REPUBLIC OF CHINA

USSR

USSR

Harbin

MONGOLIA

Beijing

Shanghai

Nanjing

Wuhan

Fuzhou

Xiamen

Hong Kong

Chongqing

Guangzhou

THE PEOPLES
REPUBLIC OF
CHINA

Yellow River

Xian

Chengdu

Yangzi River

NEPAL

PAKISTAN

Part I: Reforming the Enterprise

1 Introduction

Malcolm Warner

China is now set on a course of management reforms which will transform its industrial enterprises, and ultimately bring its economy closer to the international markets than at any time since the Liberation in 1949. It is, for example, embarking on a programme of management education on an apparently unprecedented scale as part of its 'Four Modernizations' (of agriculture, industry, science and technology and defence) policy. As a result of the post-1978 economic reforms, enterprises are now accountable for both profits and losses. This new strategy first started with 'experimental' industrial sites, after similar changes in the agricultural economy, and has been extended to state-owned firms in the urban sector. The effectiveness of such changes has, however, been limited by the lack of administrative and managerial capacities.

This volume hopes to shed light on the ways in which China is developing new organizational structures, training enterprise-managers, adapting its labour markets, and changing its business culture in order to overcome the obstacles to economic development. The material is organized into four parts dealing in turn with each of the above areas of concern.

Part One of this volume deals with enterprise reforms at both macro and micro levels. Lockett's chapter examines recent economic changes and assesses their impact on management at enterprise level, via an overview of the macro-environment and newly emerging institutional structures. Taking 1976 as a point of departure, Lockett looks at both rural and urban reforms and concludes that even a decade later such changes 'were still both limited and partial'. Even so, the emergence of the enterprise as a relatively independent business unit is a new phenomenon to be reckoned with. Factory directors will also need to behave less like bureaucrats and more like managers. In this context, political as well as economic uncertainty may increase, he concludes, for the practitioner involved in the reforms.

Child's chapter looks at enterprise reform in China, particularly examining a wide range of decision areas. The data was collected while the author was teaching MBA students in Beijing. The fieldwork concentrated on six industrial, state-owned enterprises in that city. The study particularly analyses the extent to which decisions have been decentralized to enterprise level, and the position of management *vis-à-vis* Party and Workers' Congresses within such firms. Child's chapter also provides some benchmarks derived from research on Western enterprises to measure the degree of decentralized decisionmaking found in the Chinese enterprises studied.

The next chapter, by Campbell, examines the same set of enterprises in the Beijing municipality, but concentrates on a narrow range of decision areas, namely labour management, marketing and purchasing, thus spelling out in greater detail the degree of enterprise autonomy both aspired to and ultimately achieved. He concludes that the amount of discernible change is noteworthy, but can easily be 'exaggerated'. It is still influenced by 'the traditional subordination to higher authorities and the sellers' market in China'.

Part Two of the volume deals with management education and training. In his chapter on China's 'managerial revolution', Warner discusses the evolution of management education from the fall of the 'Gang of Four' up to recent times in the context of the wider economic reforms. It looks specifically at organizational experiments such as the promotion of institutes, university departments and training centres offering management courses, based on an empirical investigation of such institutions. It looks at such efforts against the backdrop of the educational system, and discusses, amongst other innovations, the role of distance learning as seen in the work of the Economic Management Periodical University. The chapter concludes that the impact of management education is as yet hard to measure, but that the Government has given it priority. By the beginning of the Seventh Five-Year Plan, all top managers will have to have attended management training courses. Whether China can achieve its goals by 1995 or 2000 is open to debate, but the openness to management ideas from the West and Japan constitutes a major departure from the closed economy of Maoist times.

The next contribution, by Livingstone, looks at the 'Marketing' concept in Chinese economic development and its applicability to a non-Western environment. The chapter is based on the author's experience in teaching marketing to Chinese managers at the State Economic Commission Management Centre in Beijing, and sets out the results of a field-work exercise carried out by himself and his students in a department store in that city. This market research survey on four hundred shoppers assessed the products sold in this store, the layout of the floors, and the attitude of the staff. Livingstone concludes on an optimistic note regarding the positive role of the students, the cooperation of the store management and the critical reactions of the growing consumerist aspiration of the shop's clientele.

Teaching quality circles to Chinese managers is the theme of Bank's chapter. The author, an American academic at a British business school, draws parallels between the Chinese problem of poor-quality goods and how they could learn from the Japanese who were faced with the same state of affairs some decades ago. Bank notes the 'cultural fit' as the Chinese managers took to the small-group activities on the course with considerable enthusiasm. He sees the need for such inputs as 'temporary', if we look at China's technology-transfer problem in a historical perspective.

In Part Three, China's attempts to reorganize its labour market to fit the needs of its enterprises are discussed. White's chapter shows how the reforms are a 'package, the progress of each component depending on the other'. The author concentrates on the industrial state sector which has been 'the main target of the reforms'. He discusses the reduction of the state's role, the diversification of the channels of labour allocation and the establishment of the labour contract system. White concludes that a 'labour-market' has not yet been created in the state sector, but outside it there is now something closer to such a notion: the Chinese urban labour scene is still 'dualistic'.

The development of work incentives in Chinese industry is explored by Henley and Nyaw in their chapter on material versus non-material incentives. They look at the work motivation of Chinese workers in state-owned enterprises and how this has been affected by the current wage reforms, and the changing role of the Workers' Congresses. They finally present the results of a survey of work motivation in twelve Chinese industrial enterprises in five major industrial cities. This empirical study revealed material incentives first and second in terms of mean scores, but cadres placed more emphasis on non-material rewards.

Worker participation in the Chinese enterprise is the subject of the chapter by Ng and Lansbury. They show how the Workers' Congress has been renewed and revitalized as an institution in the Chinese factory since the beginning of the 1980s. The most innovative power they have has been the possibility of electing the factory or enterprise management. How far this practice has spread is still controversial. The enhancement of the trade-union role is also discussed. Recent field visits in 1985 and 1986 reveal cases where the Congress and union committees have been merged. In other cases, the authors note that ironically 'it is the Workers' Congress for which the union now deputizes'. The State, they conclude, 'remains suspicious of 'grass-roots' industrial democracy *per se*'.

Part Four of the book deals with wider themes related to China's management reforms. A Chinese contributor, Liu, discusses the problems arising from changes in ownership relations in China. In order to achieve greater efficiency and expand employment, no one form of ownership could suffice. Reforms in ownership, the author recounts, start in the countryside with the appearance of the household responsibility system, reforming the rural co-operative economy. Collectively-owned enterprises in urban areas have evolved, and individual enterprises have been encouraged, so that the nature of industrial ownership has become mixed. Problems have arisen of unequal competition and balance of public and private ownership. The biggest dilemma is how to reform the state-owned large and medium-sized enterprises. Share-ownership may be one possible solution 'under the system of ownership by the whole people', rather than encouraging individual share-purchase, concludes the author.

Can China have 'capitalist efficiency without capitalist exploitation?', asks Sklair in his chapter on the experience of the Shenzen Special Economic Zone (SEZ). He discusses this question in relation to the socialist planned economy, the role of foreign investment and its effects on the attitudes of the Chinese people. He sets out to show that 'in any transition from one mode of production to another, elements of the old and the new co-mingle'. He does not believe the Chinese conception of economic management is simply a copy of Western practice. The SEZs have a dual character, 'and management must reflect this'. Discussing corruption in the SEZ, Sklair does not believe it characterizes all of the Shenzen economy, nor will it necessarily spread. He concludes that the real question is whether 'welfare socialism' will be better at 'delivering the goods' to the Chinese man-in-the-street than 'welfare capitalism' has been, and that the Chinese authorities are in 'largely uncharted waters'.

Simon's chapter deals with the problems associated with technology transfer. He examines the special attention China has paid to the development of computers since the mid-1970s when the 'Four Modernizations' were introduced. Component manufacture is being given top priority and the main goal is to minimize dependence on foreign suppliers. But they have not as yet taken that 'critical step into the world of the informatics revolution', except perhaps for defence applications. Ultimately, 'management must make the technology work and not the other way round', Simon concludes.

The question of whether China could use greater bureaucracy is the focus of Boisot's intriguing chapter. He presents a conceptual model designed to help understand to what extent culture may play a role in creating a shock-absorber to 'soften the impact of irresistible market forces'. He tries to assess how far 'Socialism with Chinese characteristics' expresses a culture-specific strategy as opposed to a universal, ideologically-motivated one. He concludes that cultural values and beliefs and transactional strategies exert a reciprocal influence on each other. Training Chinese managers to develop new skills will not be a sufficient condition for 'making out' in the systems; the ability to operate effectively requires *more* and not less bureaucracy of a rational-legal kind in the system, he argues.

How then to assess the overall picture presented in this volume of China's management reforms? Lucien Pye has recently questioned the view that pragmatism is 'simply a pure form of rationality, untainted by cultural biases' (Pye, 1986:207). He goes on to argue that 'Chinese pragmatism has its own distinctive characteristics and is unlike pragmatism in British or American public life' (1986:208-9). Going on to deny that *pragmatic* is the opposite of *ideological*, he concludes that the former means 'somewhat narrow calculations of national interest will prevail (1986:233). It is clear that, given the cost-benefit calculations involved, the Chinese leadership will promote the courses of action which will produce results.

The question of whether management practices can be transferred from one country to another is a moot one anyway, let alone from one culture to another: China has not only its Confucian past, but a Maoist legacy which has shaped its industrialization. The full extent of the damage done by the Cultural Revolution to the education infrastructure is only just being fully realized. Now, China has changed course, with 'economics in command', it needs a better-trained workforce, and greater professional expertise at managerial levels (see Chan & Zhian, 1986). It cannot, however, simply copy the American model since this has not provided the 'right' answer even for European countries, or for those new expanding Pacific Basin economies.

In addition, the cultural assumptions underlying Western mangement concepts are alien to Chinese society at present. American culture stresses individualism, initiative and achievement; Chinese culture (like its Japanese counterpart) emphasizes collectivism, dependence and belonging, it is said (Helburn & Shearer, 1984:15). Values do not change that easily — as Western management experts in China have often found.

Is China on the verge of a 'managerial revolution', the consequences of which are hard to predict, as events (and their ideological justifications) pursue their zig-zag course? It is none the less difficult to be sure whether there is a consistent policy being pursued: the new 'pragmatism' covers many options. Since the fall of the 'Gang of Four', China appears to have broken the mould of thirty years' political history. In joining world society, it now looks outwards. If the 'Open Door' policy is here to stay, it may put too much strain not only on the economic but also on the political status quo. With decentralization, middle-level cadres may lose out, and a counter-reaction may occur. A move to greater pluralism as other interest groups try to benefit and consolidate their influence to buttress the 'Four Modernizations' line pursued by the leadership in Beijing is still problematic, given the fall of Hu Yaobang (see Warner, 1986). It is possible that the scramble for economic growth could get out of hand. There are many physical bottlenecks — energy being the most crucial — which could cause problems in the industrial sector, even if the agrarian economy continued to flourish. China thus cannot jump from a command to a market economy overnight (see Wang, 1985:18–20).

References

Chan, M. W. L. & Guan Zhian (1986). 'Management Education in the Peoples' Republic of China; With Special Reference to Recent Support by Foreign Countries'. *Management Education and Development*, **17**: 181–90.

Helburn, I. B. & Shearer, J. C. (1984). 'Human Resources and Industrial Relations in China'. *Industrial and Labor Relations Review*, **38**: 3–15.

Pye, Lucien (1986). 'On Chinese Pragmatism in the 1980's. *China Quarterly*, No. 106: 207–34.

Special Issue (1984). 'The Readjustment in the Chinese Economy'. *China Quarterly*, No. 100.

Warner, Malcolm (1986). 'Training China's Managers'. *Journal of General Management*, **11**: 12–26.

Wang, Hirijiong (1985). 'China's prospects for the Year 2000'. *Beijing Review*, 28, 14, 4 November: 18–20.

2 The Economic Environment of Management

Martin Lockett

Introduction

Behind the major changes in Chinese management analysed in this book are significant changes in the economic environment in which enterprises operate. This chapter looks at these economic changes and assesses their impact on managers at the enterprise level. It therefore provides an overview of the economic environment of management in China in relation to both institutional structures and the pattern of economic growth.

To achieve this, the chapter first outlines the major changes in economic policy in China since 1976. In the next section, it analyses China's urban economy in the mid-1980s, with a particular focus on the nature and extent of economic reform, the performance of the Chinese economy, and current economic issues. It then analyses the Seventh Five-Year Plan, which forms the background to economic policy into the 1990s. Conclusions are then drawn on the implications of these changes in the economic environment for enterprise managers.

Changes in Economic Policy Since 1976

A New Leap Forward? (1977–1978)

Developments in the Chinese economy over the last ten years can be divided into four main phases. The first, which lasted from late 1976 to late 1978, was the unsuccessful attempt to achieve rapid growth without major institutional change. In industry this was to be through the import of advanced foreign technology financed by oil exports, while in agriculture mechanization was the key. Ideologically, it was assumed unrealistically that after the fall of the 'Gang of Four' the major blocks to rapid growth had been removed.

The problems of these policies soon became clear. First, oil export revenues were not as high as expected, owing to a plateau in oil output and increased domestic demand. Foreign loans, the alternative form of hard currency finance for technology imports, were disliked for political reasons. Second, the import of major heavy industrial plants was exacerbating existing bottlenecks in the economy—notably energy, transport and building materials. Third, the balance between investment and consumption was problematic. To gain political support and increase incentives, significant wage increases and bonus payments were being introduced at the same time as the level of investment was soaring, leading to macroeconomic imbalances and inflationary pressures. Fourth, the supply and quality of consumer goods was insufficient for increased wages to act as an effective incentive in many cases. Also, agricultural mechanization plans were quickly seen to be unrealistic. While many of these problems can be seen as the results of poor planning rather than the planning system itself, the response was more radical.

Readjustment, Reform and Consolidation (1979–1980)

The shift in official policies came in December 1978 with the Third Plenum of the Eleventh CCP Central Committee. Economic policy soon shifted towards a second phase of 'readjustment, reform, consolidation and improvement', lasting from late 1978 to early 1981. Readjustment meant shifting priorities from industry to agriculture, from heavy industry to light industry, and focusing attention on bottleneck sectors. In industry reform meant moves towards the types of economic reform already implemented in Eastern Europe, notably in Hungary, giving enterprises greater autonomy in decisionmaking; using profit as an incentive and allowing enterprises to retain a portion of profit (for use in production, bonuses and welfare/housing); introducing limited competition and some direct marketing of products by enterprises; and increased but limited flexibility in labour management. Initially these reforms were concentrated in a small number of experimental enterprises, notably in Sichuan, but were then extended through a variety of economic responsibility mechanisms. Consolidation and improvement meant essentially trying to upgrade the level of management and efficiency.

In agriculture, grain and other prices were raised significantly to increase incentives for peasants—who benefited in particular from above-quota sales. Also, greater freedom was given to decide what to grow in the light of local conditions—and there were prospects for a higher return on effort. But more fundamental was the start of the 'production responsibility system', in which contracts were signed between groups or households and production teams with payment based on output. While not foreseen or intended by the central leadership, in practice a process was started whereby agricultural production changed from being organized on a collective basis to a household one.

In foreign economic relations, the idea of direct foreign investment into China was approved, primarily through joint ventures. The Special Economic Zones in Guangdong and Fujian were also approved with the official aim of absorbing foreign technology and management. Some enterprises were given greater freedom to deal directly with foreign firms as part of the reforms. More generally, the policy was that of an 'open door'—at least compared with the past.

These 'reform, readjustment, consolidation and improvement' policies therefore led to initial urban reforms and to the start of a process of radical change in rural areas. There were, however, significant problems in urban areas and industry. First, there was a conflict between readjustment and reform as readjustment was probably best achieved through central control over investment and related decisions, while reform made changing direction more difficult in the short term by giving enterprises greater financial and decisionmaking power. Second, the combination of enterprise profit retention, readjustment, decentralization to provinces and lower levels and urban food subsidies led to a major central state budget deficit through falling income from industrial profits and rising expenditure. Third, as a result inflation was rising significantly—a politically sensitive issue. Fourth, problems associated with reform arose, such as enterprises shifting to products made profitable by anomalies in the price system as well as tax evasion and fraud. These were seized upon by those threatened by reform, notably those in the middle layers of the Party and management without technical or professional skills.

Urban Reform Slowdown, Rapid Rural Change (1981—1983)

These problems resulted in a third phase, from mid-1981 to mid-1984, in which urban and industrial reforms were slowed down but rural reforms continued at a fast pace. In industry much more attention was paid to profit-sharing systems between state and enterprise which clearly benefited the state. More generally, the focus shifted from institutional reform of state-enterprise relations to 'consolidation'. Thus improvement of internal management was seen as the key to growth and efficiency. There was greater emphasis on the power of factory managers, management training, and economic responsibility systems within enterprises, such as internal contracting. Teams of officials were sent to enterprises to check up on this consolidation process. In rural areas, the shift towards household production accelerated—becoming a policy goal for everyone as opposed to a special measure for poor areas. Central control of foreign trade was strengthened after trade deficits in 1978–80, though foreign investment was still encouraged.

Renewed Urban Reforms (1984–   )

A fourth phase began in late 1984, with the Party Central Committee's *Decision* on urban reform. Thus urban reforms became a focus of attention again, with the intention of creating a 'socialist planned commodity economy' with Chinese characteristics. Again, enterprise autonomy was emphasized, with planning shifting towards a guidance as opposed to a directive role. A shift to a tax system for enterprise profits was also finalized, though in practice this is subject to administrative adjustment given the current 'irrational' price system. However, price reform was seen as an essential component of the urban reforms, though how this was to be implemented was less clear. A first step was to let many food prices float in urban areas in 1985. Change in the wage system was also foreseen, to bring pay more into line with enterprise and individual performance. The enterprise director's role was to be strengthened relative to the Party through the introduction of the 'Factory Director Responsibility System'. There was also encouragement of the private individual sector, which has grown rapidly, especially in commerce and services.

The result of these new reforms was seen from the final quarter of 1984. Industrial growth-rates shot up, reaching 21 per cent at one point in 1985. Rural industry grew even faster, and today it employs sixty million people. Agricultural growth continued, despite a reduced grain harvest. The economy was overheating, however, with inflation rising, especially in cities as a result of the decontrol of meat and vegetable prices which rose maybe 30 per cent. Investment and consumption were rising rapidly, fuelled by internal bank credit and a rundown of foreign exchange reserves as both consumer goods and capital goods imports rose sharply. The result by late 1985 was a cutback in investment, especially that outside the plan, stricter control of foreign trade, and a statement by Zhao Ziyang that 1986 was a year in which to 'consolidate, digest, supplement and improve reform'.

China's Economy Today

An official Chinese view of the economic position today was given recently by a Vice-Minister in charge of the State Commission for Restructuring the Economic System:

> Although our all-round economic structural reforms have only just started, a favourable situation has been created. A series of profound and revolutionary changes has occurred in the economic operational mechanisms and management system in our country, and our national economy has entered the most vigorous and dynamic period since the founding of the PRC [Gao, 1986].

To see if such a view is justified this section will examine three areas: the state of reforms, economic performance and current issues in the Chinese economy.

Economic Reforms

In 1986 urban and industrial reforms were still both limited and partial—in many areas these have not gone as far as those in Eastern Europe. The planning system still exerts a major direct influence, especially at the provincial and municipal levels. This is recognized by the leading Chinese economist Xue Muqiao who argues that, 'all these reforms are still at a transitional stage and have not been basically completed. We have also failed to coordinate these reforms sufficiently and satisfactorily' (Xue, 1986). The clearest area which reforms have yet to affect significantly is the price system, as enterprises still face incentives from the price system which go against efficient resource allocation and give rewards which are not necessarily based on efficiency or on satisfying consumer demands.

Overall urban reforms remain limited and in certain respects contradictory. This applies not just at the enterprise level but also with respect to state bodies. A clear case here is the tobacco industry, where local government bodies have set up their own factories to obtain tax revenue of which they keep a significant proportion as a result of administrative decentralization. According to a report by the Chinese Academy of Social Sciences, 'good tobacco processed into cigarettes will produce ten times the tax it would as tobacco. Thus the tobacco-producing areas retain as much of the good tobacco as possible in order to process it themselves'. The result of this and marketing 'loopholes' is that, 'In state-run shops one cannot buy good cigarettes while large quantities of the superior cigarettes come into the hands of small traders who raise the prices at will' (Institute of Industrial Economics, 1985). Thus the adjustment in planning power and revenue sharing between central and local government has undermined reforms aimed at improving enterprise efficiency through competition and profit incentives.

However, in rural areas, reform has gone much further and faster than in most other socialist economies, especially the shift of control in production from the collective to the household through the responsibility system. This shift to the household level has even taken place within many state farms. Land is now leased by peasants for up to fifteen years or so, though it is still owned by the state. There is in practice much greater, though by no means complete, freedom for peasants to produce what they like and to choose to some degree between putting effort into grain, cash crops, sidelines, or working in rural industry. Previous collective forms of organization are no longer effective, for example unpaid labour for capital construction projects such as irrigation. However, the marketing and price system has not changed so dramatically, while the support (and control) infrastructure for household-based production is often weak.

In the area of foreign economic relations, there has been a major change towards greater trade, but combined with previous policies of not having a continuing trade deficit. Relative to national income, the total of imports and exports has increased rapidly from 11 per cent in 1976 to an estimated 26 per cent in 1985. As a result China today is much more open than at any time in the past. In practice China has achieved its trade balance by administrative control of imports, though incentives to increase exports and reduce imports through devaluation of the renminbi have been used over the last year. Special Economic Zones—China's free-trade zones—have continued, though not without controversy, and some of these policies encouraging foreign investment have been extended to other areas: fourteen coastal cities, Hainan, and three larger zones. In practice, the focus has shifted away from the four Special Economic Zones towards the existing industrial centres of Guangzhou, Shanghai, Tianjin and Dalian. So reforms in foreign economic relations are significant though limited, with central administrative controls in evidence especially when problems arise.

Overall, reform of the economy is limited and uneven. Rural reforms in the organization of production are the most radical, while urban reform and rural marketing have not progressed as far. In comparison with other socialist economies, Chinese reforms have not yet gone as far as those in Hungary in most areas, and the Soviet Union has more freedom for workers to change jobs. So while reform as a strategy has been adopted by the top leadership of the Party, in practice much of the old central planning system still remains as a powerful force.

Economic Performance

China's economic performance since 1978 has been good, especially in comparison with most other Third World economies, particularly in agriculture. In China's Sixth Five-Year Plan (1981–5), real GNP growth was an average of 10 per cent per annum. Agricultural gross output growth was 8 per cent, excluding rural industry. This enabled China to reduce food imports substantially and feed 22 per cent of the world's population off 7 per cent of world arable land. Industrial gross output grew by 12 per cent, with light industry growing somewhat faster than heavy industry. Rural industrial growth was rapid, averaging almost 30 per cent a year, and reaching 50 per cent in 1985. Its impact on rural China was substantial as the proportion of the rural workforce outside farming rose from 11 per cent in 1980 to 18 per cent in 1985. The problem of major state budget deficits was also reduced substantially.

While growth was relatively fast, it was subject to significant fluctuation. Heavy industry has been subject to most variation as a result of the changes in policy outlined above, especially 'readjustment' in 1979–81. However, a major foreign trade deficit emerged in 1985 as a result of rapid import growth in 1984 and 1985 following relaxation of controls. The exact size of this deficit is unclear as conflicting statistics have been published by the Ministry of Foreign Economic Relations and Trade (MOFERT) and the Chinese Customs Administration. The former showed a deficit of $7.6 billion and the latter a $14.9 billion deficit. The Customs figures, which many observers reckon to be the more accurate, show a 54 per cent jump in imports. Both sets of figures show exports growing much more slowly, with the growth of manufactured exports particularly weak as a result of domestic demand strength relative to that for Chinese products internationally. Statistics for the first three quarters of 1986 did, however, show some improvement, but a substantial deficit remained.

Another feature has been the shift away from the state sector towards collective and private ownership. Collective ownership is formally similar to co-operative ownership, though in practice collective enterprises have been controlled by local government in the past. Private ownership is limited in scope, being primarily individual or household enterprises with strict (though not always enforced) limits on the number of hired workers. The collective sector has increased in importance, particularly in the generation of new employment and in growing areas of the economy such as consumer goods and services. In industry the state sector is still dominant, producing 74 per cent of output in 1985 (compared with 81 per cent in 1978), but in other sectors the situation is different. In retailing the shift from 1978 to 1985 was dramatic, with the state sector share dropping from 91 per cent (1978) to 46 per cent (1985), with collectives taking 40 per cent (previously 7 per cent) and the private sector 10 per cent (up from 0.1 per cent in 1978).

Urban private sector employment has increased significantly to 4.5 million in 1985, compared with 0.19 million in 1976, though it is still small compared with the state and collective sector employment, which totalled 123 million in 1985. In China as a whole, 11.7 million private businesses were reported in 1985, employing 17.6 million people—a growth of 35 per cent over 1984. Looking at employment generation, the record is also quite good with the urban unemployment problems of the late 1970s substantially reduced though not eliminated. Official urban unemployment rates, which are usually regarded as significant under-estimates, fell from 4.9 per cent in 1980 to 1.8 per cent in 1985.

But while much of the picture presented is good, various bottlenecks still exist in the economy. Only the difficulties with building materials appear to have been resolved to any degree, though generally growth in raw materials and semi-processed goods production had lagged behind the demands from processing industries. Energy is still a major bottleneck, especially electric power in south China where there are regular power cuts. For example, in Guangdong province it is reckoned that there is a 30 per cent supply shortfall. Nationally, electric power generation has lagged behind overall economic growth. Transport is still causing major problems, with the Army being sent into China's ports last year to ease backlogs in unloading ships. Transport bottlenecks also reinforce other problems. For example, Shanxi Province is unable to move over a third of its coal production to other areas because of transport problems. Shortages have also appeared in other sectors as a result of the rapid demand growth of 1984–5, in particular steel, for which negotiated prices rose sharply.

Thus, despite a good economic performance overall, underlying structural problems remain in the Chinese economy. Further, it is questionable whether some of the gains in the last few years can be sustained as they may be 'one-off' results of the changes in overall economic policy. Future economic performance therefore depends on whether reforms can stimulate new dynamism in China's enterprises (see Lockett, 1986).

Current Issues

The rapid growth of the Chinese economy in 1984–5 led to an accentuation of underlying bottlenecks in the economy, notably energy and transport. As these bottlenecks are in sectors with relatively long lead times between investment and results, current growth-rates are not sustainable. So while the new reforms have boosted growth, they have also increased the need for medium- to long-term planning in key infrastructure sectors. In addition they have reinforced the sellers' market characteristic of most sectors in the Chinese economy as well as raising a range of other important issues which could threaten future economic development.

The relaxation of direct planning controls has not been accompanied by effective indirect controls over the domestic economy. According to an official source, 'macroeconomic factors went out of control in varying degrees in the fourth quarter of 1984 and the following period'. In particular, credit was provided freely by the banking system to enterprises and others for investment, whether within or outside the state plan. In the final quarter of 1984, bank credit was up 164 per cent over the previous year. Often little attention was paid to the likely economic returns from projects and the banks did not effectively exercise control—especially as they lacked the experience and administrative power to refuse lending.

Wages have risen rapidly too, with some of the bank credit being used to increase wages rapidly. Again, taking the fourth quarter of 1984, earnings were 30 per cent above the level of a year before. In 1985, urban earnings were up 23.8 per cent in money terms over 1984—a real rise of 10.6 per cent. These figures also point to the inflation resulting from the overheating of the Chinese economy, particularly in urban areas. While some of this inflation is a result of deliberate reform policies (in particular the decontrol of prices of non-staple foods such as pork and vegetables), much is the result of lack of macroeconomic and financial control. It appears also that inflation may be expressed more in the private sector than elsewhere—my observations in a visit in late 1985 were that prices in private commerce were higher than elsewhere, a factor of which official price indices may not take full account. The political impact of inflation in China is significant since one of the Party's claims to legitimacy in the past was stable prices, while those groups adversely affected, including many state and Party employees on fixed incomes, could move towards opposition to reform.

This lack of effective indirect controls to replace planning in the domestic economy has strong parallels in the foreign trade field. The rapid rise in imports in 1984–5 was a result of relaxing administrative restrictions on foreign trade combined with increased domestic demand for both capital and consumer goods. Japan has been the biggest beneficiary of this import boom, notably in motor vehicles, consumer electronics and capital equipment. While the trade deficit is partly offset by foreign investment and tourism revenue, this level of imports could not be sustained without politically unacceptable foreign debt or much better export performance. However, Chinese enterprises typically find domestic sales more attractive than exports, especially as they have been able to indulge in such practices as forcing customers to buy substandard goods along with good ones—a practice on which there has since been a clampdown. A further problem has been the dramatic fall in world oil prices, as a significant proportion of China's exports have been oil. In the first quarter of 1986, the value of these exports dropped by 30 per cent compared with a year before.

The most obvious indirect control which could be used to regulate foreign trade is the exchange rate, which has not been used until recently, just as in the domestic economy effective use has not been made of levers like credit controls and interest rates. For while the official rate for Chinese renminbi (RMB) has fallen against the United States dollar from around RMB10.54/$ in 1980 to RMB3.70/$ in mid-1986, the impact on enterprises has been much less as, from 1981 to the end of 1984, an 'internal settlement rate' of RMB2.80/$ was used. Thus the effective devaluation of the renminbi against the United States dollar from the viewpoint of a Chinese enterprise has been both recent and limited, though the decline of the dollar has increased the competitiveness of Chinese exports and increased import costs for trade in other currencies. The end result of this rather limited use of indirect economic controls has been the continuing need to use administrative direct control to regulate imports and control the foreign trade deficit.

A final but important current issue is that of corruption. Last year over 200,000 cases of economic crime were tried in China, while the President of the Supreme Court stated that 'Criminal activities that seriously damage the economy are still rampant'. Most clear have been cases of outright fraud and bribery, often by Party members. While these have always existed to some extent, the opening-up of China to the outside world has increased the opportunities for such corruption, especially in the Special Economic Zones, as has the general shift in policy and attitudes towards profit-seeking. But many of the cases arise from loopholes in reform combined with inadequate regulation and the protection of those involved by superiors who might themselves be implicated.

The shift towards enterprise profit retention and the use of tax to raise state revenue as opposed to administrative control has meant great opportunities for tax evasion. This is made easier by the lack of expertise and resources in areas such as auditing and tax collection. For example, in Guangxi 'accounting errors' of ¥70 million were found between January and September 1985. Also, cadres and Party officials have set up their own businesses for private gain, using information and contacts from their official positions. The scale of some of these schemes has been surprisingly large, for example the 'Guangyu Company' case which involved senior Aeronautics Ministry cadres and others. This scheme, it was claimed, was expected to yield up to ¥100 million and included obtaining a foreign exchange loan of over $40 million from a branch of the Bank of China to import kits for 180,000 television sets from France via Hainan Island. Throughout China, such problems have become more pervasive. For example, cadres use official trips to dine out and buy cheap local goods; truck drivers trade their rationed petrol for eggs at the roadside; and a black market in foreign currency has grown more and more open.

Many of these problems can be explained as being a result of the partial nature of reforms to date. If reforms are to work effectively then relaxation of administrative controls must be accompanied—or preceded—by the strengthening of indirect ones. At the same time reforms must be co-ordinated to ensure that the incentives generated are consistent with overall goals.

China's Strategy: The Seventh Five-Year Plan

Long-Term Goals

The best-known long-term goal in China's economic strategy was that of achieving the Four Modernizations (of industry, agriculture, science and technology, and defence) by the year 2000, initially put forward by Zhou Enlai in 1964 and again in 1975. This goal of 'comprehensive modernization' so that China would 'be advancing in the front ranks of the world' by 2000 was closely associated with Deng Xiaoping, who advocated them in policy documents in the mid-1970s. However, these ideas were blocked by political opponents and the idea of the Four Modernizations next came to the fore in Hua Guofeng's speech to the 1978 National People's Congress. However, the idea of bringing China to the ranks of advanced industrial countries by the year 2000 was quickly seen as unrealistic. Taken literally, this would have implied growth of around 15 per cent a year for two decades or more, a target which few could see as possible, even given the most optimistic of assumptions. As a result, more concrete and less ambitious targets have been adopted to guide China's longer-term development.

The most immediate of these new targets is the quadrupling of the 1980 gross agricultural and industrial output value by 2000. This would bring China into the middle ranks of today's Third World, rather than being 'in the front ranks of the world' as in the original formulation of the Four Modernizations. This target would imply consistent growth in agriculture and industry combined of 7.2 per cent a year. This target is ambitious, though lower than China's industrial and agricultural growth record in the past, which was 7.9 per cent from 1952 to 1980. However, past growth was from a low base, particularly in industry, and will not be easy to maintain in the future. A problem with such a gross output value measure is that it ignores the service sector and that a net output value is a more accurate indication of economic performance.

The World Bank (1985) analysed Chinese targets of a $800 per capita GNP (in 1980 dollars) for the year 2000, which implied 5.5 per cent a year growth in per capita GDP. Its report argued that Chinese targets were well above their expectations for the Third World as a whole, as well as being higher than for China in the past. However, in periods of 'good economic management' China had reached this level of growth, while some countries, such as South Korea and Japan, had exceeded them in the past, as China did in the Sixth Five-Year Plan (1981–5), with 8.7 per cent per annum growth in per capita GNP. But, for the overall targets to be met, economic performance approaching this level must be maintained for the next fifteen years without significant faltering.

Looking beyond 2000, the targets are less precise but still ambitious. The next stage is to reach the level of an 'intermediately developed country' by 2020—around the one hundredth anniversary of the founding of the Chinese Communist Party. Finally, by 2050, around the one hundredth anniversary of the People's Republic, the goal is to have 'come close to the level of economically developed countries'. This implies continued growth at a slightly slower pace than that foreseen for the rest of this century, but still averaging per capita growth-rates of 5.5–6.5 per cent from the present to 2050, according to World Bank estimates.

The Seventh Plan: The First Step

Chinese leaders and policy-makers have therefore adopted an economic strategy committing themselves to achieving high rates of economic growth well into the twenty-first century. The Seventh Five-Year Plan represents the first step in this longer-term strategy. This is recognized explicitly in the Plan itself which sees three main tasks (China, 1986):

1. To create a favourable economic and social environment for economic structural reform . . .
2. To maintain sustained and steady economic growth . . . to prepare the required capability for continued economic and social development in the 1990s.
3. On the basis of the development of production and improvement of economic results, to continue to improve the living standards of urban and rural people.

The Plan suggests that there will be two main phases: the first in 1986–7 and the second in 1988–90. During the first phase the focus will be on macro-economic control to remedy current issues as well as on 'invigorating' state enterprises and developing lateral economic ties between them. In the second phase, there will be greater emphasis on pushing forward with structural reforms and faster growth.

When converted into overall targets for the period from 1986 to 1990, the main features of the Plan are 7.5 per cent a year average GNP growth, equivalent to 6.2 per cent a year per capita GNP growth. Looking at gross industrial and agricultural output value, the goal is for 6.7 per cent a year growth to 1990, which is slightly lower than the overall average rate needed to quadruple output by 2000. However, the good performance in the Sixth Five-Year Plan means that this rate, if sustained to 2000, would surpass the overall target. Thus, the growth-rates sought in the Seventh Plan are broadly consistent with the long-term strategy outlined above.

The targets do, however, imply a shift in direction compared with the past, in that the service sector is to assume a larger role in economic growth. Compared with other countries, the service sector is relatively underdeveloped in China, and this provides opportunities for both economic growth and employment generation at relatively low capital cost per job. The tertiary (service) sector is expected to grow at 11.4 per cent a year during the Plan—much faster than industry or agriculture. Among the areas targeted for growth are tourism, posts and telecommunications.

In agriculture growth of 4 per cent a year is planned, with rural industry continuing to grow rapidly at over 11 per cent a year. Light and heavy industry are planned to grow at the same rate of 7 per cent a year (7.5 per cent if rural industry is included). The industrial sectors areas for most rapid growth are fridges and beer, followed by soda ash and locomotives. There is also strong emphasis on shifting investment from creating new plants to upgrading existing ones, with investment in this area growing fast.

Living standards are expected to increase at 5 per cent a year, with a somewhat faster improvement in rural areas than urban ones. Within this only a limited improvement in diet is foreseen, as in the case with higher-grade clothing made from wool and leather. The growth of domestic electricity demand is another concern, and energy-intensive electrical goods—in particular heaters and air conditioners—will be constrained.

Regional Policy

One of the major innovations in the Plan is an explicit regional policy which divides China into three main areas: the Eastern Coastal Region, a Central Region and the Western Region. This marks a further move towards differential economic development in China. The Eastern Coastal Region is seen as the major export base for the future, with attention being concentrated on the upgrading of existing enterprises, the creation of new 'knowledge- and technology-intensive' industries, and the expansion of the service sector, especially in areas related to reform such as management consultancy, and financial and information services, as well as tourism.

The Central Region is seen as a base for extractive, power and materials industries, as well as promoting commodity grain and other cash crops in agriculture. In more advanced cities there will also be some features of the

Eastern Coastal Region's form of development, but if anything energy and materials-intensive industries will be transferred from the Eastern Coastal Region. In the Western Region the focus will be on agriculture, including livestock and forestry, combined with the improvement of transport links within the region and connecting it with other parts of China. Energy and mineral resources potential will be exploited selectively. A major source of technology will be transfer from the military to the civil sector, since a good part of China's defence industry is in the Western Region, for strategic and other reasons, and in the past has been kept largely separate from civil industry. The potential political implications of this in the future are substantial, both domestically and in foreign relations.

Plan Targets and Prospects

Taking an overall view of the Seventh Five-Year Plan, it is clear that while the targets are probably achievable, they do depend on progress in the critical bottleneck sectors of the economy. As argued by Wang Jiye of the State Planning Commission Research Institute, 'energy resources, transport and the raw materials industry are still the "bottleneck" which inhibits the development of the economy and, in this respect, no short-term radical improvement is envisaged'. Thus, there needs to be a combination of long-term investment to resolve the underlying problems and shorter-term measures to improve the efficiency of use of these resources.

In energy, the Plan envisages growth of only 3.4 per cent a year—well below that of GNP and industrial growth—though electric power output is planned to grow at 6.2 per cent a year—only slightly below GNP and industrial growth. The implication of these targets is that either the efficiency of use of energy must increase considerably (at almost 4 per cent a year in terms of coal-equivalent energy per unit of GNP) or China must reduce energy exports and potentially become an importer of energy with adverse consequences for the balance of trade. Plan estimates of energy saving are insufficient to achieve the necessary increased energy efficiency, though the more rapid growth of the service sector will ease the situation somewhat as this is less energy-intensive than industry. However, rising incomes will increase demand for domestic energy, even if more energy-intensive electrical goods are limited in supply. Overall meeting or exceeding energy production targets is critical to the success of the Plan, combined with major improvements in energy efficiency. Without these many Plan targets would be threatened. Similar considerations apply to transport, which also acts as a constraint on both energy and foreign trade. In addition, economic reforms which break down geographical and administrative barriers are likely to increase demand for transport.

Another potential problem area is that of foreign trade, as export growth (given unwillingness to have major foreign debt) is currently a major constraint on import growth. The Plan envisages exports growing at 8.1 per cent a year, with import growth restrained to 6.1 per cent a year, maintaining a trade deficit of about $7 billon a year from 1985 to 1990. The figures used in the Plan are those from the Ministry of Foreign Economic Relations and Trade, which as discussed above show a rather healthier picture than Customs ones which currently show a $14.9 billion deficit. The key is therefore the competitiveness of Chinese exports, in particular manufactured goods, which implies a combination of higher quality and better design and marketing, all of which will not be easy to achieve, but which should be promoted by economic reforms.

Overall, therefore, the Seventh Five-Year Plan represents the first effort for some time to lay out a clear plan for the short to medium term. Its targets fit into the longer-term strategy laid down by the Chinese leadership and are probably achievable, subject to success in key sectors, especially energy and transport. However, both the Plan and the longer-term targets imply a commitment to reform to achieve the goals of higher efficiency, as well as making sure economic growth will be a key political priority. This in turn has major implications as the focus on economic improvement will lead to higher expectations which must be satisfied to maintain support for, and the legitimacy of, the Chinese leadership and management at enterprise level.

Conclusions: The New Demands on Chinese Management

This chapter has analysed the changes in the Chinese economy which form the background to the position of enterprise-level management which forms the main focus of this book. In these conclusions the major implications of these changes will be discussed in three areas: first, the changing role of the enterprise; second, the demands placed on managers and managerial skills; and third, the political implications of reform.

The Role of the Enterprise

China's economic reforms have begun to change the role of the enterprise significantly. In the past, a Chinese enterprise was primarily a production unit whose operations were mainly determined by planning bureaux and other higher-level bodies. As a result, output targets were the most important. Today there has been a shift towards the enterprise as a business unit, in which economic results—notably profit—are the key targets for managers. Those running the enterprise have more power than before to determine how it will be run—though they are still constrained to a fair degree by the planning system and administrative bodies. But reforms have also devolved power to lower levels of government. The combination of local economic and political goals pursued by these low-level government bodies tends towards a localism in which enterprises are pushed towards local sourcing and marketing, thereby undermining competition and the creation of links between enterprises in different areas.

The social and political role of the enterprise is changing. Historically, housing and many welfare benefits have been provided by state-sector enterprises to their workers. As enterprises become more independent and responsible for their own profit and loss, more of the workers' livelihood than just wages is linked to the success or failure of the enterprise. This strong tie of workers to the enterprise impedes the development of labour mobility. Further, if, as has been proposed, enterprises are allowed to go bankrupt, then workers stand not only to lose their jobs but possibly also their houses and welfare benefits. This is recognized and elements of a state-run rather than an enterprise-run system were beginning to emerge during 1986, such as unemployment benefits for workers employed under the labour contract system. Thus the move towards the enterprise as a relatively independent business unit will mean an increasing role for the state in welfare provision.

Demands on Managers

The changing role of the enterprise implies that managers will need not only a higher general level of skill but also skills in new areas which in the past were of little value in China. Alongside this demand for new and increased skills is the need to change the internal structure and decisionmaking processes of the enterprise to adjust to the new economic environment—and to take advantage of the opportunities it provides. This was characterized by one Chinese management expert as the need to move 'from bureaucrat to manager'.

In particular, there is a need to develop processes for developing corporate strategy within the enterprise as its autonomy grows and is no longer so subject to external administrative control. Marketing is another important area in many sectors, though obtaining adequate supplies of materials and other inputs is still a larger concern in most enterprises today. Management accounting is another need as financial information becomes important to internal decisionmaking. More fundamentally, the nature of the uncertainties with which enterprise management has to deal is changing: from political and administrative decisions to the workings of markets with relatively independent actors. Overall, Chinese managers are finding themselves in a more uncertain environment, with new sources of uncertainty, and thus needing to develop a range of new skills. The rapid growth of management education in China reflects this need but there is still a wide gap between the current level and range of skills and those necessary for the potential benefits of economic reform to be realized.

The Political Dimension

While top Communist Party and state leaders now see economic development as their key goal, many middle-level officials are threatened by the changes brought about by reform. Enterprise autonomy reduces the power of those in city and provincial industrial bureaux—positions to which enterprise managers were promoted in the past. Within the enterprise too, policies of separating state administration from economic bodies, and of separating the Party from day-to-day management, threaten officials whose skills do not match those needed as a result of economic reform. Thus, the economic changes associated with reform give rise to inertia and sometimes outright opposition from those adversely affected. One such case in the mid-1980s was the widespread passive resistance by enterprise Party Committee secretaries to the 'factory manager responsibility system' in which power shifted from the Party Committee to the factory director. Managers who had taken initiatives in reform found that they were attacked when something went wrong, whether or not they were to blame.

More fundamentally, the future of China's reforms depends on the balance of power in the political leadership at the top—as well as at lower levels—as exemplified by the fall of Hu Yaobang. While a process of reform has been started, this chapter has argued that it is still limited in scope and often gives contradictory incentives at the enterprise level, especially given the lack of effective indirect controls to replace previous administrative ones. To date, most people in China have benefited from the growth and new policies associated with reform. However, the potential exists for political alliances between those adversely affected—for example middle-level cadres and contract workers made redundant—which could block further reform moves. Thus, Chinese managers face an environment with not only the greater economic uncertainty resulting from reform but also a degree of political uncertainty over whether and at what pace reform will continue.

References

China (1986). *Guomin Jingji he Shehui Fazhan Di Qige Wunian Jihua* ('Seventh Five Year Plan for National Economic and Social Development). Beijing, Renmin Chubanshe.

Lockett, M. (1986). 'Economic growth and development', in Goodman, D., Lockett, M. & Segal, G., *The China Challenge: Adjustment and Reform*. London, Royal Institute of International Affairs/Macmillan.

Gao Shangguang (1986). 'On the first year of the first battle'. *Renmin Ribao*, 26 January, in *BBC Summary of World Broadcasts*. FE/8177/BII/11–14.

Institute of Industrial Economics, Chinese Academy of Social sciences (1985). 'An investigation of the problems in the reform of the tobacco monopoly system'. In *BBC Summary of World Broadcasts*, FE/8163/C1/1–8.

World Bank (1985). *China: Long Term Development Issues and Options*. Baltimore, Johns Hopkins University Press.

Xue Muqiao (1986). 'Retrospect and prospects of the reform of the economic structure in our country'. *Jingji Ribao*, 25 January, in *BBC Summary of World Broadcasts*, FE/8184/BII/3–9.

3 Enterprise Reform in China — Progress and Problems

John Child

Introduction

Economic reform in China has since 1984 been primarily directed at 'revitalizing' the state-owned sector of industry which in 1984 accounted for 73.6 per cent of total industrial output. State enterprises have generally achieved lower rates of growth and been less adaptive to new opportunities than those under collective and individual ownership. Their level of efficiency tends to be low and many still manufacture products of outdated design.

The key features of reform at the enterprise level are contained in two responsibility systems. The first is the 'enterprise responsibility system' which envisages the decentralization of responsibility for the operation and performance of the enterprise down from higher administrative bureaux to its director. The second is the 'director responsibility system' which entails the concentration of internal executive authority into the hands of the enterprise director, subject to monitoring by its party committee and workers' congress. The intention behind these two systems is to transform what were previously little more than factories into business enterprises. Within planning and policy guidelines set out by the state, it is envisaged that the managements of these enterprises will to a much greater extent than before engage directly in market transactions following their own strategic judgements. A correct application of the term 'enterprise' would in fact be confined to economic units in which this degree of transformation has been achieved.

In this paper, we consider the salient features of the present Chinese enterprise reform model. This has to be located within the programme of economic structure reform as a whole, as well as the history of previous phases through which Chinese industrial management has passed since the 1949 revolution. We then examine and discuss evidence of its progress and problems drawn directly from state-owned enterprises. With the two responsibility systems in mind, the paper first considers the extent to which decisions have been decentralized down to enterprise managers and, second, the position of management in relation to Party and workers' organs within enterprises.

Previous Phases of Chinese Industrial Management

The system of Chinese industrial management has passed through *four* major phases since the foundation of the People's Republic in 1949, of which the last is the particular concern of this paper. Following the transformation to socialist ownership, a centralized planning system was established along Soviet lines. This passed down to units of production through provincial and municipal administrative levels. Larger factories in the priority heavy industrial sectors normally had executive authority concentrated in the hands of their directors—the so-called 'one director management system'. This system contributed to substantial advances in heavy industrial output during the 1950s and the essentials of its planning and administrative structure remain in place today. It was, nevertheless, an imported approach relying heavily upon bureaucratic top–down direction which did not fit happily with either of two existing traditions that favoured greater participation by local Party officials and worker spokesmen. The first of these was the revolutionary 'Yanan' tradition of mass mobilization, high ideological consciousness and the key role of Party activists. The second stemmed from the industrial tradition of work teams led by gang bosses. In the less capital-intensive sectors of industry, an indigenous 'Shanghai system of management' in fact continued to operate; this involved a major role for the collective leadership of the Party committee and significant participation by shop-floor work teams. The Soviet model was therefore incongruous with Chinese ideology and tradition. It relied, moreover, upon the availability of a substantial body of technically-trained managers which China did not possess at the time, and this constraint also spoke for broadening the base of contribution to decisionmaking (Littler, 1985; Xie, 1985).

Party cadres and workers expressed increasing dissatisfaction with the Soviet system of one-man factory management. Reforms in 1956 and 1961 strengthened the role of factory party committees and workers' collectives respectively. Factory directors were placed under the leadership of Party committees and became responsible for carrying out decisions made by those committees. Workers' congresses acquired rights to review managerial actions. The higher-level planning system, however, remained intact. Although this second phase was in turn terminated by the Cultural Revolution in 1966, it was restored after 1976 and still constitutes the formal system of management in many enterprises.

While the motives behind the Cultural Revolution are still a matter of debate, it is apparent that Mao Zedong chafed at the limitations placed on his personal leadership both by the aftermath of the disastrous 'Great Leap Forward' and by the development of a bureaucratic administration which routinized his charisma. His strategy referred back to that developed during the anti-Japanese and civil wars in the revolutionary bases of the Yanan period, namely the mobilization of a mass nationwide movement combining direct workers' control guided by ideologically-primed local Party leaders with loyalty to a charismatic, rather than bureaucratic, central leadership. The Cultural Revolution was *inter alia* intended to discredit and remove the layers of administration and industrial management which intervened between the working class and its leader. Lockett's (1985a) study of the Beijing General Knitwear Mill, officially regarded as a model factory during the Cultural Revolution, suggests, however, that radical changes to previously established managerial structures and reductions in staff numbers were in practice short-lived.

Since late 1978 the Chinese authorities have moved into a fourth phase of industrial management which has evolved through experiment as a very conscious learning experience. This programme of 'economic structure reform', together with inherited structural and behavioural characteristics, has shaped the present pattern of enterprise management.

The Economic Structure Reform Programme

In December 1978, the Third Plenum of the Party Central Committee decided on a major programme of reform for the structure of the Chinese economy. This programme became identified with the 'Four Modernizations' of agriculture, industry, science and technology, and defence. While more immediately it was an attempt to rebuild the economy after the depletions of the Cultural Revolution, the reform programme represented a reaction both to the perceived shortcomings of that period and a desire to transcend the limitations of the Soviet-style centralized system developed between 1950 and 1957.

The Cultural Revolution was seen to have dissipated incentive and responsibility for economic performance through egalitarianism, the weakening of management, the general devaluation of expertise and the claim that ideological fervour and inspired leadership could substitute for technical knowledge. The mass mobilization of workers against the authority structures upon which central direction depended had led to chaos and destructive factionalism. The older, Soviet-style system was not, however, regarded by the 1978 reformers as an appropriate model to which to return. Although this was acknowledged to have played a role in establishing a base of heavy industry, it was now viewed as too rigid. Its heavily administrative approach confused the functions of government and enterprise, imposed undue uniformity and suppressed initiative, failed to adapt to changes in market demand, and did not link rewards to economic performance (Huan, 1985).

So the search began, via a series of experiments, for a structure of economic management which combined incentive and responsiveness with the maintenance of overall central planning and control, through a blend of market and bureaucratic transactions. This is the so-called 'dual structure'. The stages through which the reform developed have been detailed by Oborne (1986) and only the key developments are mentioned here. The first reform experiments in agriculture and industry were instituted in Sichuan, home province of both China's 'Chairman' and Prime Minister. The agricultural reform was based on the household 'responsibility system' whereby land is contracted to peasants, and on various incentive policies linked to permitting higher levels of commodity production for the market. This raised production significantly and spread rapidly.

As is continually stressed by the Chinese, urban industrial reform is a much more complex matter. It has developed through a longer process of trial and error which still continued. The key elements have been the administrative delegation of powers to the provinces and municipalities, the decentralization of responsibility for performance to enterprise managers, and a controlled receptivity to foreign capital and technology.

By mid-1979, over one hundred provincial-level state enterprises in Sichuan were authorized by the central government to assume new powers over production and the marketing of products. A system allowing some retention of profit was introduced to create a link between enterprise performance and reward. There were new forms of investment financing and opportunities for enterprises to use depreciation funds were improved. By 1980, most provinces had initiated pilot experiments in enterprise management covering a total of some 6,600 state enterprises.

In 1981 there was a recentralization of decisionmaking with respect to the allocation of inputs and the distribution of products, especially in heavy industry, which had suffered a 5 per cent decline in ouput that year. A drain on foreign exchange reserves also led to the centrally imposed postponement or cancellation of many contracts for foreign equipment. The government now decided to keep more direct administrative control over key allocative and distribution decisions, but at the same time to apply a form of the responsibility system which had been successful in the agricultural sector. This was intended to clarify responsibility for success and failure at all levels of the industrial hierarchy down to factory workers. It was complemented by a contract system allowing for direct inter-enterprise transactions. By the end of 1982, this reform was being tried out in over three thousand state-owned enterprises.

Although governmental planning and control of state-owned industry were retained, the bureaucratic apparatus was streamlined at this time. There was a reduction from ninety-eight to fifty-two in the number of ministries and commissions. The State Planning Commission and the State Economic Commission were given more direct responsibility for enterprise planning and control, with many decisionmaking powers, including finance and investment, being delegated to provincial authorities. The local branches of foreign trade corporations were given wider powers to negotiate directly with overseas trade partners. In March 1982, selected cities were designated to pioneer urban economic restructuring, particularly to decentralize enterprise management and create conditions for more effective market transactions.

The State Council decided, in May 1984, to expand the decisionmaking powers of state enterprises in *ten* areas, including production, sales, pricing of non-quota products, disposal of assets, organization, personnel and bonuses. In October 1984, a directive was issued increasing enterprise autonomy, releasing certain enterprises from central ministry control and permitting some prices to float. Enterprises could now officially charge market prices for production achieved in excess of their plan quotas. At the same time, a decision to make enterprises responsible for profits and losses was accompanied by a fiscal reform under which they would be allowed to pay taxes on profits rather than have to remit all profits to the government. Retained profits could be used to pay bonuses and/or pay for new construction or renovation, which increased the incentive for profit maximization. Proposals were also announced for a law under which enterprises could be declared bankrupt, and the experimental sales of shares in enterprises began.

In October 1984, the Party Central Committee adopted a major policy document on 'China's Economic Structure Reform'. This document was an attempt to build upon experience with the economic reform programme, to reaffirm its 'pressing necessity' and to expound a 'systematic' and 'all-round' policy to be applied generally through the industrial sector. The most important focus in this blueprint is on *enterprise management reform* allied to a greater role for market forces and complementary reforms in the fiscal and pricing systems. The main themes of this important document are now summarized (page numbers to the English version given in the References).

Modernization is again firmly restated as the rationale for reform, the key to which lies in the 'invigoration' of urban industrial enterprises which alone account for over 80 per cent of the state's tax revenue (pp. 8–9). The main requirement for injecting vitality into enterprises is seen to be an extension of their decisionmaking powers so that they can respond to market forces and provide incentives. The major defects of the existing economic structure are summarized as follows:

> No clear distinction has been drawn between the functions of the government and those of the enterprise; barriers exist between different departments or between different regions; the state has exercised excessive and rigid control over enterprises; no adequate importance has been given to commodity production, the law of value and the regulatory role of the market; and there is absolute egalitarianism in distribution. This has resulted in enterprises lacking necessary decision making power and the practice of 'eating from the same big pot' prevailing in the relations of the enterprises to the state and in those of the workers and staff members to their enterprises. The enthusiasm, initiative and creativeness of enterprises and workers and staff members have, as a result, been seriously dampened and the socialist economy is bereft of much of the vitality it should possess [pp. 5–6].

The new policy envisaged an extention of enterprise decentralization within a system of governmental planning in which the mandatory element was reduced in favour of guidance plans and where control was exercized through economic regulators rather than administrative fiat. Within this revised framework of state planning and control, enterprise management was now to take on significant new responsibilities (p. 10). These were:

1. to decide on enterprise operations and organization, including 'flexible and diversified forms';
2. to plan its production, supply and marketing in tune with market mechanisms;
3. to set prices within limits prescribed by the state;
4. to retain and budget certain funds;
5. to decide on recruitment, personnel and reward policies.

Enterprises would become 'independent and responsible for their own profit and loss and capable of transforming and developing themselves . . . [acting as] legal persons with certain rights and duties' (p. 11). Their directors would assume full responsibility for their performance under a unified management system. This is the so-called 'director responsibility system' which replaces the previous system of managerial responsibility to the enterprise Party Committee.

The document particularly stresses the need for city governments not to interfere in enterprise management or to create barriers to inter-enterprise contracting (p. 21). All government organs were enjoined to see their role as providing services to enterprises rather than treating them as their private dependencies (p. 23). They also had to 'eliminate such bureaucratic maladies as organisational overlapping, over-staffing, vague delimitations of functions and endless wrangling' which handicapped the effective operation of enterprises (p. 23). Within enterprises, managerial adherence to Party principles and policies was, however, to be ensured by enterprise Party organizations, while workers were to have the right to examine major decisions and articulate their interests through congresses and trade unions (p. 25). These policies were expressed in terms of establishing 'correct relationships' between enterprises and the state, and between enterprises and their members (p. 9).

The document envisages the continued opening of China to external market transactions and even more the removal of barriers to such transactions within the country (p. 31). Internal market barriers are seen to hamper the growth of production and its rationalization. Exposure to market competition would 'lay bare the defects of enterprises quickly and stimulate enterprises to improve technology, operation and management' (p. 22). It is recognized that efficient markets operate through the price mechanism, and that the centralized system of price control should therefore be relaxed (p. 17).

A regulation approved in September 1985 by the State Council on 'Strengthening the Vitality of Large and Medium-Sized State Enterprises' confirmed that the assumption of strategic powers by enterprises within the guidelines of state plans and policies should be formalized by a 'responsibility contract' between the enterprise director and higher authority. The same regulation stated that enterprise plans should be drawn up with reference to market conditions and urged that 'enterprises should change from production oriented operation to production and marketing oriented operation' (*People's Daily*, 20 September 1985).

At the level of declared policy, the Chinese economic structure reforms express a firm belief that efficient and rapid modernization requires a decentralized management system that is exposed to market forces and is capable of adapting to them. They retract bureaucracy from a directly controlling to a guiding and ring-holding role, and require the dissolution of local fief-like protective preserves.

Enterprise Reform in Practice

The evidence on the progress of enterprise reform presented here was gathered in September and October 1985. By this time the macroeconomic problems which China had experienced during the previous twelve months had grown to a point where they threatened the reform programme as a whole. These problems could readily be ascribed to a loss of control consequent upon the shift from central bureaucratic regulation towards decentralized market socialism. Indeed, it later transpired that senior conservative Marxist critics had, in the Party special delegates' meeting held in September 1985, blamed the economic reform programme and the 'open door' trade policy for the economic strains and corruption which had emerged. Subsequently, certain of the powers delegatd to local administrative authorities, including authorization of technology imports, were withdrawn, as were those officially decentralized to enterprises under the reform relating to borrowing money, factory enlargement, increasing output, raising wages and buying foreign equipment.

More recently, however, government leaders have reaffirmed that the reform programme will continue to go forward, albeit with stronger central management of the economy. Articles appearing in the officially-sponsored *Beijing Review* during the summer of 1986 strongly reaffirmed the need for reform to continue, expressing, for example, the 'demand' of enterprises for more power (16 June: 6–7), criticizing the harassment of reforming managers by local officials (28 July: 5–6), and even reprinting a 1979 speech by Chen Yun, one of the reform's leading critics, in which he cautioned against neglect of the regulatory role of the market (21 July: 14–15). This suggests that reform will remain official policy for the foreseeable future, and lends continuing relevance to investigation of its progress on the ground. Moreover, the more immediately obvious problems have been those of a macroeconomic nature and much less is understood about what has been achieved in applying decentralization through the responsibility system down to where it is really intended to have results, the enterprise itself. Even if the problem of macroeconomic control is eventually solved, difficulties may remain in actually implementing the reform locally. Both the general experience of managing top–down change, and the enduring cultural and institutional factors in the Chinese context, give rise to the expectation that the implementation of decentralization to the enterprise and its engagement in market transactions will be subject to severe constraints, even when it has the strong backing of central government (Boisot & Child, 1986). The demise of Hu Yaobang has cast a shadow over the future of the economic reform, but official policy still emphasizes the 'open-door' policy.

The most detailed source of information comes from field-investigations conducted with the aid of industrially-experienced Chinese Master of Business Administration (MBA) students within six state enterprises located in Beijing. Initially, the writer visited each enterprise and interviewed its director and/or a deputy director, accompanied by two European faculty colleagues working at the Management Centre of the State Economic Commission (details regarding such management-education initiatives are provided in the chapter by Warner, later in this volume). Interpretation during these visits was provided by Chinese faculty colleagues. Teams of six students per enterprise then collected detailed information on decisionmaking and on the role of directors as part of a wider investigation into management and work organization which the writer directed.

A foreigner faces obvious difficulties in securing valid information on the internal workings of Chinese enterprises. Quite apart from the problem of language and meaning systems, there is also the tendency to provide a mere gloss to someone who is a double outsider—both to the enterprise and to the country. The virtue of working with teams of mature indigenous students lies in their ability to approach much closer to the real situation prevailing within enterprises. The student teams had already conducted two studies within the same enterprises earlier in the year. They had built up an extensive network of informants and had generated goodwill through the practical assistance these projects had afforded. Prior to undertaking the fieldwork from which data presented here are drawn, the students had taken the writer's course in organizational analysis in which relevant concepts and methodology were reviewed, and they also received specific training for the research project. The writer remained in close contact with the students during the fieldwork period. He also gained additional background material through interviewing other managers, former Party secretaries, researchers and management education faculty, as well as visiting additional enterprises engaged in joint ventures.

Table 3.1 presents information on the size, status and industrial sectors of the six enterprises. In order to preserve their anonymity, their products are not precisely identified. Within Chinese state-owned industry, enterprises are designated as large, medium or small, depending on their output, asset value and numbers employed. There were at the time 291 large and medium

Table 3.1 Profile of six Beijing state-owned enterprises

Product Category (P)	Date of Foundation	Total Employment 1985	Sales Turnover 1984	Net Profit Before Tax 1984	Retained Profit After Tax (%) 1984	Official Size	Quota (Q) or Profit Target
			Y'000	Y'000	Y'000		
A. Automative	1966	3,883	204,525	53,368	6,566 (12.3)	M	Q
B. Audio-visual	1973	2,200	183,308	12,702	3,097 (24.4)	M	Q
C. Heavy electrical	1956	1,869	23,362	4,766	924 (19.4)	M	Q
D. Pharmaceutical	1973	957	27,104	3,971	n.a.	S	P
E. Audio	1955	848	24,942	4,661	1,724 (37.0)	S	P
F. Electrical switchgear	1955/58	718	6,101	1,472	237 (16.1)	S	P

state enterprises within the Beijing municipality and 833 small ones. Three of the enterprises studied were classified as medium and three as small. A significant concomitant of this classification lay in the enterprise's upward reporting relationship. While each formed part of a municipal-level holding company, the small enterprises had stronger formal ties to the Beijing Economic Commission (the municipal economic planning agency) than did the medium enterprises who enjoyed relatively stronger links with the higher-level corporations responsible for their industry. This implies that the smaller enterprises were subject to greater local economic control, a theme to be explored in greater detail by one of my colleagues teaching with me in Beijing, in a subsequent chapter.

1. Enterprise responsibility: managerial decisionmaking

Information was gathered about the extent of decentralization to the enterprises and delegation within them of forty-eight decisions. These decisions relate to the main areas of activity normally found in an enterprise, namely marketing, production and contingent functions, purchasing, finance and investment, organization, R&D, employment and personnel. A full list of these decisions is given in the Appendix to this paper. The method of assessment used is based on that developed in the 'Aston Programme' of organizational studies; it particularly focuses on the extent to which decision powers are passed down a hierarchical structure and it also permits an evaluation of decentralization through comparison with findings from other countries.

Table 3.2 shows the decisions for which authority was withheld from some or all of the six enterprises. This provides a preliminary indication of the extent to which enterprise responsibility has developed. Several points are immediately apparent. First, the extent of decentralization was far from uniform among the different enterprises, and this raises the question of what might lie behind the variations. Second, decentralization had been withheld in certain areas, including the pricing of products subject to quota plans approved by higher authorities, the determination of investment levels, the size of the employment establishment, and the level of basic salaries (both workers and cadres are paid monthly). Third, decisions on internal organization, production and contingent functions, and most purchasing matters had now been decentralized. The progress of reform in the direction of enterprise responsibility was therefore rather mixed. The managers in all six of the Beijing enterprises reported, however, that there had been some relaxation in the control exercised by their higher authorities, the holding companies or municipal bureaux, and it is necessary to examine the picture in greater detail.

All official documents and statements on economic reform express the intention that enterprises should engage directly in market transactions and be responsive to market conditions. Three of the Beijing enterprises, however, were still obliged to supply the greater part of their outputs on a quota basis to designated outlets. They were the larger enterprises producing economically more strategic goods and whose plans were closely integrated into national plans for their industries. To a substantial degree their activities and transactions were still governed by higher bureaucratic authorization rather than by their own ability to respond to market opportunities. Nor could their managements determine the prices of quota products which remained well below market levels. For example, the automotive enterprise produced 70 per cent of its output on a quota basis and another 15 per cent according to a 'guide plan' which it had to discuss with the National Automotive Industry Corporation and the Beijing Economic Commission: it could sell one half of guide plan production (i.e. 7.5 per cent), plus the remaining 15 per cent to the market. In 1985, it was able to secure up to Y28,350 per product on the market, which was 75 per cent higher than the fixed quota price of Y15,950.

Nevertheless, these three enterprises had been able to increase the non-quota proportions of their output which could be marketed with a degree of managerial discretion. Two could determine the prices of their non-quota products within a broad discretionary band and the third, the audio-visual products manufacturer, could decide whether or not to offer discounts on the 10 per cent of its output which it sold directly to customers. The other three enterprises had been given profit rather than output targets, and two of them could vary their product prices. Overall, then, four of the six enterprises were now able to set prices within limits for at least some of their output, and a fifth enjoyed some discretion over discounts.

Prices had, however, become a sensitive social issue by 1985 because of inflation, and this meant that any decision to raise product prices was in practice liable to evoke external criticism. The price reform, which is an integral part of the economic reform as a whole, suffered a setback at the time, with restrictions on pricing being reimposed. Managers in the Beijing enterprises which had enjoyed some freedom of pricing reported that in practice the municipal price bureau was making it increasingly difficult for them to raise prices.

It was also evident that inexperience and a lack of information were holding back the freedom which the enterprises now enjoyed to develop their own marketing policies. With the exception of the automotive manufacturer, which was constrained by the national planning of marketing territories, each enterprise could, for output not subject to quota, determine the type of oulet or customer to supply, the priority of different orders and deliveries, and the geographical spread of its marketing territory. In practice, however, market information was still not being gathered and analysed on a systematic basis, and considerably larger staffs were allocated to the task of securing supplies than to marketing products.

Securing supplies in a shortage economy, hampered further by an under-developed communications and transport infrastructure (cf. World Bank,

1985), was in fact a problematic area of market transactions for which the enterprises had in practice to assume even more responsibility than was officially intended. All of them could now select their own suppliers for non-strategic items. Where the quota system applied, this was supposed to guarantee supplies necessary to meet quota output levels. The term 'supposed' is used advisedly, since management were still left with the headache of actually ensuring that supplies were delivered on time and to required quality. There is a serious lack of co-ordination between enterprises which are linked by the production cycle but dependent upon the planning of different ministries, and in a shortage economy little pressure can be exerted upon a recalcitrant supplier. Five of the enterprises were also able to determine their own procedures for purchasing, including the terms of contract.

It had been officially claimed that the 1984 fiscal reform would be a significant step towards enterprise responsibility and revitalization. Under this reform, enterprises would pay taxes on their profits rather than having to remit all profits to the government. Retained profits could be used to pay bonuses, support welfare provisions and pay for new construction or renovation, and this local autonomy was expected to increase the incentive for profit maximization. Official statistics indicate that, in 1985, 81 per cent of state-owned enterprises adopted this system of substituting tax payment for profits delivery (*Beijing Review*, 24 March 1986: 29). However, the great bulk of enterprise investment still needs to be financed out of the governmental 'investment fund', leaving relatively little to the responsibility of enterprise management. For once taxes have been paid to the state and municipality; as little as 15 per cent may be left to be retained by the enterprise. The percentages of total profits for 1984 retained by the six Beijing enterprises ranged between 12 and 37 per cent (see Table 3.1). This retention has to finance bonus payments and welfare provisions, leaving possibly no more than 5 per cent for investment expenditure at management's discretion. A regulation restricts the per annum allowance for depreciation to 5 per cent, half of which has to be remitted to the holding company. There are also restrictions on the purchase of equipment requiring foreign exchange. The decentralization to enterprises of responsibility for investment decisions is therefore extremely limited.

The October 1984 policy document on economic structure reform envisaged that enterprises would enjoy flexibility in their employment policies. Employment and personnel matters are subject to social criteria such as the reduction of unemployment 'waiting for work' among younger people, and they are understandably sensitive in a workers' state. In four enterprises the directors were now formally able to initiate the return of unsatisfactory workers to the 'labour market' through dismissal. Dismissal of permanent workers is, however, a delicate matter in a workers' state, on which directors would in practice normally secure the approval of the enterprise party committee, if not higher authority.

Table 3.2 Decisions for which authority was withheld from some or all enterprises
× = authority withheld

Decision	A	B	C	D	E	F
				ENTERPRISE		
Marketing						
Price of products in quota plan	×	×	×	no quota	no quota	no quota
Price of non-plan products		×			×	
Type of market served	×					
Marketing territories	×					
Purchasing						
Procedure followed					×	
Investment and Accounting						
Level of investment	×	×	×	×	×	×
Choice of capital equipment		×				
Scope of costing system	×				×	
Personnel						
Recruiting workers					×	
Recruiting supervisors					×	
Recruiting managers		×	×	×	×	×
Selection methods					×	
Size of total establishment	×	×	×	×	×	×
Workers' basic salaries	×	×	×	×		×
Cadres' basic salaries		×	×	×	×	×
Dismiss worker			×		×	
Dismiss cadre		×	×		×	
Quality						
Extent of product inspection			×			
Total of decisions with authority withheld	7	9	9	5	12	5

Several managers expressed interest in the possibilities of increasing the numerical flexibility of their enterprises by employing a larger proportion of contract-workers who could be laid off at the termination of their contracts. The government is now preparing to extend the contract system of employment which only covers 3.5 million workers, or under 5 per cent of the urban workforce at present (*China Business Report*, 13 August 1986: 1; *Beijing Review*, 15 September 1986: 16–17). In none of the six enterprises did management enjoy the power of numerical flexibility by being able to determine the size of its employment establishment. Although with one exception the enterprises could decide to recruit more workers and decide on selection methods used, management will often find when seeking new recruits from the municipal labour bureau that the bureau attaches the condition that the enterprise takes on more people than it requires, and quite likely these people will not possess the requisite skills or capabilities. Nor is it usual for enterprises to determine the basic salaries of cadres or workers, which are generally fixed according to a standard grading system. Regulations limit the ratio of bonus to salary payments through tax penalties, while the ability to link bonuses to individual performance is limited by poorly-developed work measurement techniques and a persisting ethos of egalitarianism.

Enterprise managers now had the authority to adjust their organization structures by altering the responsibilities of departments and creating new roles within them. But they still found themselves hemmed in by government regulations such as the one which states that every managerial post must have a deputy, even though the specific situation may not warrant this. The ability of directors to reconstitute and integrate the typically large number of functional and staff departments also remains limited in practice. Functional departments seeking to preserve their standing and staffing have been supported by their counterparts in holding companies who are wary of allowing enterprise line managers to rationalize their dependencies. It is not uncommon therefore to come across considerable organizational duplication and serious problems of inter-departmental co-operation. One of the six Beijing enterprises, for example, had three separate quality control departments and another had two technical departments. As might be expected, there was a confusion of responsibilities and rivalry between them. Lockett (1985b) has similarly identified poor co-ordination and unclear responsibilities as among the problems of Chinese management.

Prior to the reform, Chinese enterprises were essentially just factories in which performance criteria were orientated to production plan fulfilment. Their longest span of experience has therefore been in the management of production and related functions, and they inherit the tradition which resurfaced during the Cultural Revolution, whereby work groups and their leaders participated in many operational decisions. Decentralization of production and operations decisions had been the practice before the reform, and this was found in all six enterprises, with the one exception that the scope of final production inspection was set out by higher authority in the case of the automotive manufacturer. The annual production plans worked to were decided by enterprise directors or vice-directors in charge of production, and their targets typically exceeded those contained in the official plans that had been submitted to higher authority. The intention of this shadow-system is, first, to lower the expectations placed on the enterprise from above and, second, to earn a larger retainable profit which can be spent on welfare provisions and bonuses.

Decisions on operational matters tend to be delegated within the organization. In the engineering factories (automotive, heavy electrical products and electrical switchgear) which were divided into separate workshops with intervening buffer stocks, the scheduling of each shop was normally decided by its manager. In the other, more integrated plants this was decided by the production vice-director; in the audio products firm, by the director. In most of the enterprises, decisions on allocating work among the available workers and on the equipment to use were taken by work-group leaders who used to be elected but now approximate to the Western concept of appointed first-line supervisors. The choice of work methods was also made within each shop: in three enterprises by work-group leaders, in two by shop managers, while in the automotive enterprise this could be decided by at least some of the workers themselves. When discussing this relatively high level of autonomy within enterprises, Chinese informants pointed to a continuity with the legacy of workgroup control encouraged by the Cultural Revolution. Personal visits to the sites suggested that the very limited application of scientific management and costing techniques also preserved workshop autonomy from control systems and staff intervention. This is itself partly a legacy of the hostility to formalized expertise displayed during the Cultural Revolution.

Although the policy of enterprise responsibility had taken effect in the decentralization of certain decision areas such as internal organization and marketing, higher authorities still controlled the key parameters of investment, product pricing and overall employment. (For further detailed discussion of these areas, see the next chapter, by Campbell.) One should recall, however, that the six Beijing enterprises were subsidiaries belonging to holding companies rather than whole companies in the Western sense. It is not unusual for subsidiaries in capitalist market economies to require higher approval for their investment proposals or to have to remit their profits to the owning group. With this in mind, and in order to place the Chinese case into a wider perspective, Table 3.3 compares the level of autonomy which the six Beijing enterprises enjoyed to take twenty-three of the decisions studied with the same measure applied to manufacturing firms in Canada, England and the United States. Whereas the English and American samples included a mixture of principal units and subsidiaries or branches of parent companies, the Canadian firms were all subsidiaries. The average size of the Chinese sample falls approximately halfway between the larger average for the English 1967/8 and American samples and the smaller average for the English 1962/3 and Canadian samples. This should be borne in mind when interpreting the table since studies of Western manufacturing enterprises have tended to find that decentralization and delegation increase with the size of firm (cf. Child, 1973; Pugh & Hinings, 1976).

Surprisingly, in view of their location within the still-continuing bureaucratic infrastructure of a centrally planned economy, the sample of Beijing enterprises displays a comparable level of overall decisionmaking autonomy to the Canadian and later English sample, and a higher level than the other Western samples. There is no evidence from this comparison to suggest that the Chinese enterprises enjoy significantly less *overall* responsibility than has been the case with their counterparts in the West.

A supplementary assessment is also possible from the information given in Table 3.4 on the overall centralization of decisionmaking. This measures the extent to which decisionmaking is concentrated in the upper levels of

Table 3.3 Level of decisionmaking autonomy in six Chinese manufacturing enterprises compared with four sets of Western enterprises

Enterprises	Level of decisionmaking Autonomy*
location; date of study; number	
Beijing, PRC	
1985 (N = 6	19.7
Birmingham, England	
1962/63 (N = 24)	14.9
Birmingham, England	
1967/68 (N = 25)	19.2
Ohio, USA	
1968 (N = 21)	17.9
Toronto, Canada	
1969 (N = 24)	19.5

*Number of decisions which can be taken within the enterprise without reference to a higher authority out of a standard list of twenty-three decisions. For details see Pugh & Hickson (1976:52–3, 73–4). Source of data on Western enterprises: McMillan et al. (1981:Table 3.2).

organizational hierarchies, *including* the possibility that it is restricted to a higher authority. Overall scores are derived from data on a standard set of thirty-seven decisions which were contained in the set of forty-eight investigated in the Beijing enterprises (cf. Pugh *et al.*, 1968). The table compares overall centralization in the Beijing enterprises with that found in samples of firms from Hong Kong, Japan and the United Kingdom. The Japanese and British firms were all manufacturing, but only nineteen of the fifty-three from Hong Kong were. The majority of the Japanese firms were subsidiaries or branches, while nearly all of the Hong Kong and British ones were principal units. The Hong Kong firms were all Chinese-owned and managed. The average size of the British sample was close to that of the Beijing enterprises; that of the other samples was appreciably smaller. With these elements of non-comparability in factors which are known to affect the assessment of decisionmaking centralization, interpretative caution is required. It is nevertheless worthy of note that the overall centralization of decisionmaking in the Chinese enterprises was not so much higher than that of the British sample and was similar to that of the Hong Kong sample which consisted mainly of independent and whole companies, albeit of small size on average. The Japanese firms were on average more centralized than those from Beijing, though one has to recall their smaller average size.

There is again no evidence here to suggest that the overall level of centralization reported by the Beijing firms is appreciably greater than that found in other countries. Nevertheless, responsibility is still being withheld from management in key areas and overall assessments such as those pre-

Table 3.4 Overall centralization of decisionmaking in six Chinese manufacturing enterprises compared with enterprises in Hong Kong, Japan and the United Kingdom

Enterprises	Level of Overall Centralization*
Beijing, People's Republic of China (N = 6)	110.2
Hong Kong (N = 53)	109.9
Tochigi Prefecture, Japan (N = 50)	122.1
United Kingdom, national (N = 55)	98.4

*Higher scores denote greater centralization, based on an analysis of a standard set of thirty-seven decisions. Scores derive from a scale referring to lowest level in the organization to which decisions are delegated where 5 = above the chief executive or factory director; 4 = chief executive or executive board level (including factory party committee in China); 3 = head of range of departments (e.g. production director); 2 = head of single department or workshop; 1 = supervisory level (or appointed workgroup leader in China); 0 = operative level. Being a standardizing measure, this scale does not necessarily equate exactly to the number of hierarchical levels in a particular organization, but in each organization studied hierarchical positions are carefully assessed in relation to the scale.

Source: United Kingdom and Japan—K. Azumi & C. J. McMillan (1981). 'Management Strategy and Organization Structure: a Japanese Comparative Study' in D. J. Hickson & C. J. McMillan (eds), *Organization and Nation: The Aston Programme IV*. Farnborough: Gower, Tables 9.5 and 9.6. Hong Kong—S. G. Redding & D. S. Pugh (1985). 'The Formal and the Informal: Japanese and Chinese Organization Structures', paper presented to the Conference on Enterprise and Management in East Asia. University of Hong Kong, January.

sented mask a somewhat different distribution of responsibility across decision areas compared to that which tends to be found in capitalist countries. Comparison with data available from Japanese, West German and British manufacturing firms on individual decisions suggests that the Chinese enterprises delegate production and work allocation decisions further down their hierarchies than do German and Japanese firms (cf. Child & Kieser, 1979; Azumi & McMillan, 1981). They also delegate representational duties more than in the other countries, though in China representation may be more purely formal than elsewhere. On the other hand, pricing and employment decisions, with their direct social implications, are considerably more centralized than in the other countries and this significantly limits the extent to which enterprise managements can pursue effective marketing and labour policies.

The policy of enterprise reform has been introduced on a wide scale only for a relatively short period and it may reasonably be argued that we are presently witnessing a period of transition and learning. There has undoubtedly been significant resistance from local authorities to the granting of more initiative to enterprises within their purview and to a rationalization of their own multiple bureaux whose separate rationale was based upon their detailed regulation of specific areas of enterprise activity. This is recognized publicly by government spokesmen who complain about 'meddling in enterprise affairs' (interview with Tong Dalin, *China Daily*, 12 April 1986: 4) and 'too many authorities lording over the enterprises' (an official of the State Economic Commission quoted in *Beijing Review*, 14 April 1986: 27). Thus, even though some decentralization of decisionmaking has been achieved, the implementation of such decisions may still continue to be frustrated. We have argued elsewhere that this constraint stems from more than just a matter of administrative structuring, for, at the local level in China, there exists a web of diffuse multiple dependencies between the municipality and the enterprise which reflects the historical importance of the local community and is sustained by local networks of personal obligation and trust (Boisot & Child, 1986). It will not be easy for enterprises to break out of that web in order to assume a relatively independent role as players in a national, and possibly international, market-place.

2. Enterprise director responsibility

A major principle in the enterprise reform programme is that the performance responsibility decentralized to enterprises will be placed upon their directors who therefore require the authority to carry it out. This is expressed by the so-called 'director responsibility system' which shifts enterprise leadership from party committees to directors. The unification of authority it implies is, however, seen by the reformers to contrast with the earlier and relatively short-lived Soviet-style system of one-man management in that it is intended to incorporate a continuing role both for party and workers' organs. Indeed, the contribution of workers' congresses and their representatives to 'democratic management' is to be developed [see chapters in Part Three of this volume].

Translating the principles of the new system into practice is likely to take time and to be influenced by local factors. The leadership system in the great majority of state-owned enterprises at the end of 1985 remained one in which their directors were subject to the overriding authority of the enterprise party committee. The activity level of workers' congresses appeared to vary considerably. After providing some further background, this section examines the situation prevailing in the enterprises to which the writer had access.

Following increasing resistance from Party cadres and workers to the Soviet-style system of unified managerial authority, reforms in 1956 and 1961 introduced the system by which the role of enterprise directors was to execute decisions made by the party committee. Workers' congresses were also established in at least some enterprises after 1961. During the Cultural Revolution both these provisions were abandoned, though various other types of representative bodies, usually excluding staff members, did play a significant role up until the early 1970s (cf. Lockett, 1985a). After 1976, the leading role of the enterprise party committee was restored under a system of 'unified leadership under the party committee' in which the director and functional managers reported directly to the party committee. Depending in practice on their motivation and capacity, party secretaries could under this system perform a general management role in which they chaired policy meetings, dealt directly with departmental heads, and called departmental meetings (Fang, 1985).

Regulations issued during 1982 and 1983 ushered in a second stage in the recent development of leadership within state-owned industrial enterprises. This is the so-called 'system of director responsibility under the leadership of the party committee'. It identifies managerial tasks and recognizes the need for these to be undertaken through adequate structures of management. Usually vice-directors were appointed for major functions who now reported to the director rather than to the party committee. Under this system, however, the director remains responsible to the enterprise party committee which takes upon itself the discussion of business and production policies. He or she has to date had no formal authority independently of the party committee, although this situation is expected to change (see *Beijing Review*, 3 November 1986: 4).

Although the two principles of party committee leadership and democratization of management through the role alloted to workers' congresses express the rationale of the party as the leading organ in a workers' state, reformers in the Chinese government increasingly recognized that this system could run into practical difficulties. Responsibility for enterprise performance was diffused by the collective nature of party committee decisionmaking. A clear distinction between party business and enterprise administration was lacking, with the result that the party committee and its secretary in particular became the source of authority for both functions. The party secretary, if conscientious, became overloaded; otherwise managerial leadership went by default. The result in either case tended to be that decisions were delayed, directors lost motivation or decided to adopt low profiles, and the management process was generally impaired. Moreover, the ability of the committee to function as an organ to supervise the implementation of party and governmental policy was impaired by the pressures upon it to deal with immediate business problems (Fang, 1985; Xie, 1985).

The October 1984 policy decision on 'China's Economic Structure Reform' emphasized that the contingencies of modern industry required a unitary system of management:

Modern enterprises have a minute division of labour, a high degree of
continuity in production, strict technological requirements and complex
relations of co-operation. It is therefore necessary to establish a unified,
authoritative and highly efficient system to direct production and conduct
operations and management. This calls for a system of the director or
manager assuming full responsibility [1984: 25].

Under this new 'director responsibility system', enterprise directors are no
longer responsible to party committees but rather to the state through
holding companies and municipal or provincial bodies. Indeed, party organizations in enterprises were now called upon to 'actively support directors in
exercising their authority' (p.25), while retaining a supervisory role with
respect to the implementation of party and state policies. Although this is the
first instance of official approval for a unitary management system since
adoption of the Soviet model in the 1950s, it is claimed that the continuing
roles of party and workers' congress distinguish it from that earlier precedent
(Xie, 1985).

The central authorities had in April 1984 approved the trial implementation of the director responsibility system in six cities. The October 1984
Central Committee decision on economic reform signalled the intention to
popularize the system throughout state enterprises nationally. Articles on the
new system appeared at regular intervals in the journal *China Entrepreneur*
which was established under the auspices of the State Economic Commission
in 1985. The journal claimed that, by June 1985, 22,211 enterprises had
already adopted the system (Issue No. 9:6).

Beijing was one of the cities selected for early trials of the director
responsibility system. Of the six enterprises discussed in this paper, three
were operating the new system while the other three retained the second-
stage system whereby their directors were responsible to their party committees. Information was also available from three joint venture enterprises
which had the new system in place. This contrast permits the two systems to
be compared in both formal and operational terms.

The transition from the unified leadership of the party committee to the
stage-two system of director responsibility under the party committee's
leadership appears to have led to the clearer designation of material activities
around the formulation of plans for the enterprise, adjustments in its
organization, proposals to appoint middle managers, internal transfers of
workers, organizing production, purchasing and sales, and rewarding employees. The party committee's activities in examples of the stage-two system
include examination and approval of business plans (before these are passed
to higher authority), interviewing and approving candidates for promotion
suggested by the director, approving rewards suggested by the director,
discussing and deciding on major issues and problems in the enterprise, and
applying ideological pressures to employees including those aimed at improv-

Table 3.5 Main tasks allocated to the Director, Party Committee and Workers' Congress in the audio-visual products enterprise

Director
 1. Formulating strategic plan
 2. Examining and approving new product plan
 3. Examining and approving operational plan
 4. Assigning capital allocations
 5. Organizing production system
 6. Approving purchasing and sales contracts
 7. Adjusting organization
 8. Proposing middle management appointments
 9. Transferring employees
10. Employee motivation

Party Committee (of which the Director is a member)
 1. Discussing and deciding on enterprise strategy and development
 2. Discussing and deciding key problems in the factory
 3. Assessing cadres, rewards and approving appointments as suggested by the director
 4. Reinforcing the ideological education of employees, with particular reference to their productive performances
 5. Discussing and publishing applications of the Party's line and policy
 6. Strengthening the ideological and organization position of the Party within the enterprise

Workers' Congress
 1. Discussing the strategic and annual plans
 2. Examining the director's annual report
 3. Analysing the enterprise's economic and production situations
 4. Appraising managers, suggesting appointments to and removals from office
 5. Suggesting measures to improve task performance
 6. Pressing for improvements in working conditions and welfare

ing their performance. By way of illustration, Table 3.5 lists the main tasks formally allocated to the director, the party committee and the workers' congress in the audio-visual products enterprise.

It was apparent how the system of responsibility under the leadership of the party committee could set considerable limits to the director's power. In the heavy electrical products enterprise, the previous director had been removed under pressure from the party secretary and long-established cadres 'with deep seats in the company' when his attempts to tie down responsibilities for performance and to reform managerial practices became too uncomfortable. The director of the electrical switchgear enterprise had not even taken up the powers granted to him under the system. He was an engineer with no experience in management. He could not join the party committee since he was not a party member. Managerial initiative effectively remained with the party secretary who had been the previous director for a span of twenty years and who had only been rotated out of that post because of the new policy of promoting younger and qualified persons into management. Over that time he had built up personal friendships with many of the middle-level managers who continued to reciprocate loyalties with him. In this enterprise the director himself stated that he had to secure the agreement of the party secretary to any significant decision.

Adoption of the director responsibility system by the other three Beijing enterprises had increased the scope of the director's decision powers, though by varying amounts. In the audio products enterprise, which adopted the system at the beginning of 1985, it was reported that the only difference after nine months lay in the fact that the director could now decide on the appointment and removal of middle-level managers. The automotive enterprise, which was one of the first in the country to adopt the system in 1984, had extended the director's authority to encompass managerial appointments, salary increases, dismissal of workers (subject to the social sensitivities discussed earlier) and approval of the overall production plan. The role of the party committee appeared to have become highly reduced in the pharmaceutical enterprise. Here a good deal of the initiative which had been seized by management was ascribed by various informants to the personal determination of the university-educated lady director. Significantly, she enjoyed sponsorship from a higher level, including her selection to attend a six-month executive course staffed by American faculty. The constraints on management in this enterprise were now perceived to emanate from its holding company rather than from internal opposition.

The scope of managerial powers in joint ventures clearly represents a special case because of the direct involvement of foreign management. They are worthy of note since, judging by the three joint ventures on which information was collected, this category of Chinese enterprise embodies the least constrained system of internal managerial authority. The economic reform programme has encouraged joint ventures and they have become instruments for change in the enterprise management system. All three joint ventures involved Chinese state enterprises with a preceding history of operations. For them, entry into the joint venture provided a major stimulus to change.

In one of the joint ventures which had been formed in 1980 there was neither Party secretary nor workers' congress. The managing director was an expatriate appointed by the foreign partner. He had full responsibility and authority, with all departments reporting directly to him. The foreign partner considered that having the authority to manage was a major factor in the success of a joint venture in China. The second joint venture had only been officially approved in mid-1985, though the foreign company had previously had a Chinese partner in running its representative office. The general manager of this joint venture was a Chinese American. His deputy-general manager was a Chinese national who was also in charge of Party matters. It was stated that he would 'make arrangements' to select the company's trade-union leader. There was a separate Party secretary in the third joint venture company who saw his role, according to the Chinese director, as 'helping the director to use his powers better'. The example given to support this statement concerned the improvement of worker motivation through the Party secretary's moral persuasion. The Party secretary also served as the trade-union leader since no workers' congress had yet met to elect representatives. Senior management openly declared their wish to avoid taking that step towards democratization.

As Lockett & Littler (1983) have described in detail, it was official policy after 1978 to reinstate workers' congresses and to encourage the election of managers, particularly those below, but not necessarily excluding, the director. Regulations issued in June 1981 envisage that workers' congresses consisting of elected representatives of the workers and staff of an enterprise will take part in decisionmaking in order to supervise management. The main powers of a workers' congress were to be (1) to scrutinize the director's production plans and budgets; (2) to discuss and decide on the use of enterprise funds for welfare and bonus provisions; (3) to decide about proposed changes to the management structure, payment system or training; (4) to supervise managers to the extent of making reports to the higher authorities; and (5) to arrange the election of managers (Lockett & Littler, 1983: 695). The October 1984 decision on 'Economic Structure Reform' regarded workers' congresses and the enterprise trade union structure emanating from them as a democratic counterweight to the consolidation of managerial authority through:

> examining and discussing major decisions to be taken by the enterprises, supervising administrative leadership and safeguarding the legitimate rights and interests of the workers and staff members. All of this expresses the status of the working people as masters of the enterprise [1984: 25].

The right to elect managers was, however, no longer mentioned and in contrast the document introduces the criterion of expertise, advocating the promotion of younger personnel who are capable of acquiring and applying the knowledge now required by modern industry (ibid., pp. 32–3).

None of the directors of the six Beijing enterprises had been elected; all had been appointed by the holding companies. Current practice was that managers lower down the organization were also appointed. If they were recruited from outside the enterprise, the holding company made the decision; if promoted from inside the enterprise, the decision normally required the director's approval. Even first-line supervisors ('workgroup leaders') were no longer elected by their work groups, as had been previous practice. It would be usual for managerial appointments below the director to be discussed with the Party committee and the committee would have to approve these where it still exercised formal leadership. Moreover, whereas directors previously enjoyed tenure of office, they are now appointed on limited-term contracts which can only be renewed twice. In large state-owned enterprises, directors are given four-year contracts, and in medium or small enterprises, two-year contracts (Xie, 1985).

From May 1984, the appointment procedure for directors was widened to include the possibilities of consultation within the enterprise, recommendation from within the enterprise, and invitation of outside candidates. The appointment of the director in the pharmaceutical enterprise provides an example. Holding company staff met with middle managers to sound out their opinions on suitable candidates, and the views of the Party secretary and trade-union leader were also solicited. The holding company then made the appointment. This particular enterprise had also held an election to put forward potential candidates for future directorial appointments for the holding company to hold on file.

The reported frequency at which workers' congresses met ranged from 'two or three times a year' to nil. Table 3.5 listed the tasks formally undertaken by one of the active workers' congresses, in the audio-visual products enterprise. However, the only reported instances of active participation by worker representatives in decisionmaking concerned personnel issues. In the automotive enterprise a managerial proposal to change the payment system was submitted to workers' congress representatives following approval by a joint meeting of management with party officials, trade-union officers and the youth league leader. In the audio-visual products enterprise an instance was cited where a reduction in profit had reduced workers' and cadres' bonuses, leading to a complaint by the workers' congress. In such circumstances generated by disappointing performance, the workers' congress, exercising its supervisory role, could demand the director's dismissal, though this had not in fact happened. In several enterprises it was also said that the leading congress deputy, in his or her capacity as trade-union leader, became involved in discussions on managerial appointments.

Overall, the enterprise director responsibility system is still in a state of evolution and is probably at present taken to its furthest extent in joint ventures. Although the system of leadership which is formally in operation undoubtedly affects the boundaries to managerial authority, local factors appear also to be influential. These include the experience and personality of the director and Party secretary, the network of supporting relationships and upward channels of influence they may command, and the mutual accommodation they reach accordingly. The role of the workers' congress as a platform for democratic management is muted, except on occasions where the interests of employees are directly concerned. It may come to play a more active part if and when issues of contention arise around the flexible incentives and possibilities of contract non-renewal which are envisaged in the government's labour system reform approved by the State Council in September 1986.

Conclusions

The managements of Chinese state enterprises are being accorded a greater degree of responsibility in areas such as marketing and purchasing, and they appear to be learning how to use this, albeit slowly. In line with the stated intention of the reform programme, this enables them to increase their direct involvement in market transactions and to decrease their dependence upon plans formulated at a higher level. However, the situation on the ground appears to be considerably more varied and problematic than is allowed for by official specifications of enterprise reform, even though these do recognize the complexities of the urban industrial sector.

A variety of accommodations to the problematics of relations between subsidiary companies (or divisions) and controlling groups have been identified in capitalist countries and in this respect the Chinese case is not exceptional (cf. Brooke & Remmers, 1970; Grinyer & Spencer, 1979). One school of thought seeks to account for such variations primarily in terms of the different environmental and operational contingencies which have to be accommodated in a given situation, and it therefore looks to discover predictable relationships which apply to many organizations. Others regard the configuration of powers and responsibilities between levels as the product of historical and contemporary features that are unique to each organization and which are more substantially cultural and political in their nature.

Certain aspects of the distribution of decision powers among the Beijing enterprises hint at accountable regularities of a more general kind: for instance, that enterprises more strategically located in terms of their contribution to national plans for key products, such as the automotive company, will be granted less autonomy than others in respect of marketing policy. This kind of inter-enterprise variation in responsibility is consistent with the official reform line that 'concrete forms of the responsibility system [should be] suited to their specific conditions' (Communist Party of China, 1984: 24) and expresses a clear contingency perspective.

It has also become apparent, however, that the present state of economic reform at enterprise level cannot simply be ascribed either to official intentionality or to strategic and operational contingencies. Specific local factors are significant. Not least among these are the connectedness and disposition of key factors within the multiple power networks described by the enterprise's plural internal organs and its several higher authorities. There were several examples indicating how the operation of the director responsibility system was shaped by the situated power enjoyed by a single individual or by mutual accommodation between major factors, as in two of the joint ventures. While reliable evidence was not available on the operation of such factors in relations between the enterprise and higher authorities, commentary in the Chinese press points to them having a key bearing on the autonomy that enterprise management is effectively able to secure.

The threads of connectedness and reciprocated relationship (*guanxi*) draw upon a deep well of Chinese traditional culture. Chinese tradition is a third fundamental which, alongside central socialist planning and increasing exposure to the regulative role of the market, must enter into any analysis that strives to account for behaviour in Chinese industry and, in that respect, for how reform is actually working out. An attempt has been made elsewhere to lay certain foundations for such analysis, and it is beyond the scope of this paper (Boisot & Child, 1986). What may be said here is that the tendency of the Chinese reformers to contrast their programme with centralized bureaucratic regulation in the Soviet tradition, or of some Western journalists to frame the situation within a markets versus hierarchy perspective, is not sufficient. It overlooks that texture of tradition which gives rise to the distinctively 'Chinese characteristics' which are, if anything, reasserting themselves now that they have returned to ideological acceptability.

There is clearly a need for investigation into Chinese enterprise reform which extends further in both depth and coverage of cases. Additional enlightenment of the way that the two responsibility systems operate will require access to the dynamics of relations firstly between enterprises and higher authorities, and secondly among the leading groups within enterprises. Such investigation will need to be sensitive to cultural and informal features, and it should go well beyond the exposure which has so far been permitted to foreigners. It is a project which thus lends itself to collaboration with the emergent body of Chinese researchers.

References

Azumi, K. & McMillan, C. J. (1981). 'Management Strategy and Organisation Structure: A Japanese Comparative Study', in D. J. Hickson & C. J. McMillan (eds) *Organisation and Nation*. Farnborough, Gower.

Beijing Review (24 March 1986) 'Communiqué on the Statistics of 1985 Economic and Social Development': 27–33.

Ibid. (14 April 1986). 'Reform Guarantees Fulfilment of New Plan': 26–28.

Ibid. (16 June 1986). 'Enterprises Demand More Power': 6–7.

Ibid. (21 July 1986) 'Planning and the Market by Chen Yun': 14–15.

Ibid. (28 July 1986) 'Reformers Merit Moral Support': 5–6.

Ibid. (15 September 1986) 'Labour Reform: Making a Dint [sic] in the 'Iron Rice Bowl'": 16–17.

Boisot, M. & Child, J. (1986). 'Efficiency, Ideology and Tradition in the Choice of Transactions Governance Structures—The Case of China'. Unpublished paper.

Brooke, M. Z. & Remmers, H. L. (1970). *The Strategy of Multinational Enterprise*. London, Longman.

Child, J. (1973). 'Predicting and Understanding Organisation Structure'. *Administrative Science Quarterly*, 18: 168–85.

Child, J. & Kieser, A. (1979). 'Organisation and Managerial Roles in British and West German Companies: An Examination of the Culture-Free Thesis', in C. J. Lammers & D. J. Hickson (eds), *Organisations Alike and Unlike*. London, Routledge & Kegan Paul.

China Business Report (13 August 1986). 'Move Towards Free Labour Market': 1.

China Entrepreneur (September 1986). 'Problems that Must be Clear and Solved when Promoting the Director Responsibility System': 6.

Communist Party of China (1984). *China's Economic Structure Reform—Decision of the CPC Central Committee (October 1984)*. Beijing, Foreign Languages Press.

Fang (1985). Interview by the writer with Mrs Fang, former Party secretary in a construction company, September. (Full name withheld to preserve anonymity.)

Grinyer, P. H. & Spencer, J. C. (1979). *Turnaround—Managerial Recipes for Strategic Success*. London, Associated Business Press.

Huang Xiang (1985). 'On Reform of Chinese Economic Structure'. *Beijing Review*, 20 May: 15–19.

Littler, C.R. (1985). 'Work outside the Capitalist Framework: The Case of China', in R. Deem & G. Salaman (eds) *Work, Culture and Society*. Milton Keynes, Open University Press.

Lockett, M. (1985a). 'Cultural Revolution and Industrial Organisation in a Chinese Enterprise: The Beijing General Knitwear Mill 1966–1981'. *Templeton College Management Research Papers*, 85/7, Oxford.

Lockett, M. (1985b). 'Culture and the Problems of Chinese Management'. *Templeton College Management Research Papers*, 85/8, Oxford.

Lockett, M. & Littler, C. R. (1983). 'Trends in Chinese Enterprise Management 1978–1982'. *World Development*, **11**: 683–704.

McMillan, C. J., Hickson, D. J., Hinings, C. R. and Schneck, R. E. (1981). 'The Structure of Work Organisation across Societies', in D. J. Hickson & C. J. McMillan (eds), *Organisation and Nation*. Farnborough, Gower.

Oborne, M. (1986). 'Industrial Organisation in China', paper presented to Conference on 'Chinese Culture and Management' organised by The *Economist*. Paris, January.

Pugh, D. S., Hickson, D. J., Hinings, C. R. & Turner, C. (1968). 'Dimensions of Organisation Structure'. *Administrative Science Quarterly*, **13**: 65–105.

Pugh, D. S. & Hinings, C. R. (eds) (1976). *Organisational Structure: Extensions and Replications*. Farnborough, Saxon House.

World Bank (1985). *China: Long Term Issues and Options*. Washington, DC.

Xie Yu Jao (1985). Interviews by the writer with Mr Xie, Enterprise Administration Bureau, State Economic Commission, Beijing. 30 September and 5 October.

Appendix

List of Decisions or Responsibilities Investigated

Marketing
1. introducing a new product
2. the price of products: in the plan
3. the price of products: outside the plan
4. the type of market to supply (type of outlet, type of customer)
5. the geographical spread of selling (in China, exporting, etc.)
6. the priority of different product orders and deliveries

Purchasing
7. which suppliers of materials to have
8. the procedure for purchasing (e.g. whether to ask for several quotes, order quantities, terms of contract)

Production and Work Allocation
9. the overall production plan (annual) adopted
10. the scheduling of work (up to one month) against given plans
11. the allocation of work to be done among the available workers

12. which machines or equipment are to be used
13. the methods of work to be used (not involving new expenditure)
14. when overtime will be worked

Quality Control
15. what items will be inspected (including what %)—inward supplies
16. what items will be inspected (including what %)—completed products

Work Study
17. which production operations will be work studied (have industrial engineering applied)

Maintenance
18. the maintenance schedule or procedure

R & D
19. what research and development work will be done (i.e. how much and what priority)

Investment and Accounting
20. the level of expenditure on new capital equipment
21. the type or make of new capital equipment
22. what will be costed: to which items the costing system is applied
23. what unbudgeted money can be spent on capital items
24. what unbudgeted money can be spent on revenue/consumable items

Staffing
25. the numbers of workgroup leaders/supervisors
26. appointing workers from outside the factory
27. appointing supervisors from outside the factory
28. appointing managers from outside the factory
29. the size of the total workforce
30. the total numbers of managers above work-group leader level
31. the promotion of production workers
32. the promotion of work-group leaders/supervisors
33. the salaries of production workers
34. the salaries of cadres
35. the methods for selecting new workers and cadres

Discipline
36. dismiss a worker
37. dismiss or demote a supervisor or manager (cadre)

Training
38. the training someone will have

Welfare
39. what welfare facilities and how many are provided

Organization Structure
40. altering responsibilities/areas of work of non-production departments
41. altering responsibilities/area of work of production departments
42. creating a new department
43. creating a new non-production job
44. creating a new production job

Office Systems
45. the design of office systems (including use of computers)

Representation of Management
46. who is the most junior person who can deputize for the Director in his absence?

Who is the most junior person who can represent management in:
47. discussions with the Party Secretary
48. discussions with the Trade Union leader (or Workers' Congress leader)

4 Enterprise Autonomy in the Beijing Municipality

Nigel Campbell

The economic reforms in China, so successful in the agricultural area, are now influencing the industrial sector at an accelerating pace. Almost every day China's leaders exhort factory directors to take more responsibility and improve the performance of their enterprises. On 11 September 1985 the State Council approved some new regulations to improve the vitality of large and medium-sized enterprises. The fourteen regulations included more autonomy for state enterprises from municipal authorities and government departments and more decentralized management within the large enterprises.

The purpose of this chapter is to present a 'snapshot' of the extent of autonomy enjoyed by six state enterprises in the Beijing municipality in the autumn of 1985. How far do the managers of these enterprises control their own destinies? To what extent are they still tied to the apron-strings of municipal authorities and government departments?

The opportunity to study this question arose out of the author's involvement as a visiting professor with the China–EEC Management Training Programme, which operates in close collaboration with six Beijing enterprises. The research was carried out in parallel to that undertaken by Child (see previous chapter). The impetus for the research arose out of meetings with the factory directors when they were asked in what areas they would like additional freedoms in order to develop their factories more successfully. The answers varied over a wide area, including pricing, recruitment, and salaries and bonus and prompted further discussion of these questions with the Chinese faculty at the Training Centre, followed by thorough analysis of documents describing the six enterprises, which the students had produced, as part of their course-work (for background on management training in China, see Lindsay and Dempsey, 1983; Warner, 1986; Warner, in this volume).

This chapter attempts to analyse what freedom the managers have in six state enterprises to make certain important business decisions, going into greater detail on a number of selected areas than the previous chapter. The decisions covered in this chapter are listed below.

Labour	– Recruitment
Management	– Punishment and Dismissal
	– Incentives—salaries and bonus
Marketing	– Pricing
	– Selection of customers and amount sold to customers
	– Product range
Purchasing	– Choice of suppliers and price paid.

This is not an exhaustive list. For example, financial decisions about the retention and use of profits, bank borrowings, and access to foreign exchange are excluded. One reason for excluding the financial decisions is that in this area there may be less difference between Chinese enterprises and subsidiary companies in the West. In the West, subsidiaries are usually subject to strict financial control. In the Norcros group no individual subsidiary can borrow money or retain its surplus cash. The superficial similarity between a Chinese factory and a subsidiary in a Western industrial group makes it tempting to try and draw comparisons between the two. This chapter deliberately avoids this opportunity, which is of doubtful validity, and would, in any case, require a separate chapter of its own. Rather, the aim is to provide as accurate a picture as possible of what is actually happening in rather more detail than the previous chapter, in the six enterprises which will provide a benchmark for subsequent work.

The chapter starts with a brief introduction to China's labyrinthine planning system. This is followed by an account of industry in the Beijing Municipality, which provides the setting for a description of the six Beijing enterprises on which this study is based. The results of the analysis are then presented in the following order: first, labour management; second, marketing; and third and last, purchasing.

State Planning System

With all the attention given in the popular press to Deng Xiaoping's economic reforms, it is easy to forget that China is still very much a centrally planned economy. (See Barnett, 1981, Richman, 1969). Figure 4.1 is a simplified diagram of the reporting relationships between state and collective enterprises and their various higher authorities. The Chinese use the word 'shanji danwei' for higher authority, which, strictly speaking, means 'upper unit'. In this chapter the term higher authority is used to convey the combined direction and control which is part of the Chinese bureaucratic hierarchy.

Reporting relationships

In Figure 4.1 some state enterprises report directly to central ministries, while others report through municipal (Beijing, Shanghai and Tianjin) or

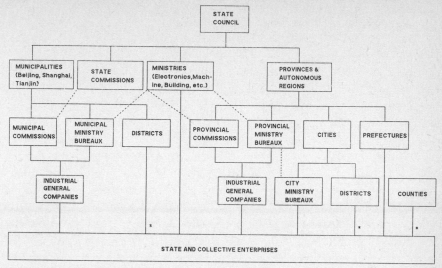

Figure 4.1 China's state planning system

provincial authorities. The first level below the State Council is made up of municipalities, provinces, ministries and state commissions. At the next level, Figure 4.1 shows that the three municipalities and provinces have commissions and ministry branch offices, often called bureaux, correspond-ing to those at the national level. These commissions and bureaux supervise industrial general companies, each of which, in turn, controls the activities of a number of factories and research institutes. As Figure 4.1 illustrates, most enterprises report to two higher authorities, which in turn report to two ultimate masters—a technical ministry and a State Commission, usually the State Economic Commission.

Municipalities control district organizations which supervise smaller enterprises, which are normally organized as collectives. In the provinces the major cities are also divided into districts; and some of these districts have ministry bureaux looking after state enterprises in that city. Outside the cities the prefectures control state enterprises directly and collective enterprises through their county sub-divisions.

A specific example of reporting relationships is found in Figure 4.2 which shows how the Beijing Recorder and TV factories fit in with the Ministry of Electronics and with the State Economic Commission. It is clear, from the figure, that subordination is an important principle in China. Every enter-prise must be subordinate to some higher authority. The same applies to individuals and it is normal when you meet someone, for the first time, to ask which *danwei* (work unit) he or she belongs to.

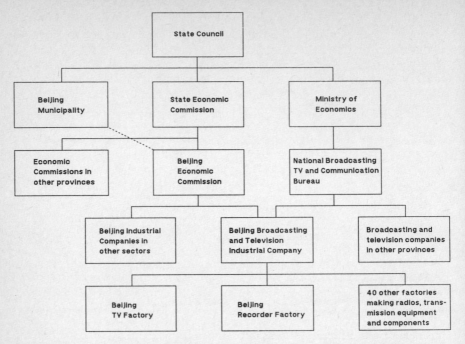

Figure 4.2   Higher authorities for television and recorder companies

Setting plans and targets

Before the economic reforms started, state enterprises were just production units, completely subordinate to a higher authority which provided the finance, took the sales income, and decided all details of the production plan. In other words, all decisionmaking power was concentrated in the hands of the higher authority.

In the case of the Recorder and TV factories, the Beijing Economic Commission issued financial targets for profit, tax and output to the Beijing Broadcasting and Television Industrial Company (BBTIC). BBTIC also received quantity targets from the Ministry of Electronics through the National Broadcasting, TV and Communication Bureau. These covered production and sales, and included allocations of materials, components and foreign exchange.

With these two inputs and taking account of provisional plans submitted by the Recorder and TV factories, BBTIC made its own comprehensive plan and issued it to each factory under its jurisdiction. Until 1984 each factory had twenty or more targets or indicators on which it had to report regularly, normally every month, but sometimes every day. Although the process of economic reform started in 1978 and experiments with state enterprises had been going on for some time, it was not until May 1984 that the State Council formally announced that state enterprises should have more authority in ten aspects, including planning, sales, prices, purchasing, disposal of assets, organization, and wages and salaries. Although the number of targets and indicators has now been reduced, the principle of subordination to a higher authority remains. Of course subsidiaries in the West are also controlled by their parent company, but in the West the emphasis is more on financial control and less on output targets and there is no equivalent of the daunting hierarchy of levels all the way up to the State Council.

In addition to the reporting system the BBTIC controls the activities of the factories by enforcing the technical and quality standards laid down by the ministry, by its allocation of components and raw materials, by auditing the operations and by controlling the prices which the factories can charge.

Official Categories of Materials

In China all materials are now divided into three classes. Class I is for basic raw materials, such as steel, coal and aluminium—vital for the nation's economy—and rice, wheat, grain and fuel—vital for people's livelihood. State enterprises which require these materials in large quantities must apply to their higher authority which will then allocate them a quota to be obtained from specific suppliers. However, increasingly these quotas only amount to 40–60 per cent of what the enterprise needs. The balance it must obtain by itself. Class II materials, such as standard components, tools and other important industrial products, are obtained by the enterprise by direct contact with the appropriate material supply company. Finally, for Class III materials, the enterprise can make direct contact with the producer without any intervention by official bodies.

Industry in the Beijing Municipality

The six enterprises with which this chapter is concerned are all in the Beijing municipality. Beijing, like the other major cities of Shanghai and Guangzhou, holds the same position in China's administrative structure as a province. The municipality has an area of 16,800 sq. kms and in 1983 the population was 9.3 million.

Beijing is an industrial as well as an administrative centre. In 1983, industry accounted for 70.9 per cent of the municipality's output, compared to 8.6 per cent for agriculture. A construction boom is under way, which contributes 11.7 per cent to Beijing's output, with the balance made up of commercial activity, transport, post and telecommunications.

In 1983 most of Beijing's 1,690,000 industrial workforce were employed by state enterprises, but there were also collective enterprises, a handful of enterprises jointly owned by collectives and the state and two joint ventures.

Table 4.1 Industrial statistics—Beijing municipality, 1983

	Number of Enterprises	Output Rmb (billions)	Number of Employees
State Enterprises	1,124	20.10	1,152,000
Collective Enterprises	2,874	4.79	527,000
State Collective Enterprises	11	0.10	10,000
Foreign Joint Ventures	2	0.03	1,000
Total	4,011	25.02	1,690,000

Source: Beijing Municipality

The employment and output statistics for these enterprises are given in Table 4.1.

As the data in Table 4.1 indicate, the collectively-owned enterprises are much smaller than the state enterprises. For the most part they are small factories set up by the communes making handicrafts, light industrial products, or undertaking sub-contract work for state enterprises. One large and prosperous commune close to Beijing was reported to have three hundred small factories and to be deriving a good part of its income from their output.

The Six Beijing Enterprises

The six enterprises which form the basis of this study were drawn exclusively from the state enterprise sector, and were the same firms as those covered in the Child study (see previous chapter). Based on output, the value of fixed assets and the number of production machines, state enterprises are classified as large, medium and small. In Beijing in 1983, there were 291 large and medium enterprises, the others being classified as small.

Obviously, six enterprises cannot be representative of a total population of over one thousand. Thus, the sample included two medium-sized, but no large enterprises. The activity of the six enterprises covered trucks, pharmaceuticals, switchgear, televisions, tape recorders and transformers. There was no enterprise making chemicals or textiles, although in 1983 these sectors represented 20 per cent and 16 per cent respectively of Beijing's industrial output. The machinery sector, which formed 28 per cent of output, was better represented by the truck, transformer and switchgear enterprises.

Factory directors' perception of problems

Table 4.2 is an analysis of the responses to an open-ended question about the areas in which the factory directors would like additional freedom. Of the seventeen points mentioned, nearly half relate to labour problems of recruiting and dismissing workers and setting wage levels. Each company mentioned one or other as a problem and two companies mentioned both hiring and firing and lack of flexibility in setting wage levels.

Greater freedom to set price levels was mentioned by three companies. These companies wanted to increase their margins by raising prices. Two companies mentioned that they wished there were fewer restrictions on what they could do with the financial surpluses they generated. One of these companies would also have liked to be able to retain more of the foreign exchange generated by its exports.

Two companies indicated that they would like greater freedom to select suppliers. In one case the director explained that they had wanted to obtain a component from West Germany, but had been unable to do so because of a lack of foreign exchange. In China, obtaining supplies is far more difficult

Table 4.2 Freedom desired by factory directors
Question: In what areas would you like more freedom?

Freedom is wanted to:	Number of mentions	Number of times mentioned first
Recruit and dismiss workers	5	2
Set wage levels	3	—
Set prices	3	1
Use their financial surplus	2	2
Select suppliers	2	—
Determine type and quantity of products produced	1	1
Use foreign exchange they generate	1	—
Total	17	6

Source: Company interviews

than selling the product; in consequence, purchasing departments are normally larger than marketing ones. Finally, one factory director was concerned about restrictions on the type and quantity of products which his enterprise could produce. The higher authority had assigned the production of a certain range of products to his factory and he was not allowed to make products assigned to other factories, nor to develop product variations, without permission.

To summarize, enterprise directors attach most importance to having greater freedom in the recruitment, dismissal and control of their workforce. This is similar to the results obtained by Child (see previous chapter). Next, they would like more freedom to set prices and to dispose of the surplus which they generate. Since labour management questions seem most important, they are discussed first.

Recruitment and dismissal

From the interviews with the factory directors it is clear that this is one of the most important areas in which they would like additional freedom. Strictly speaking, recruitment can be divided between replacing employees who have left or retired and adding to the number of employees. Usually there is no problem in getting permission to replace employees and very often this is done by employing a relative of the person who retires, or by recruiting from the relatives of other workers. In fact, because of the unemployment problem, quite a number of workers in their fifties will retire early in order to give their children an opportunity to get a job.

Where the company is expanding and needs additional workers, it can obtain them by applying for them through the higher authority, or it may obtain additional staff from its own training school, or some school jointly administered with the local authority. Finally, there are other informal methods.

The normal method is for the factory to ask its higher authority to allocate additional workers to meet its needs—which could be for graduates or just production workers. The extent to which the factory can then actually choose from the workers who are available depends on the relationship between the factory and its higher authority. Sometimes they may simply have to accept those people who are allocated. In other cases they may be able to look at the files of the potential recruits and have some influence over which ones come to their factory. If you want to have the best student you may also have to accept one who is not so good!

The second method is for the factory, if it is large enough, to establish its own technical training school which would recruit students from the local middle school. After graduation, most of the students will work in that factory. If the factory is too small to have its own training school it may nevertheless be able to recruit from a training school established by its higher authority for the purpose of providing recruits in the factories under its control. These schools normally train people to be technical workers or middle-level managers (see Warner, 1986). Another possibility is for the factory, instead of, or in addition to having its own training school, to run a vocational high school jointly with the local authority. Again this provides a source of recruits.

In addition to these normal methods of recruitment there are, of course, a number of informal methods which the factory can use to obtain the qualified staff it requires. For example, the factory directors or senior managers may be able to get permission to recruit relatives or other people because of their personal connections. In addition, there have been reports of factories making payments to the university in order to get the opportunity to select the best students.

The greatest freedom in recruitment is where the factory only seeks to employ temporary workers such as cleaners, porters and people to prepare the hot water for tea. Such people can be recruited without restriction so long as the total number of employees in the company does not exceed the agreed figure. The small collective enterprises such as restaurants and small factories on the commune can usually recruit directly since the numbers involved are quite small in relation to total employment in China.

Dismissals

The situation in China with respect to dismissals is changing quite rapidly and regulations are not applied uniformly throughout the country. The most recent change has been the introduction of a category of employee which is referred to as a contract employee, to distinguish him/her from permanent employees. Basically, permanent employees are those who were recruited before the end of 1985: they still belong to those who 'eat from the iron rice bowl'. They are almost impossible to dismiss unless they commit a crime and are sentenced by the court, or fail to come to work for several months. Even if they work badly or create trouble it is very difficult to get rid of them. The only thing the factory can do is to change their job to a less attractive position and perhaps also reduce their salary.

On the other hand, those recruited after the end of 1985, other than college graduates, are referred to as contract employees. They have the same salary and conditions as the permament employees, but when they join they have to sign a contract which states that they can be dismissed if they break the disciplinary rules, etc. This contract normally has a three- to six-month probationary period and then it is renewed every two or three years, assuming that the employee continues to work satisfactorily. Since this system is new there is not yet much experience of how it will operate, but it is unlikely that companies will be easily able to cancel the contract unless there is some serious misbehaviour.

Salaries and bonus

There are many different types of worker in China. The two most common are cadres and workers, but there are also teachers, technicians, soldiers, and so on. This section concentrates on salaries and bonuses for cadres and workers, but unfortunately the distinction is not very clear. It is possible for two people doing the same job to be in different categories—one cadre and one worker; and many workers earn more then cadres. In general, cadres are better educated and undertake administrative jobs.

The salary system in China is very complex. Basic salary depends on a person's grade. In state enterprises there are eight grades for workers, fifteen grades for technical personnel and twenty-five grades for cadres. This grading system was established soon after 1949 and is still being used. The basic salary is then adjusted by one of eight regional allowances to compensate for cost-of-living differences in different regions. There are eight differ-

Table 4.3 Workers' and cadres' salaries

WORKERS								
Grade	1	2	3	4	5	6	7	8
Salary ¥	34	41	49	58	69	82	96	112
CADRES								
Grade	25	24	23	22	21	20	19	18
Salary ¥	36	41	49	56	64	73	84	96

Source: Company interviews

ent regional adjustments. In addition, there are adjustments by ministry, so that workers in heavy industry get a further supplement. Collective enterprises have the same grading system, but the basic salaries for workers are usually a little lower than in state-owned enterprises (salaries for cadres are the same). The two salary levels overlap and the grades are separate. A cadre with a high salary will have a low grade, whereas a worker with a high salary will have a high grade.

There is another type of salary supplement which is called a 'floating salary'. This was introduced in 1984 and applies only to employees with more than six years' service. These employees got an increase in salary of one grade, equivalent to an average of ¥7 per month. This salary addition only continued to apply if the employee stayed in the same factory. In other words, it was designed to prevent too many people from moving.

In 1985 it was announced that if a person occupied a responsible post and was in charge of other people, then he would receive an additional supplement based on his job level, provided that his work group performed its tasks correctly. Thus, in the Switchgear factory the director receives a responsibility supplement of ¥25, the deputy-director ¥20, the section chief ¥15, the group head ¥5 and the vice-group head ¥4.

Up to 1983 the bonus payments were controlled by the state. However, in 1984 a bonus tax was introduced, such that if the total bonus in a year exceeded two and a half month's worth of the salary bill, the enterprise would have to pay tax on the extra amount. In 1985, the limit was raised to four months, and a progressive tax was introduced—100 per cent tax for bonus equivalent to more than four months' salary, and 200 per cent for more than five months' salary. While the total amount of bonus is controlled by these regulations, the factory has some flexibility in how the bonus is distributed where there are a number of workers in a workshop. It is usual to have a system of points related to different aspects of the job. For example, there may be points for output, quality, cleanliness, timekeeping, and so on. The manager in charge of the workshop will award points for each of these qualities to each worker every month and this will determine the worker's bonus. On the basis of these points, the worker will either receive a first-class, second-class or third-class bonus. The workshop manager normally receives the average bonus of his work group.

The bonus calculation for cadres is somewhat different since they receive a fixed bonus as a percentage of salary related to the job they are doing. For example, the factory director would receive 50 per cent of his salary as bonus, the deputy-director 45 per cent, the section chief 40 per cent, the technician 25 per cent and the section worker 15 per cent.

It is evident from this discussion that there is a difference between the bonus arrangement for workers and those for cadres. The workers' bonus is more directly related to their performance than the bonus given to cadres who receive it automatically. One of the problems with the bonus system is that a bonus of at least ¥10–20 per month is becoming so common that everyone expects to receive it automatically; only a bonus of two or three times this amount is now likely to motivate people to work hard.

This brief summary confirms the restrictions that apply to all state enterprises. They do not give the factory director much flexibility in motivating his workforce. Fortunately, there is an alternative, since it is important to appreciate that a person's total remuneration is made up of salary, welfare payments, fringe benefits and bonus.

In the transformer factory the proportions are similar except that the cadre receives more of his remuneration in fringe benefits (housing, transport, etc.) and less in bonus. In practice, it seems that it is easier to provide a good employee with some extra fringe benefits rather than try to get him some additional bonus. Fringe benefits are less carefully controlled than bonus and salary payments.

Marketing

Marketing (and applied behavioural science—see Wong, 1979), it must be remembered, is a relatively new subject of both study and practice. In the early part of the twentieth century many manufacturers could sell all they produced. There was no need for a special emphasis on selling. Nowadays, however, production exceeds supply and firms must compete for the customer's attention. China is forty to fifty years behind the West and, consequently, marketing is very under-developed (see Livingstone, in this volume).

Seller's market

In the main, factories can sell all their output and managers have had little need to worry about what the consumer wants. The truck company even went so far as to put a notice in the newspaper telling customers that it did not have any spare parts! The same company is described as acting as an emperor in front of all its customers. It spends less than one-thousandth of one per cent of sales on marketing. This may seem rather extreme, but the situation has arisen because up to 1984 over 99 per cent of the truck factory's sales were allocated by the state plan. Each year the central planner organizes a trade fair to which only one distributor from each province is normally admitted. The truck factory and the distributor each receive a copy of the official allocation form and the only negotiation is about the delivery schedule.

In a seller's market customers are struggling to find a way to obtain the products they need. To avoid inconveniencing the transformer factory, one of its main customers set up a transformer repair centre to solve problems of quality!

Friendly competition

Where more than one company does supply the market, competition is often muted or non-existent. Again, this applies more to industrial than consumer products. A few years ago in Beijing there was a great demand for certain types of transformer which could not be met by the Transformer factory. The Dalian and Ningbo transformer factories were therefore invited into the market by the Beijing municipality. The three companies share the market peacefully. Historically, China has never encouraged competition, hence the party directive to 'fill a vacancy and complement each other!'

In addition to stifling competition between regions, the municipal or provincial authorities are quite capable of obstructing competition in their own area. Again, the example is from the Beijing transformer market. In addition to the Beijing Transformer factory there is another small transformer company called Tongxian Transformer factory which has a similar product range. Despite the fact that the products of this factory are of poor quality, the Beijing Power Supply Bureau must still buy from them. The municipal authority instructs them to do so to prevent the firm going out of business.

Marketing in the Six Enterprises

Although China is backward in its development of marketing, Chinese products must still be priced, promoted, packaged and distributed. Furthermore, new products must be developed or existing products improved. In the West, the managers of independent companies are free to make their own decisions. Even when the company is part of a closely-knit group, marketing decisions are normally left to managers on the spot, with sister companies encouraged to trade with each other on an arms-length basis. Of course the situation is different in a centrally planned economy. This section attempts to spell out how much freedom the six companies have acquired under the economic reforms.

The Recorder and Switchgear factories sell three-quarters of their output direct to end-users; for the transformer company the proportion is one-third, while for the other three the great bulk of sales goes to state wholesalers. The low importance given to marketing and selling is reflected in the insignificant sums devoted to marketing expenses and the small number of salesmen employed by even the largest firms.

Pricing

Before the economic reforms, all prices were set by the state. For example, in the engineering industry when a new product was launched, the ministry calculated its average cost among all the producers, decided an average profit and added them together to set a price for all the enterprises. Enterprises had no power to change the price, no matter how the cost or demand altered. The price was fixed and it lasted for many years. This pattern of stable prices still persisted up to 1984 for tape decks, recorded cassettes, travel switches and light trucks. Where prices have changed they have as often as not gone down, as in the case of televisions and pocket radios; only those of electromagnetic clutches have increased slightly. This indicates the high degree of control still exercised by the state over prices.

Some form of price control still exists in all factories. Either prices have to be agreed with the higher authority or they can only be changed within prescribed limits. It is clear that the economic reforms have so far led to only limited changes and, judging from the six Beijing enterprises, there is a great variety in the regulation and in the ways in which they are applied. Where price flexibility is allowed, it is usually 20 per cent of the agreed price. This flexibility applies to the products of the Pharmaceutical Switchgear factories: often the higher authority will allow the factory to make price reductions, without consultation, but price increases require permission! Where the product moves through a distribution channel, then the margin available to wholesalers and retailers is also controlled.

In some circumstances the factory can sell its surplus production, the extra produced over plan targets, at genuine market prices. Thus, the market price of light trucks is ¥28,350, compared to the state price of ¥15,950. This huge differential reflects the unsatisfied demand and the fact that in 1984 the Truck factory only had one hundred out of 14,600 trucks to sell on this free market. The situation is different for the Transformer factory which can only sell its surplus at 20 per cent above the state price.

Several firms mentioned that another way to get a higher price was for the firm's products to be awarded a quality prize. Regular assessments take place, usually organized by a technical department of the ministry concerned. Manufacturers can then charge 20 per cent more for the winning products than their competitors. In a seller's market the extra price flows through directly as profit and allows the firm to pay higher bonuses to managers and workers. Managers at the Television factory had set themselves a target of winning the quality prize in the next year or so.

During the interviews questions were asked about the firm's freedom to change prices following product improvements or to set the price for new products. In both cases the firm can suggest a price to its higher authority, but must wait for approval before implementing it. Undoubtedly, approvals are being given more quickly but the controls still exist.

The general impression is of the pervasive influence of price controls. Even in the transformer factory, the director reported that the state was in the process of introducing a system to control the pricing of non-standard items. Freedom to set prices was probably greatest in the pharmaceutical firm and they had used their freedom effectively to push a competitor out of one market and to enhance their profit margin in another area. However, this is an isolated example and it will probably be many years before we see pricing being used normally as a competitive weapon.

Product Policy

Before the economic reforms, as has already been explained, the planning authorities made all the decisions and the factories simply produced what the planners decided on. Since 1984, there has been a gradual loosening of central control, but each factory's higher authority is still actively involved in decisions about the product range which the factories under its supervision will manufacture. This is obviously necessary in the case of companies like the Beijing Broadcasting and TV Industrial Company, which has more than twenty different factories under its supervision. A competitive free-for-all between these companies is a possible development for the future but it has certainly not yet arrived. These restrictions are particularly irksome for the TV factory which, for some time, has wanted to produce television sets with remote-control switches and has also wanted to expand into the market for video cassette recorders. It has been refused permission to do this by its higher authority. Equally, it has been refused permission to stop the production of black-and-white televisions.

Another example is in the Switchgear factory, where the management felt that it took too long for their proposed new product to get into the development plan of the ministry. The Switchgear factory is the leading supplier of travel switches in China and they wanted to develop a new type of travel switch and felt that they were asked to wait longer than was necessary before this was approved. In the case of the Switchgear factory it is not simply approval from the ministry that is necessary, the factory must also obtain the approval of the municipal authorities. This requirement for dual approval is one of the bureaucratic features of the existing system which will come under increasing pressure as the economic reforms continue.

Although there are restrictions on new product development, there are also some incentives. In the Recorder factory a new tape deck will be exempt from taxation for two years.

Another example of state intervention is found in the transformer market where the ministry has decided that only certain types of energy-saving transformers should be made and from 1986 onwards the Transformer factory will have to comply with this central decision.

Choice of Customers

There are considerable differences between the six factories in their freedom to choose their customers. At one extreme, the Truck factory has almost no choice and delivers 99 per cent of its output to state supply companies. The Transformer and TV companies also sell two-thirds of their production to state wholesalers. On the other hand, the Recorder and Switchgear factories are much less dependent on their products being distributed through state wholesalers and they have direct dealings with individual customers and the opportunity to develop direct relationships with them. For example, in the case of the Switchgear factory there are three or four trade meetings each year attended by the machine-tool manufacturers, materials suppliers and other interested companies. The switchgear factory takes advantage of these meetings to promote its product directly to the end-users and to make sales contracts with them. In fact about 35 per cent of annual sales are secured at these meetings. The balance of sales is made as a result of direct visits to customers to introduce the company's products. The Switchgear factory's salesmen travel throughout China and have sold everywhere other than Tibet and Taiwan. In constrast, the TV factory really only has freedom to choose customers in the Beijing area, where they can use a small portion of their output—about 10 per cent—to improve their relationships with suppliers and the higher authorities. Despite the restriction on the TV company from selling products other than to the main wholesalers, it has had to set up a national repair and service centre in order to make sure that the Peony brand has a good reputation throughout the country. The Recorder factory also does a lot of its business through trade meetings and, whereas before 1983 all contracts for tape decks were signed at the two trade fairs organized by the ministry, the Recorder factory is now able to arrange its own meetings and to invite customers to visit it.

Purchasing

Every company needs to buy raw materials, components, and capital equipment. To get what you need is especially important in China since it is still a seller's market. As explained earlier, the Chinese government has divided all materials into three classes. Class I is for basic raw materials such as steel, coal, aluminium and cement—vital for the nation's economy—and rice, wheat grain and fuel—vital for people's livelihood. Materials in this class are subject to comprehensive central control and in principle all output is strictly allocated. Other important industrial materials come into Class II and factories must apply for their requirements to one of the material supply companies. Finally, to obtain Class III materials, factories can negotiate directly with the supplying company. To understand what is really happening in China as far as purchasing is concerned, an example of purchasing materials in each category follows.

The Recorder factory needs steel, so it presents its requirements to the Beijing Broadcasting and TV Industrial Company (BBTIC) for the amount of steel needed for next year's production. After a few months the factory is given a quota from the authority. With this quota it is entitled to receive steel at a certain price. It does not know who will be the supplier, nor the quality of steel it will receive. The buyer and seller do not meet. One advantage of the quota system is that the price of the steel is low and the quota is not transferable. Fortunately, the Recorder factory's quota is usually sufficient. Otherwise, it would have to buy steel on the market from a steel plant which had produced more than the state plan. The price could be double the quota price; in Chinese, this is the so-called 'negotiable' price, though it is not really negotiable to the buyer!

For products in Class II such as small motors and magnetic heads, the BBTIC, in conjunction with the National Bureau, organizes two meetings every year for buyers and sellers. The Recorder factory attends these meetings and tries to get agreement for the supply of its requirements to avoid the difficulties of trying to get suppliers to deliver extra later on. Its engineers test different suppliers' products, considering specifications, quality and price. When the engineers have decided from whom they wish to buy, the purchasing department signs the contract to fix the delivery details.

Resistors, capacitors, semi-conductors, etc. come into the third class. Here the purchasing manager has much more freedom to choose suppliers. The price, location of supplier, delivery and quality will be important when making a buying decision. In principle the factory has complete freedom; in practice the factory director may feel that he has to buy from certain suppliers known to have good relationships with higher authorities or other influential people.

To purchase from abroad the factory must have the necessary foreign exchange. If the factory exports, it is allowed to keep a small part of the foreign exchange earned, which it can then use at its own discretion. Otherwise it must apply to higher authorities to get a foreign exchange quota. For example the TV factory imports colour tubes from Matsushita. To get the foreign exchange, it can apply for a quota to both the Beijing Municipality and the Ministry of Electronics. If it receives the quota, the next step is to buy the foreign exchange from the Bank of China. However, the factory also needs permission from the ministry to import the display tubes. The TV factory can contact Matsushita, but only through the Electronic Technology

Import and Export Corporation. In the discussion with Matsushita, the TV factory is responsible for technology negotiation and the import–export corporation deals with prices and other trade terms. The final cost to the factory includes customs duties and commission for the import–export corporation.

Thus, the freedom of the factory to choose suppliers and to negotiate the price paid depends on the type of material purchased. The factory has the least freedom for Class I and the most for Class III materials. One way for a factory to mitigate its dependence on suppliers is to establish good relationships by supplying them with television sets on the tacit understanding that this will ensure a favourable quota or preferential delivery. A significant proportion of the TV factory's output was distributed as part of this kind of back-scratching exercise.

Conclusions

Chinese industrial reform is accelerating, but the amount of discernible change can be exaggerated. It is not a revolution but a structured period of evolution (see Lockett & Littler, 1983). The restrictions enforced by the centrally planned economy in labour management, marketing and purchasing still, for the most part, hold firm.

The conceding of power to state enterprises is under way. It remains influenced, however, by the traditional subordination to higher authorities and the continued seller's market in China.

In the sphere of labour management, the greatest changes surround dismissals. The lack of uniformity in the application of the appropriate regulations provides problems. The Chinese remain inexperienced in the usage of labour-related laws. It seems unlikely that companies will be able to cancel an individual's contract unless they seriously misbehave.

Despite the various methods of recruitment, Chinese managers are still unable to freely select their staff. They are similarly limited in the matter of wage levels and bonuses. The latter issue is clouded by the number of different classifications for employees and the general expectation that all workers will receive a bonus.

Inevitably, in a seller's market, marketing remains under-developed. The prospects of a chaotic free-for-all are slim when one considers the Chinese idea of 'friendly competition' which involves rival companies acting more like satisfied bedfellows than highly-charged competitors.

The broadening of choice cannot be easily integrated into the Chinese workplace. Companies generally have a limited choice of customers and a purchasing power restrained by state quotas and price control rather than commercial rationale. It will be some years before pricing and marketing will be used effectively as commercial weapons.

References

Barnett, A. Doak (1981). *China's Economy in Global Perspective*. Washington DC, Brookings Institute.

Lindsay, C.P. & Dempsey, B.L. (1983). 'Ten painfully learned lessons about working in China'. *Journal of Applied Behavioural Science*, **19**, 3.

Lockett, M. & Littler, C.R. (1983). 'Trends in Chinese Enterprise Management 1978–82'. *World Development*, **11**: 683–704.

Richman, B.M. (1969). *Industrial Society in Communist China*. New York, Random House.

Warner, M. (1986). 'Managing human resources in China'. *Organization Studies* (in press).

Wilson, R.W. (1970). *Learning to be Chinese*. Cambridge, MIT Press.

Wong Siu-Lun (1979). *Sociology and Socialism in Contemporary China*. London, Routledge & Kegan Paul.

Part II: Developing Management Skills

5 China's Managerial Training Revolution

Malcolm Warner

Introduction

Can business schools be transplanted from West to East? The answer is both 'yes' and 'no'. China, for example, is currently experimenting with a variety of management training ideas—as indeed it needs to. When we realize that the number of industrial managers to be put through training exceeds the total populations of Switzerland and Norway added together, the size of the problem becomes evident. Managing China's attempt to raise its average living standards to US $1,000 a head by the year 2000 will be no easy task.

Confucius once praised a prosperous province he was visiting, commenting 'What a flourishing population!' A disciple asked 'When the population is flourishing, what further benefit can one add?' The Master replied 'Make the people rich'. To which the acolyte responded, 'When the people have become rich, what further benefit can one add?' Said Confucius 'Train them' (1979: 119–20). Perhaps the Master's logic ought to be turned on its head, for training may well be a precondition for achieving prosperity.

China has several bottlenecks in its economy: a major one is the lack of adequately trained human resources. The educational debris of the 'Cultural Revolution' still litters the road to higher living standards, although, as we shall soon see, many changes in education and training are afoot. A major restraint on technology transfer from the West (and Japan!) is the shortage of professional managers at all levels, especially in market-related disciplines. Given the existing 'Four Modernizations' (of agriculture, industry, science and technology, and lastly defence), is the attempt to alleviate the shortage of trained managers, a 'Fifth' Modernization?

Any discussion of China's training needs must be placed against the backdrop of the educational system. To compensate for the years of the 'Cultural Revolution', there has been a period of expansion since 1976. The number of higher educational institutions has grown from two hundred in the early 1950s to over one thousand in 1986. Student University enrolment comes to over one and three-quarter million, of whom over 87,000 are graduate students and over five hundred are doctoral candidates. But China has a low percentage of graduates *vis-à-vis* even Third World states, let alone advanced economies.

Chinese universities and institutes are now expanding and educational reforms are being implemented to change not only the quantity but also the quality of education. Decentralization of the management of learning is also under way and pedagogic innovations are being encouraged. The distribution of graduates and their assignment to jobs is being drastically changed to overcome the rigidities of a state-controlled manpower system. But much more needs to be done.

'Train Them'

China needs to train its managers on a 'revolutionary' scale, if only to keep pace with the economic reforms introduced by the post-Mao leadership (see Warner, 1986: 326–42). Since 1979, China has gone through a period of economic upheaval as it opened its doors to the outside world. The 'Cultural Revolution' had of course caused great dislocation and imbalance in its economy during the period 1966–76, while the aftermath subsequently saw targets set too high, in 1977 and 1978, as official sources now readily admit. Agriculture was then given greater priority, together with light as opposed to heavy industry. The 'responsibility system' was brought in, first in the rural and then in the urban sector, decentralizing management decisionmaking in effect. The Sixth Five-Year Plan, which ran from 1981 to 1985, set out technological and organizational changes, not withstanding an all-round reform of how managers were to be trained (see Table 5.1).

Deng Xiaoping, China's leader, wanted rapid results: 'If the cat catches mice, it doesn't matter if it's black or white', he once remarked. Managers can now catch their requisite quota of mice, without their factory party-

Table 5.1 Chronology of Chinese political and economic changes

1921	Chinese Communist Party (CCP) established
1931	Japanese invade Manchuria
1945	End of World War Two
1949	The 'Liberation': the Communists take power
1960	Break with the Soviet Union
1966	Start of the Cultural Revolution
1976	Death of Premier Chou Enlai, and after this Chairman Mao
1978	The launch of the new economic reforms
1979	Setting-up of Chinese Enterprise Management Association
1980	Trial of the 'Gang of Four'
1981	Sixth Five-Year Plan (1981–5)
1981	Decision to send all economic cadres on at least one course in enterprise management
1984	New reforms in enterprise management in urban factories start officially
1986	Seventh Five-Year Plan (1986–90)
2000	Target-year of 'Four Modernizations' for gross GNP to reach $1,000 (at current prices) per capita

committee amateurs looking over their shoulders. In order to attain this end, the Premier, Zhao Ziyang, added his authority to the reforms and exhorted

[all] cadres engaged in economic work [to] . . . conscientiously learn economic management and modern science and technology . . . [In addition] all enterprises and institutions should train their employees in a planned way. To obtain practical results the content and requirements of such training should vary with the posts and ages of employees. From now on, in recruiting workers and staff members, the enterprises must provide pre-job training for candidates and enlist those who have done well in examination. This is to ensure the quality of workers and staff, labour-discipline, production-safety and good condition of equipment in factories and mines. [Zhao, 1984: I].

A major problem of technology transfer, whether we are dealing with 'hard' or 'soft' varieties, is whether to choose an external model, or at least one or more of its components, at all. If a country chooses to 'import' a foreign institution, practice or behaviour, it has to select an appropriate one for its level of economic or industrial development. Moreover, this importation has to fit its own cultural norms if it is to work well. If a country wants to change its way of running its economy, it has to look elsewhere for ideas as to how to prepare its managers for the new rules of the game and provide them with appropriate techniques to manage the new technology it imports. The managers also have to learn how to respond to the market signals which internally and externally characterize the relatively more open economy on hand.

As the Chinese move away from a command-style economy, they now look elsewhere for training models, turning to North America, Western Europe and South-East Asia. Discussing which route China should copy in its economic reform, and hence management structure, Chinese experts often point to a variety of influences, both from the 'capitalist' West as well as the 'socialist' East. Of the latter, no single Eastern European Country is favoured, least of all the Soviet Union. Yugoslavia, often scrutinized by 'reformers' in both the present, as well as post-Cultural Revolutionary periods, is not referred to without criticism: it is felt, for example, that the state there does not enjoy sufficient control over the economy. The success of the decentralized Hungarian economic model is sometimes spoken of favourably by some economic experts, with the Bulgarian and Romanian cases noted but less frequently praised.

The influence of the Soviet model on Chinese management is clearly tempered by the negative experience of the period after the break with the Soviet Union in 1960. Today, there is no desire whatsoever to learn from the Soviet example among Chinese management educators, even if they appear to be willing to look at the experience of many other countries. Admittedly, a number of Chinese, management educators and managers studied in the Soviet Union in the early period of Communist rule in China. Soviet personnel at that time were the main—possibly the only foreign advisers there. None the less, apart from the last vestiges of Soviet industrial-bureaucratic structure and practice still to be found in Chinese enterprises, the policies guiding management have now decidedly taken another course.

In the light of such changes, we must now see how China is tackling the problem of developing institutions such as business schools to professionally prepare a generation of better-trained managers. As a start, a co-ordinating body for management education in China was set up by the State Economic Commission to oversee the new policy, namely the Chinese Enterprise Management Association (CEMA).

It is predictable that, in order to diffuse new management ideas and create a forum at both national and local levels for managers, a national association should be established. Like the British Institute of Management (BIM) and similar bodies in other countries, such an association would play an important role in not only promoting 'management', but *legitimizing* its function in a society where until recently the very word itself was ideological anathema. The Chinese Enterprise Management Association was therefore a vital step in both creating a new status for managers as well as stimulating a climate in which 'management' as a set of ideas could flourish. Its main goals are:

> the modernization of production technology and that of management [as] indispensable and mutually promoting parts for modern industrial development. Modern industry needs a scientific management system. The purpose of Chinese Enterprise Management Association [CEMA] is to study and deal with problems in the system and methods of management and the related economic policies. [It further aims] to improve enterprise management, enhance management capability and serve socialist modernization and construction through its activities. [CEMA, 1983: I].

Management is to be included as a branch of science, and governed by its own laws. Only by 'running the enterprise in a scientific way will it be possible to bring into full play the potentialities of the manpower and material resources, and to gain greater economic results (CEMA 1983: I). To achieve these ends, CEMA runs such lecture courses as 'How to be a Good Factory-Director' among other activities (examples of its meetings can be seen in Table 5.2).

Founded in March 1979, CEMA brings together leading officials and experts in industry, government and research, as well as universities. It is run as a non-profit making entity, but its funds inevitably involve a government subsidy. The Association clearly enjoys high status and is usually the first stop for VIP delegations of foreign businessmen visiting Beijing. The organization of CEMA is based on a central headquarters in Beijing, with local associations around the country. It has over two thousand group associates, over four thousand individual members and over three thousand enterprise-associated members. CEMA's Governing Board is serviced by sixty staff of the central Secretariat in six main departments.

Table 5.2 Examples of meetings sponsored and organized by CEMA

Topics	Participants	Papers
Experiences and Lessons of China's Enterprise Management in the past 30 years	156	50
Behavioural Science and Enterprise	110	32
Tasks of Enterprise Management in the Readjustment Period	180	60
Raising the Productivity and Economic Results of Enterprises	130	40
Rationalization of Industrial Structure	75	53
How To Be A Good Factory Director	144	40

The plans that CEMA has in mind for Chinese managers were put to me by Zhou Wei-Ling, who runs their Liaison Department. He had previously received his training in the West in the early 1980s on a prestigious Sloan Programme Fellowship at Massachusetts Institute of Technology (MIT) in Cambridge, Massachusetts. His background appeared to be *atypical* of most of the other experts I encountered in China, and indeed this was the only formal occasion when the services of the interpreter were redundant. It was a rare event in another sense, namely that both of us seemed to be 'on the same wavelength', discussing management and management education.

A major problem encountered by myself and others investigating the management reforms in China is that all too few people, even experts, speak English (or indeed any other foreign language), although some of the older scholars and practitioners spoke Russian, which they had studied in the 1950s. However, an increasing number of young professionals have mastered English either at interpreters' school, or through study abroad, and are now being given additional training in the management field to enable them to act as intermediaries and help with contacts with foreigners. Since 1978, 36,000 students have been sent abroad, mostly to North America, Western Europe and Japan.

In 1981, the Government decided that middle and senior managers should be trained on at least one 'course' (however short) in enterprise management. The major target group was to be those employed at such levels, referred to in the Chinese terminology as senior cadres, in manufacturing, transportation and communication sectors overseen by the State Economic Commission. Subsequently, three dozen or more university-level academic institutes were re-established after their demise during the Cultural Revolution, and twice this number of departments in universities and similar bodies were set up.

Several experiments in on-the-job training distance-learning were also launched, to which we will return later.

At present, over 350,000 managers of various kinds are attending such courses. Examinations were also to be introduced for all managers, as described above, and a Qualifications Commission was set up. In 1984, candidates in ten major cities took the trial exams, and the first national comprehensive ones went ahead in August that year. To take the exam, senior cadres have to go on a three-month course. By mid-1985, 60,000 managers had taken this route. There are now over seventy-five higher training institutes of economic management, and around five hundred schools of economic management which provide on-the-job training. The former offer one- to two-year full-time training courses (with a diploma), with fifty to a hundred participants each. In addition, respective ministries have their own training centres.

It is clear that an expansion of on-the-job training for managers is inevitable, not only because of the economies involved but also because closely linking theory and practice is an essential part of the official philosophy of management training. Distance-learning is a major prop in this strategy. There is considerable motivation for self-study, and this can be constructively channelled into distance-learning and adult educational channels, potentially to great effect in the long run, and at low cost to the economy.

Spreading The Word

Thus far, the Chinese Enterprise Management Association has set up a network of 'business school' type activities involving:

(a)   Institutes/Universities
(b)   Institutes with specialized courses
(c)   Big corporations' and ministries' own training centres
(d)   Television correspondence schools/periodical university and self-study courses
(e)   New MBA courses now offered in selected training centres, for example:
   Dalian   (involving the State University of New York at Buffalo)
   Beijing   (with the support of the EEC)
   Chengdu   (helped by the Canadian Aid Commission)

The aims of the policy outlined above are threefold. First, to create a top team of management educators, and to raise the standard of the training infrastructure nationally. Second, to avoid simply copying the United States model and take advantage of the experience with the 'Second World', rather than relying on links with either superpower. Third, to create graduates who are versed in the practice and language of international business, as English is to be the lingua franca of the course, to work with Western European and (through the language link) with North American multinational corporations in joint ventures. There will inevitably not be enough graduates at this high level to go round and there will thus be a conflict between the needs of the business and teaching sectors, it is argued. At present, China's 'business schools' turn out about 5,000 trained managers in total, at any level of recognizable professionalism, although the figure is closer to 30,000 if lower-level courses are included. Even if the entire output of MBA graduates were to go into teaching, however, it would only amount to numbers in the low hundreds over the next decade. The number of Ph.D. graduates in management would be smaller, even in several years' time.

Training management teachers is now a top priority. The MBA programmes at Beijing, Dalian, Chengdu and elsewhere are helping to produce teachers of management who in some cases are already replacing foreign professors brought in to set up the programmes. There are other programmes, such as the Tianjin Enterprise Management Training Centre's programme for teachers which is sending teacher trainees to Japan in rotation. There is a similar programme in Shanghai, collaborating with the Federal Republic of Germany. None the less, the total potential output of teachers remains low—perhaps in the low thousands in the period up to 1990. Bringing in foreign experts is expensive, and few speak Chinese. Most are therefore brought in as a stop-gap solution.

How then to reach the 'mass' of managers at low cost? A new network was set up in 1983, popularly known as the 'Periodical University', or to give it its full name the 'Economic Management Periodical (Joint) University'. It appears to operate in a similar way to the British Open University, although with less reliance on audio-visual materials than other media-based courses in China. It has an enrolment of 10,000 managers a year, for the three-year course. Of these, about seven in ten are middle managers. In addition, China launched a nation-wide television educational channel in July 1986, which is planned to carry vocational educational programmes in the evenings.

As it is very short of experienced management teachers, China uses recent distance-learning graduates as much as possible. One major heavy-industrial corporation, for example, enrolled a hundred students in order that many of them could later become 'in-house' instructors. The company initially bought 2,000 sets of teaching materials for this training purpose for the three years and eight courses. In addition to buying the monthly 'periodical', each person participating pays ¥50 to enroll. This is not an inconsiderable sum since it is not far short of the average monthly industrial wage. In addition, the student's employing enterprise pays a similar amount.

Against this background, the British Open University and CEMA have been discussing a joint venture to produce distance-learning material for Chinese managers in both Mandarin and English. The scale of China's problem in training its vast number of managers underlies the attempt to bypass traditional 'chalk and talk' methods by using a 'high-tech' approach by which a few highly-skilled faculties could diffuse case material via distance-learning media, backed up by in-house support at factory level. It is early days, however, since China has not yet entered the era of widely distributed video-recorders and video-disc players!

It is hard to evaluate the work of CEMA, but its national scope, its professional goals and the breadth of its interests are ambitious. None the less, as an umbrella organization for improved management education in such a vast country, it clearly will have an uphill struggle given the magnitude of its task. New managers' clubs are, however, proliferating. Linked with CEMA, for example, is the Young Enterprise Managers' Association (YE-MA) which has started to run local training-programmes, and the China Enterprise Directors' Association (CEDA), which held its first national conference in the winter of 1984.

Books on management are in great demand. On a recent visit to China, I saw specialized sections in provincial bookshops devoted to texts on management information systems techniques. The titles at least were in English, referring to business applications of Cobol and Fortran, as well as Visicalc, for example, although personally-owned computers are still restricted to a minority. China is producing its own PC models, however. The best-known is called the 'Great Wall' (see Chapter 13 for further details).

In attempting to diffuse and popularize new business ideas in China, CEMA has published two dozen or so new books with sales of over four million; for example, *Management Teachers' Reference* in seven volumes, *Teaching Material of Dalian Management Training Centre* in eight volumes, *Special Edition on Practical Management Techniques of Japan*, as well as an *ABC for a Team-Leader*, and so on.

Each month, CEMA publishes a more accessible review called *Qi Ye Guan Li*, namely *Enterprise Management*, which has a national circulation of over 200,000 copies per issue. In 1982, the *Harvard Business Review* signed an agreement with CEMA's journal to allow it to feature translations of any HBR articles, past or present. It has sent a copy of all issues since 1982, and will send future ones. The HBR is already published in six languages, and will now have an edition in Mandarin. CEMA has also published the *Chinese Enterprise Management Encyclopedia*, the first ever to appear in the People's Republic of China. Work on the encyclopedia started in the early 1980s, and CEMA was made responsible for its editing and publishing by the State Economic Commission. The editing committee comprised senior officials and specialists from all over China, with twelve subcommittees, in Beijing, Shanghai, Tianjin, Guangdong, Hebei, Shaanxi, Sichuan, Liaoning and elsewhere. The purpose of publishing the encyclopedia was 'to systematize the evolution of enterprise management in China, sum up experience and introduce management concepts and techniques developed both in China and abroad, thus providing a comparatively comprehensive and appropriate reference book to managers, management teachers and researchers'. (CEMA,

1985:4). An initial print-run of a quarter of a million copies of the two-volume encyclopedia has been decided on by its promoters.

Another new CEMA-sponsored development is the China Enterprise Management Consulting Company which was ratified by the State Economic Commission, and founded in Beijing in August 1984. Professor Pan Cheng-lieh, Deputy Secretary-General of CEMA, becomes the General Manager of the company. Under the leadership of CEMA, the company will provide the consulting service to both foreign and Chinese organizations and train managers and consultants for those enterprises. The purpose of the company is to update enterprise managements, increase their economic effectiveness and help them modernize. The company also wishes to develop contacts with both foreign and Chinese consulting companies, organizations and research institutes.

Preparing Top Managers

Directly linked with CEMA is the Beijing National Training Centre, set up by the State Economic Commission in 1979, and serving most of China's cities and provinces (its full name is the Management Training Centre for Economic Cadres of the SEC). As an openly elite institution, it aims to be the main training centre for *top* managers. Its goal is to update the capabilities, in the shortest time possible, of people already in high industrial positions, and of those who will later have top jobs. The Beijing Centre mostly deals with people equivalent to directors of large state-sector corporations, namely senior public-sector personnel. The younger MBA candidates will be preparing for these jobs as they reach their mid-career stage, and will be expected to be fluent in English. The Centre has twenty full-time teachers, forty to fifty working part-time, with VIP guests brought in from time to time. The curriculum is modelled on Western lines.

In addition to this Beijing 'business school', another school is active at Dalian, called the China National Training Centre for Industrial Science and Technology Management. It provides both postgraduate and executive instruction, and started operation in 1980. It runs a six-month seminar for 150 factory directors, and others of similar status. Since October 1984, it has also provided a two-year Masters' programme, in co-operation with the State University of New York at Buffalo. To date, over one thousand managers have passed through its doors on post-experience courses. Since the Dalian Centre was a pioneer, it has had to confront at an early stage the pedagogic obstacles to training Chinese managers unused not only to the Western 'content' of courses, but also to the 'process' involved in importing the new techniques. It is not surprising that management 'development' has provided no bed of roses, when introduced into a Chinese cultural context.

Chinese managers need training which is appropriate to the ideological and cultural norms (see Pye, 1986: 231). The Dalian Centre provides a good example of the problems of foreign-expert aid. To start with, all the courses were taught by American professors, but by 1986 many executive courses will be taught by the Chinese staff. Over the last five years, over seventy-five American senior academics have taught there, including the Nobel laureate Professor Lawrence R. Klein of the University of Pennsylvania, a distinguished econometrician. Apart from the Chinese state bodies involved, the United States Department of Commerce co-manages the project. The teaching programme is planned bilaterally, which helps its adaptation to Chinese norms. The curriculum now not only includes Western business concepts and practice, but also a course called 'Chinese socialist economic theory and economic laws'.

Problems To Be Faced

The main problems stemming from many of the 'business school' experiments described above, as seen by CEMA, seem to be as follows:

(a)   The Chinese academic infrastructure is still not yet able to cope with the training implications of the economic reforms.
(b)   The Chinese like everything too formally structured and 'on the blackboard'.
(c)   Active interaction needs greater emphasis, athough it is said to have worked at the Dalian Training Centre.

The Chinese are also experimenting with on-the-job training for middle and senior managememt: for example, CEMA sponsors seminars taught by foreign experts—the Japanese in particular offer training of consultants at factory-level. Several European countries, such as France, West Germany, Italy (and Sweden) have also provided help.

Chinese management teachers, in turn, are exhorted to learn from Western capitalist practice and, noting the good points (so the official line goes), match these with their own to create a specifically Chinese 'mass' model of management education. The priority areas involved are mostly specialist, such as:

— finance and accounting;
— management information;
— managerial economics;
— enterprise management.

Some say 'organizational behaviour' should be added, but its inclusion is controversial. A number of university centres have set up departments in this area of study, such as Jiaotung University, Shanghai. To date, courses dealing with behavioural science have been taught in sociology faculties, as opposed to management departments. The basic division in behavioural subjects between psychology and sociology is not favoured by some in the academic Establishment, who see it as all part of sociology (Wong, 1979). There is also the same rivalry as in the West as between 'hard' and 'soft' approaches in management studies.

To encourage the development of a corporate identity, a professional body for teachers of management in China was set up in 1980, known as the 'Chinese Association of Industrial Enterprise Management Education'. Its purpose is to encourage the improvement of the teaching of management and research in its component fields. Professor Liu Chunquin, who teaches at the Institute of Industrial Economics, is its Permanent Secretary. With seventy-six universities and institutes associated nationwide, it has three categories of membership: first, general universities; second, specialized colleges (which focus on technology and engineering; third, financial and other relevant institutes.

How then to compare the Chinese and British ways of training managers? First, and most obviously, there is the binary organization of the system in each country, namely the split between university and post-experience sectors, although both overlap to some degree. Second, the length of courses in the respective sectors is roughly comparable to their British equivalents. Third, the size and organization of several training institutions is broadly similar. Fourth, the curricula-headings resemble our own, at least in terms of the type of topics studied.

The Chinese system, on the other hand, differs from both the British (and American) models in both *quantity* and *quality*. Since it had little previous experience, it tried with hardly sufficient resources to build an *indigenous* set of programmes in order to better cater for local needs. With the very large numbers of managers to be trained, and the lack of an initial infrastructure of management education, the problems are considerable. In starting to move towards a 'mass' system of management and industrial training (see Table 5.3 for a comparison with other national models), they are trying to train their very top economic cadres first, but at the same time they desperately need many others as the 'trainers' of tomorrow. A 'mass' post-experience pro-

Table 5.3 National management education models

Stages	Time	Country	Model	Intake
Early	18th century	Britain	Initially In-house, now University/ Business Schools	Narrow
Intermediate	19th–20th century	France	Grandes Écoles	Narrow
		Germany	Technical Univ.	Intermediate
		USA	Business Schools	Intermediate
Late	early 20th century	Japan	Univ./In-house	Broad-based
	mid-20th century	USSR	Econ./Eng. Inst.	Broad-based
	late 20th century	China	Univ./Inst.	Mass-based?

gramme with in-house training and distance-learning thus seems to be a necessity in the long term.

What are China's prospects for the year 2000? China expects a population of 1.2 billion; of this, a college and university graduate population of 10 million; and a national output of US$1,200 billion. Moreover, 'China's long-term policies should aim for simultaneous development of the economy, society, science and technology and ecological balance' (Wang, 1985:20). In order to achieve these aims, it is vital that management-training plans succeed in the intervening period. It is hard to predict if there is a strong likelihood of these ambitions being fulfilled.

Summing Up

Chinese management training has a long way to go to remedy the educational 'fall-out' of the Cultural Revolution. Even now, far too many Chinese managers lack formal qualifications commensurate with their responsibilities, and this must remain a major constraint on the implementation of the new economic reforms. Indeed, in the broadest sense, China lags behind in industrial training. With the new economic reforms, it is essential that managers be trained to cope with the new enterprise-level decisionmaking powers envisaged (Tian, 1986: VII). However, major discrepancies will separate the explicit aims of the reforms and the quality of management at factory-level—let alone the political uncertainties (MacDougal, 1986: 26). Whilst considerable priority is now being given to management education, it still only affects relatively limited numbers of China's vast cohorts of managers. It is as yet too early to discern positive results.

We can hardly conclude that the impact of management education on China's economy has been an instant success, but the Government at least has given it top priority and considerable resources. During the Seventh Five-Year Plan (1986–90), it is hoped all top managers will have received systematic management training. Whether the Government can achieve its ultimate economic goals by 1995 or 2000 has yet to be seen, but the openness to 'pragmatic' management ideas from the West and Japan constitutes a major break with the closed society of the Maoist past.

References

CEMA (1983). *Chinese Enterprise Management Association.* Beijing, CEMA.

CEMA (1985). *Newsletter (Special Supplement).* Beijing: CEMA.

Confucius (1979 edn). *The Analects (Lun Yu).* Harmondsworth, Middlesex: Penguin Books (trans. with an introduction by D.C. Lau).

MacDougal, Colina (1986). 'The forces of Marxist reaction at large'. *New Statesman*, 3 October: 26.

Pye, Lucian W. (1986). 'On Chinese Pragmatism in the 1980s'. *China Quarterly*, No. 106, June: 207–34.

Tian, Jiyun (1986). 'On the present economic situation and restructuring of the economy'. *Beijing Review*, **29**, 6, 10 February: VII.

Wang, Huijiong (1985). 'China's prospects for the Year 2000'. *Beijing Review*, **28**, 44, 4 November: 20.

Warner, Malcolm (1986). 'The Long March' of Chinese Management Education, 1979–84'. *China Quarterly*, **106**, June: 326–42.

Wong, Siu-Lun (1979). *Sociology & Socialism in Contemporary China*. London, Routledge & Kegan Paul.

Zhao Ziyang (1984). *Report on the Work of the Government*. (Delivered at the Second Session of the Sixth National Peoples Congress, 15 May 1984), 16 pp.

6 The Marketing Concept in China — A Qualified Acceptance

James M. Livingstone

In the course of the new economic reforms, official Chinese views on marketing have swung from almost blank condemnation to enthusiasm tempered by nervousness. In discussing the possible role of the marketing concept in Chinese economic development, therefore, three important caveats have to be entered.

Economic change does not occur overnight in China, nor is its acceptance by managers in state enterprises either instantaneous or wholehearted. Some managers are indifferent, some hostile, many frankly apprehensive at the strange new environment which is being created (see Lockett, 1985).

Implementation is likely to be piecemeal and sporadic. As a general rule, the further away from Party headquarters in Beijing, the more the decision to implement reforms, including the introduction of competition and a marketing environment, is left to the local authorities: implementation is at best piecemeal and often progress may be by omission rather than commission, i.e. co-operatives may market aggressively, and are allowed to do so by default rather than by fiat (see Chastain, 1982; Feuchtwang & Hussain, 1983; Garratt, 1981).

Even if and when the marketing concept is widely accepted in China, many aspects of Western marketing will remain inappropriate, or unacceptable. Marxist China is significantly more puritan than hedonistic—a poor country with a protected local industry, i.e. a seller's market dominated by scarcity rather than over-abundance of choice (see Feuchtwang & Hussain, 1983). Not least, it is a closed society in the information sense, with advertising by poster or television relying on a blunderbuss effect rather than targeting; and where, as one student suggested, the only realistic manner of acquiring a sampling frame for local consumer market research would be to enlist the co-operation of the local police station, as the only source of information.

The context of this chapter is based substantially on the author's experience of teaching marketing to cadres within the State Economic Commission Management Centre in Beijing, during a period in 1985, visits to state enterprises which co-operated in the project, and some insights into consumer reactions from a very crude market research survey of a Beijing department store. It is, therefore, an account of the views of a relatively small number of students, of cadres in their mid-thirties, engineers by training who

had suffered badly during the Cultural Revolution and were strong supporters of reform: of a smaller sample of enterprise managers some ten to
twenty years older, who had long experience of the system both before and
after the Cultural Revolution, but whose professional qualifications were
probably not great: and a somewhat impressionistic view of some shoppers,
acquired in translation at second hand. An empirical assessment would be
that the students represented the hope of a better-educated and more
questioning generation of future leaders, while the managers were more
representative of Chinese management today—the management that has
to implement the reforms.

The remainder of this chapter looks at some of the lessons which may very
tentatively be drawn from the three sources, the students, the managers and
the shoppers. It is not proposed to described in detail the content of the
marketing course taught, on a fairly conventional MBA marketing syllabus:
but, what was more necessary than with Western students, was an attitude to
marketing, rather than a detailed knowledge of sophisticated techniques (see
Livingstone, 1986a and 1986b).

Problems in Teaching Marketing

There were clearly a number of potential pitfalls on the ideological side. The
lectures and examples were, as far as possible, presented in ideologically
neutral terms, but the situation was not eased by the fact that there was a
degree of confusion among the Chinese staff and students about the extent to
which the new economic reforms being pursued by the Government were, in
effect, changing the ground rules. To what extent, for example, could one
assume that enterprises would in future have some discretion in fixing prices,
choosing their own suppliers, and finding their own customers?

As has been remarked, the Chinese economy has operated substantially as
a seller's market, where virtually any product has a guaranteed sale, usually
within the same municipality or province. Even where an enterprise or a
customer was supplied with products of an unacceptable standard, it was
difficult to reject them because any loss of goodwill on the part of the supplier
could have unfortunate effects on future supplies.

Three other less anticipated phenomena were quickly identified. The first
was that the ideological and cultural system tended to produce a situation
where personal responsibility was minimalized. There were relatively few
rewards for outstanding individual effort, but more obvious punishments
where an individual's actions were disapproved of by his or her work unit or
the community in general. China in this sense is not a risk-taking society, and
this was marked among the students who in general had experienced
considerable personal hardships during the Cultural Revolution. Indeed, it
could be argued that the biggest risk the students themselves had taken in
recent years was to apply for a place in the course which might seem a route

to rapid promotion. The students had been sought by press advertisements which encouraged them to apply for a place without, if necessary, the prior agreement of their work unit, on the basis that, if they were accepted, the State Economic Commission would negotiate their release by the work unit (see Garratt, 1981; Jones, 1984; Lindsay & Dempsey, 1983).

The second factor in the situation was the degree of verticalization and in consequence sub-optimization in society. There appeared to be little interest in or knowledge of other institutions even within China, outside the work unit or the ministry in which an individual worked. This appeared even to be reflected in the provincialization of the economy. Before the economic reforms, regions and municipalities were almost autonomous city states, accepting the authority of Beijing and the Central Committee of the Communist Party, but more concerned with their relations to the central authority and within their regional boundaries than with other parts of China. Work units and the institutions above them tended to maximize their own advantage, rather than assume a national view. Enterprises traded with other local enterprises, and even if the same product was available from another source or at better quality elsewhere in China, it was not very easy to secure alternative sources or customers. The factors of verticalization, the relatively weak financial disciplines created by a situation where costs and profits alike were absorbed by the state, and a relatively poor infrastructure effectively destroy the theory of China as a market of one billion individuals. More realistically, it is a string of semi-isolated communities mostly near the coast, based on the cities and municipalities.

The third factor is the enormous importance of personal relationships, rather than strict adherence to organization charts. The Chinese administrative system works in part in terms of authority, in part in terms of *guanxi*, i.e. influence and personal friendship and obligation. The equivalent in relation to the foreigner is probably the concept of the 'Friend of China' who is acceptable. But the practical effect is that in Chinese terms it is difficult to get clear-cut, quick decisions based on impersonal relationships, or relationships based on respect for qualifications, in which the state of friendship between the two parties is not really vital. Negotiations in this sense could be prolonged and frustrating; but the obverse side of this was probably that, as confidence builds up, the strain on the foreign teaching staff will become progressively less over the five years during which the EEC project is to run (see Lockett, 1985).

The Marketing Course

The structure of the course was fairly orthodox: an introduction to the Marketing Concept: Market Research: Product Policy, Advertising and Promotion: Pricing Policy: Packaging: Distribution: and International Aspects of Marketing. The major problems, however, were likely to be in developing materials to reinforce the textbooks which were of limited relevance, having been written in a Western context; at the same time to co-ordinate with the other two subjects being taught simultaneously, in order to emphasize the fact that all three subjects were interdependent facets of the general management situation; and to meet the need for 'hands-on' experience, as far as this was practical (Livingstone, 1986b).

Another problem which loomed large in the first week or two, but which declined with increasing familiarity, was the teaching style. A Chinese acquaintance had previously remarked to the author, *vis-à-vis* teaching, 'We Chinese have good ears'. Traditional Chinese educational methods have depended on very intensive rote-learning and repetition (and if one considers the problem of learning to read and write the minimum of several thousand ideograms which even a moderately literate Chinese has to master, the merits of the system are obvious). Nevertheless, an environment where the students on an MBA course, with a wealth of practical experience behind them, would simply listen attentively, take notes, and if required reproduce these notes without comment or interpretation, would have been unacceptable in Western MBA training. It did not come easily to the students to express any degree of difference of opinion with their professors, and they were clearly highly anxious to avoid creating a bad impression by disagreeing with the foreign instructors. They had to be persuaded that their own experience was highly relevant and that they were not in the classroom to engage in a one-way communication between teacher and student. It took some time, but by the end of the first module a more relaxed attitude, and a readiness to express individual views, had begun to appear. The students were beginning to enjoy the course.

In a sense, however, marketing and the Marketing Concept was arguably a fuzzier concept to teach in an alien culture than, for example, more quantitative courses in accounting and production. Marketing did initially cause more anxiety to the students than more overtly quantitative disciplines.

In spite of the orthodox nature of the Marketing Course structure, the course began in a slightly unorthodox way. The instructor, having introduced himself, simply chalked up on the blackboard the Chinese expression *zhuyi*. This, and its Japanese version which also uses the Chinese ideograms, is a familiar traffic sign in both countries. It simply means 'Caution', 'Beware' or 'Be Careful'. When the students had absorbed the symbol, the instructor made the point that it was essential to beware of a too facile application of Western techniques in marketing to China. Marketing techniques were not textbook formulae or cookbook recipes which could be applied indiscriminately to conditions anywhere. An elementary point perhaps, but one which has to be emphasized again and again in any non-Western developing country. On this occasion the point was made at perhaps inordinate length, and the ideogram was repeated in later weeks when necessary, to emphasize that Western techniques and Western textbooks had to be used with extreme care, not simply memorized and applied.

The first three-hour session thereafter consisted of the distribution of a series of statements or opinions about the lives of men and women in Western Europe which were broadly true in all of the (then) ten members of the European Community, followed by a discussion. These statements/assertions were intended to bring out the implicit assumptions about society on which American or European textbooks were based. They were not likely to appear in such textbooks because they could in effect be taken for granted by the authors and their Western readers.

The intention of the discussion was to drive home the point already made about the danger of assuming that what was true of one society in marketing terms was necessarily true of others; a secondary point was to illustrate that most of the statements, although superficially social or political, could readily be reinterpreted as clues to market segments, among elderly people, for example, or followers of specific hobbies developed in cultures with considerable leisure, etc.: to emphasize in fact that there was no homogeneous market, but an almost infinite number of market segments in a society which might be identified and catered for.

All of this and the comments on the Marketing Concept, as it could be applied in China, were less concerned with hard facts than with beginning the process of getting the students in a frame of mind to challenge assumptions about what was possible in Chinese markets or indeed the status quo which appeared to prevail in a given market situation.

The need for such a 'stirring up' was graphically illustrated by the other activities which were being carried out in parallel with the formal lecturing. Each student group of five or six had, it has been noted, been allocated for the next two years to one of the six enterprises which had agreed to co-operate. As a first stage before even being introduced to the enterprise, each group had been required to produce a sectoral report on the industry represented by the appropriate enterprise. What emerged from these first reports was evidence of extensive research for information, but a totally uncritical acceptance of the optimistic picture of the industry which emerged. The students had not appreciated that a chart showing a steady growth of the production of motor vehicles, but which aggregated everything from earthmoving vehicles to saloon cars, was meaningless; or that an equally rosy picture of the steady growth in the output of tape-recorders in China, which did not distinguish between the total assembly of imported components, production with local content, or production of locally designed and produced units, was of little value. Nor could, for example, statements of consumer satisfaction from producers, but not from the customers, always be accepted as objective fact. During the presentation the students were given a fairly severe interrogation about the detail of the statistics they had presented, simply to reinforce the point that an enquiring frame of mind, rather than uncritical acceptance of statements (including statements made by foreign experts such as the faculty members) was a *sine qua non* of progress in a Western style of management education (see Garratt, 1981; Lindsay & Dempsey, 1983).

The course was now developing along orthodox lines so far as subject matter was concerned. The problem was to set tasks for the student groups which would simultaneously test their comprehension of the lecturers and the accompanying limited readings from Western textbooks on the one hand, and the need for immediate relevance to Chinese conditions, on the other.

For the first three weeks of the course, much of the student workload in all three subjects was centred on a very familiar product—the bicycle. There are some four million bicycles in Beijing and the students arrived every morning at the management centre on a variety of bicycles, from a humdrum battered machine to the Rolls Royce of Chinese bicycles, the Flying Pigeon. The first exercise was simply to compel students to think in terms of possible market segments for a new type of bicycle, by requiring them to produce up to twenty market-research type questions on what the man or woman in the Beijing street wanted in a bicycle. It was paralleled to the Accounting and Production courses by related exercises on the same bicycle theme.

The second exercise expanded the bicycle theme. The groups were each given a special-interest bicycle magazine together with a brochure containing specifications of the Sinclair C5—an electric three-wheeled vehicle launched in Britain some four months previously—and some background material on its possible market. They were then asked to produce a customer 'profile' for the magazine and questions about a possible market strategy for the Sinclair vehicle. The answers required from the students were less important than the lessons to be learned, namely the need to identify market segments for a product, including a magazine, and awareness of an ongoing (and potentially risky) decision to launch a brand-new product, which was incidentally taking the manufacturer into a wholly new market with all the attendant risks and possible rewards of product diversification. The timing of the Sinclair C5 launch was particularly apposite because it was manifestly not a textbook case but a current situation, the results of which were likely to be available long before the MBA course had finished.

This material had been prepared in advance, but it was clear that in this relatively new management education field some decisions would have to be made in mid-stream, so to speak, and such a situation developed at the end of the first week, to be implemented during the next four weeks. A stroll round Beijing at the end of the first week not only showed how rapidly the economic situation had changed even during the two years since the author's previous visit; more importantly, it identified a large Western-type departmental store, which was to prove an excellent subject for 'hands-on' experience by the students in carrying out consumer market research.

Details of this Market Research project and the results are to be found in a separate publication, but, in brief, the management agreed to a survey being carried out, and during the next month, in addition to all the other work in hand, the student teams found themselves preparing and revising a questionnaire, learning in the process the problems of setting questions and coding questionnaires, before administering the questionnaires to over four hundred shoppers during the seventh week of the course—a highly educational experience for all the students concerned (see Livingstone, 1986b).

To return to the situation by the end of week three, the theme of the bicycle was now dropped because the students were becoming more and more involved in preparing for the enterprise audit which was to occupy all their time in week six. Again, it was important that all three topics taught in the module should be co-ordinated; what in effect the students were going to have to do was to examine the enterprises, using the Western techniques they were being taught, and to reproduce as far as possible, in terms of inputs and outputs, the activities of the enterprises in Western terms. As an aid to the process, the students were given a tentative series of questions, from which they were to derive questions which would be more appropriate in the Chinese context, and which they would use to carry out an audit of the enterprise.

It has to be admitted that, initially at least, the question-frame issued to the students had only limited success. As one participant remarked, it was regarded as an Imperial Decree to be implemented without argument, and it was only after the students reported back on their deliberations after some ten days, and were fairly ruthlessly criticized for failing to develop the original questions, that they realized how much success or failure in the enterprise audit would depend on their own efforts.

In the meantime, however, apart from the student's work on readings, preparing the Market Research Questionnaire, and the audit questions, the lecturing programme continued. The students who had felt rather underworked during the first week were beginning to appreciate the degree of concentrated work which was required in a Western-type MBA. At this stage, i.e. during discussion on advertising, another 'hands-on project' was introduced, to be developed at a later stage in terms of packaging. The instructor had brought to China six sets of fifteen examples of British packaging, varying from detergent packets and breakfast cereal containers to processed food—both British and foreign—cigarette packets, etc. Seventeen features had been identified and numbered on one or two of the packages. The students were required first to identify the features on the other packaging material, and over the next week or two to collect as many specimens of the equivalent Chinese packaging for comparative purposes. By the time the class were ready to discuss packaging in week seven, they were in a position to make some judgement on which features of the British packaging were desirable or acceptable in the Chinese context: they were also asked to reverse the situation and discuss what lessons might be drawn for British manufacturers from Chinese packaging. Although the intention was to collect questionnaires on the packaging, pressure of time and the imminence of the final examination in the event precluded this, and a general discussion had to be substituted.

To revert back, however, week six consisted of research and the gathering of material inside the enterprises for the audit. In week seven, in addition to lecturing and preparation of the report on the enterprise audit, students carried out their market research survey in the department store. In week eight, the presentations were made on the results of the enterprise visits, and the examinations were held. Finally, some weeks after the end of the module, and before the next module began, each group had to produce a detailed report on the enterprise visited, on the lines already indicated.

The Reactions of the Students to the Marketing Concept

·As a teaching exercise, the course appeared to be very successful; how far, however, will the lessons learned be applied by the students and their contemporaries? In commenting on the response of the students to the marketing concepts, two or three qualifications have to be made. What has been described here was the first marketing module in the course, delivered to students who had had the most limited exposure to marketing, and that mainly through somewhat undirected local advertising, and with no experience of the world outside China. It certainly had the appeal of novelty both as a subject and in the way it was taught. Nevertheless, there appeared to be a great measure of enthusiasm—and indeed the major problem was to prevent over-enthusiastic and indiscriminate application of the concepts. There can be little doubt that an attitude of receptivity to marketing concepts is virtually innate in the Chinese character, and short of a complete volte-face on the new economic reforms, the students, in so far as they represent the future senior managers of China, are likely to be highly receptive to the marketing concept. It is ignorance of progress in the area in the outside world, not antipathy to the concept, which limits the application of marketing concepts to the Chinese situation.

The Managers

If it is dangerous to project generalizations from a group of students, it is probably even more so in the case of a handful of enterprise managers who had been persuaded or coerced by the State Economic Commission into co-operating. Two assumptions could be made. The first was that the enterprises involved—six in all from a broad range of industries—probably represented the more efficient end of the spectrum, in so far as they were being opened up indirectly to foreign inspection; the second was that the *quid pro quo* for their co-operation was the expectation that they would benefit from advice and exposure to the foreigner (see Lindsay & Dempsey, 1983).

So far as relative confidence in opening their doors to foreigners was concerned, it was fairly clear that the managers, in spite of their confidence, had considerable concern about what was involved, as and when they moved from a situation of captive suppliers and captive customers to a competitive situation, and it was not clear that all the implications had been thought through. The managers had, for example, no idea of how prices might be set in a competitive situation, nor did there appear to be any clear guidance from the centre.

A summary of the pre-reform conditions as they applied to the individual enterprise before the new economic reforms (in many cases still applicable today) demonstrates the problem (see Lockett, 1985). Prices of inputs and outputs were fixed by the state, nominally in consultation with the enterprises: effectively, both the suppliers of inputs and the customers for the product at these fixed prices were nominated by the state. Competition in terms of quality or price was largely unknown. Poor-quality supplies could in theory be rejected, but it would be a bold factory manager who did so: it was far simpler to pass the quality problems on to the customer, and, if the manager is sufficiently conscientious, try to persuade or bribe the supplier to do better next time.

Profits could theoretically be made if quotas were exceeded, but the scope in the absence of extra materials, overmanning and a labour-force where the power of recruitment or dismissal was effectively out of the hands of management, meant that in many cases there was little scope or incentive to try to improve the situation. Effectively, both profits and losses were going to be absorbed by the state. In capitalist terms it is often argued that, other things being equal in a competitive situation, profit is a measure of efficiency. No such measure can be employed given the financial conventions existing in the Chinese enterprise, where financial information, let alone discipline, can most politely be described as sketchy.

The second point relates to the benefits perceived as arising from exposure to foreign experience. It is almost certain that virtually all Chinese enterprises would like some link with a foreign partner, whether licensing, joint venture, or anything else that might give access to the outside world. The prestige of the foreign enterprise is high, quite unrealistically so, and the foreign connection is seen as the solution to a wide range of problems, which are, in truth, probably insoluble in the given ideological environment. There are a number of reasons for this: foreigners are seen to be universally rich, and presumably it is their business skills which have made them so. They understand not only the processes of advanced production technology, but that mysterious and frightening attribute, how to survive and prosper in a competitive environment, at which the new economic reformers hint. The prestige of foreign products is enormous, even to the point where locally-produced household goods will be given foreign-sounding names (e.g.

Toshibo), presumably in the hope that the more gullible purchaser will be misled. Above all, there is the implication that a foreign connection will give access to foreign markets and hard currency.

There are, however, two problems. The first is one of over-expectations of the benefits of the association, a situation which can give rise to disillusionment. The second is more subtle: it is the difficulty of convincing Chinese enterprises, not only that there must be two-way benefits from such arrangements, but that the benefits to the foreigner must be very specific. It is not difficult to envisage deals which can be made on joint ventures—licensing, technology transfer and the like—even in situations where the recipient of the foreign expertise would find it impossible to pay the foreigner in acceptable (i.e. convertible) currency. They are buy-back deals, simple barter, payment in component parts and the like. But it appears to be very difficult in discussions with enterprise managers who are not familiar with such methods to get them to think through why the benefits to the foreigner must be spelled out. When pressed on the issue, Chinese managers, in the writer's experience, tend to take refuge in generalities about the huge potential that the Chinese market represents, all very general and 'iffy', but hardly bankable. The point is not easily verifiable, but it seems likely that Chinese managers can appreciate instinctively that they are almost inevitably going to gain from the infusion of foreign experience, even if the nature of the gain is not immediately understood and quantifiable; and equally, they know that such moves carry official blessings. It is possible that, without thinking through the problem, they in turn assume that the foreigner will not really require to know what the specific benefits are likely to be: they may even assume that an individual foreign company will engage in a joint venture or similar arrangement because its government has also told the company that it is ideologically correct to do so.

One of two things may happen. Either the foreigner who has committed himself as a matter of faith to a project may find that any advantages that follow are non-bankable; or the foreign enterprise, along with its Chinese partner, will seek to exploit these segments of the Chinese market, which in one way or another already have access to foreign currency, rather than help to develop Chinese export potential. In the first case, the intentions of the foreign company are frustrated: in the second the intentions of the Chinese government are frustrated. But in both cases the Chinese enterprise still gains in getting new technology and its share of foreign currency—another interesting variant of sub-optimization, which can be avoided only if the Chinese government can lay down clear, unambiguous and specific conditions, on export requirements, etc., that are still generous enough to make the project worthwhile for the foreign partner.

In summary, it can be said of the managers that they are cautious survivors and it may well be that it will take a younger generation of better-educated cadres to implement marketing concepts more wholeheartedly, based on their knowledge of Western techniques, and above all, with a critical ability to decide which of these techniques can sensibly be applied to China (see Lockett, 1985).

The Chinese Shopper

Before commenting on the implementation problems and results of the market research survey, it is worth re-emphasizing the practical difficulties of conducting orthodox consumer market research in China. The proposed use of police records as the most practical method of obtaining a sample-frame has been cited. What emerged in general was not so much hostility as some difficulty on the part of the Chinese authorities not directly involved in working out the possible consequences. The initial reaction was that the store authorities would not be able to assist and that, in any event, shoppers would be highly suspicious about being questioned. What emerged, however, was that the store administration was very co-operative and obviously pleased at the prospect of acquiring more detailed information on their customers and that the latter, far from being suspicious, were queueing up to be given the chance of expressing their views.

Well over four hundred shoppers were interviewed by students in the course of one week, using a questionnaire substantially designed by themselves, but lacking the in-depth treatment which would have been possible in the West; shortcomings included, of course, the lack of experience of the students, who had to put together a questionnaire within a few weeks of being on an elementary marketing course, with no opportunity for testing by a pilot survey, or data-processing facilities to facilitate subsequent handling.

The survey produced a substantial number of tables, which unfortunately could not be processed in any statistically sophisticated way because of the rough-and-ready way in which information had been acquired (see Livingstone, 1986b). It is not possible, for reasons of space, to reproduce them here, but one or two results, surprising or not, are worth commenting on. The first is that in spite of the headlines about rich peasants and the fact that many customers had travelled a long way to visit what was certainly the most advanced store in Beijing, it was the party cadres—in Western terms the nearest China would have to an establishment—middle-class group of shoppers who were most clearly identified as the major customers.

Finally, a summary of three of the tables is shown below. These were:

1. Comments on the products sold, in terms of price, variety and range, quality, fashion and aftersales service (Table 6.1).
2. Comments on the layout of the store (Table 6.2).
3. Comments on the attitude of the staff (Table 6.3).

The results may appear to be very critical of the stores and the products, but at least two positive elements emerged. First, as has been noted, the management were very co-operative and were clearly anxious to improve the

Table 6.1 Comments on products sold in store

		Total
Prices		
	Favourable	—
	Unfavourable	14
	Mixed	1
Variety/Range		
	Favourable	9
	Unfavourable	138
	Mixed	5
Quality		
	Favourable	1
	Unfavourable	9
	Mixed	1
Fashion		
	Favourable	—
	Unfavourable	22
	Mixed	1
Aftersales Service		
	Favourable	1
	Unfavourable	1

Table 6.2 Comments on layout of store

	Total
Broadly Favourable	1
Broadly Unfavourable	64

Table 6.3 Comments on attitude of staff

	Total
Broadly Favourable	8
Broadly Unfavourable	38
Mixed	9

services they were offering; and it may well be that the critical reaction of the customers to many of the products will give the management a tool to demand better-quality products from their suppliers. By the very nature of the Chinese situation today, it is the producers, not the retailers, who have the power, and the store was in a sense the recipient of criticisms of shortcomings which were not their fault. Second, the customers are increasingly self-assured about their right to demand better products; and arguably it is only competition implicit in the marketing concept that can move Chinese industry along the road to satisfying the needs of its customers. In that sense, marketing is not against the ideological interest of China's rulers, but a means of delivering satisfaction to the Chinese people (see Cheung, 1982).

In summary, the students, the store management and the critical reaction of customers represented a strong hope for the future of the Chinese economy, the present managers, and the cautious realities of marketing in China today.

References

Chastain, E. E. (1982). 'Management: The Key to China's Development'. *Management International Review*, **22**, No. 1.

Cheung, S. N. S. (1982). *Will China go Capitalist?* Hobart Paper, No. 97, London, Institute of Economic Affairs.

Feuchtwang, S. and Hussain, A. (eds) (1983). *Chinese Economic Reform*. Croom Helm.

Garratt, B. (1981). 'Contrasts in Chinese and Western Management Thinking', *Leadership and Organization Development Journal*, **2**, 1.

Jones, L. R. (1984). 'Perspectives on Management in the PRC'. *International Journal of Public Administration*, September.

Lindsay, C. P., & Dempsey, B. L. (1983). 'Ten painfully learned lessons about working in China'. *Journal of Applied Behavioural Science*, **19**, 3.

Livingstone, J. M. (1986a). *Marketing in China*. Academy of Marketing Science Conference, Anaheim, California, April/May.

Livingstone, J. M. (1986b). *A Market Survey of a Beijing Departmental Store*. Occasional Paper No. 1, School of Management and Finance, The Queen's University of Belfast.

Lockett, M. (1985). *Culture and the Problems of Chinese Management*. Templeton College, The Oxford Centre for Management Studies.

7 Teaching the Chinese About Quality Circles — A Personal Account

John Bank

> At last an official unlocked the cell to give him breakfast. He searched him again before escorting him to a testing room, where a panel of scholars sat at a long table. BaBa stood with his face to the wall and his hands clasped behind him. In this position he recited by heart from the Three Character Classics, the Five Classics . . . and the Thirteen Classics by Confucius's disciples; the examiners also threw in some five-word poems. He had been afraid that nothing would come out of his mouth, but once the first words, many of which he had kept ready on his tongue, broke forth, the rest came tumbling out, like water, like grain.

> Maxine Hong Kingston (1981: 29–30) *China Men*

The Japanese engineer I met over breakfast in the Friendship Hotel in Beijing misled me. Speaking from his own experience as an engineer working in the capital who was also teaching Chinese engineers, he said: 'You'll never get them to brainstorm; they'll write down everything you say and memorize it; they won't even ask question.' His words inspired in me fears of a failed mission. Without participation from the management students it would be impossible to teach the theory and the practical application of quality circles. Brainstorming and other problem-solving techniques were essential to the course. Without an effective training programme, chances were slim that the managers from across China who attended the sessions would launch quality circles in their manufacturing and services sectors. The engineer also expressed his amazement that an expatriate American who had never been to Japan would be sponsored by the British Council to go from London to Beijing to teach the Chinese about 'Japanese working methods'. His point was well taken. But it was the Chinese themselves who had selected the topic of quality circles from a smorgasbord of business subjects placed before them by the Cranfield School of Management at the Cranfield Institute of Technology early in 1985.

In May, a delegation of three senior lecturers from the Commercial Cadre Institute of Beijing and their interpreter arrived from Beijing to visit the Cranfield Institute of Technology and to develop further academic and cultural links between the two educational institutions. During their three-week stay they gathered facts and impressions about management education, business and industry in Great Britian and also helped to plan a reciprocal visit from the Cranfield faculty the following September/October. In addition to quality circles, they chose management information systems as a second topic for the seminar in Beijing.

At my request to provide necessary training material for the quality circle seminar, the interpreter, Li-jiu Zheng, undertook to translate an 80,000 word book of training materials for quality circles (written by Mike Robson).Waiving all copyright considerations, as had been their custom, the private printing of the book on rough paper appeared in time for use in the seminar. (There is a plan to bring China in line with other modern nations on copyright although the government does not see the issue as a high priority. In the past when authors of academic and business books were even told of the desire to have their books translated and printed officially in Chinese no payment was offered.) The managers had, then, an excellent training manual in their own language, but would they brainstorm?

In the afternoon of the first day of the course after a slide lecture on lateral thinking and brainstorming as an alternative to analytical thinking for organization problem-solving, I unwrapped several packets of 'Blu-tack' and passed chunks of the bluish clay-like substance among the managers. (A year earlier I had seen the product in stationery stores in Hong Kong in a Chinese package, but no one in the group admitted to having ever seen the product.) 'We are going to brainstorm the *uses* of 'Blu-tack', I said confidently. A hand shot up: 'First tell us more about the *properties* of this wondrous substance' came the request. No information was given. The interpreter took her place at the flip-chart and the brainstorming began slowly and gathered momentum, producing bursts of laughter from the group, the test of a successful session.

Brainstorming is a technique for obtaining a large number of ideas from a group of people in a short time. Invented by an Englishman, Alex Osborn, during the 1930s, the technique requires that the participants suspend judgement and criticism, let their minds freewheel and strive for a great quantity of ideas. The ideas put forth are written large on flip-chart papers and posted around the room as they accumulate. Later, after the session, the ideas are incubated and subjected to criticism. This particular session ended with nearly two hundred uses for the strange substance 'Blu-tack' in the twenty minutes allotted to the exercise. One of the wildest ideas was to use it to repair the Great Wall of China. Another wild idea was to create a 'Blu-tack' bowl to replace the Iron Bowl. Against the predictions, the pivotal quality circle techniques had been accepted.

The need for quality circles in China is manifest to indigenous managers, to ordinary consumers and even to visiting tourists. Poor product quality and poor quality service are widespread. The more extreme cases break into print at times. The *China Daily* frequently berates the inferior quality of Chinese goods and services, particularly when unsafe products cost lives and poor services lose foreign currency. In one account the paper reported that an entire group of American tourists checked into a new joint-venture hotel and checked out twenty minutes later because standards of restaurant hygiene and service were unacceptably low, despite the shining new facilities.

In a 'seller's market' situation concern for customer satisfaction is almost non-existent. Surly service from disgruntled clerks, some of whom are 'underemployed' and feel trapped in low-level jobs, is a common experience in Chinese department stores. 'Putting people first' or 'The customer is king' are foreign ideas to most Chinese engaged in the service industry. Owing to a bomb scare on our flight from London to Beijing the flight was delayed over four hours while all the baggage was removed from the jet and passengers identified their luggage on the tarmac in Bahrain. The delay meant that we arrived at our hotel in Beijing a few minutes after 9 p.m., the cut-off time for dinner without reservation. We were treated to the spectacle of our Chinese hosts having to fight with hotel staff to get food on our table, while nearby a group of actors who had arrived after us, but apparently with a reservation, received normal service.

The state-run travel bureau in China provides many examples of bad service. Most visitors to the country must deal with the travel bureau and pay its high fees because of language problems or the red-tape procedures established by the Government. Visas must be obtained, airline and train tickets bought far in advance, good hotels at a premium require advance bookings. The scope for error is enormous, especially given the dearth of computers.

The following actual conversation between a traveller and a travel agent illustrates the problem.

Traveller: Are there any flights from city-B to city-C next Monday, which is exactly one week from today?'

Agent: 'Yes, I think so.'

Traveller: 'Could you then get a ticket for an afternoon flight on that day?'

Agent: 'No, it is not possible.'

Traveller: 'Why not? There are still some seats available, aren't there?'

Agent: Yes, but I cannot buy one for you here. Since you will be taking off from city-B, you can buy the ticket only from our city-B branch.'

Traveller: 'Could you at least give them a call to make a reservation for me, please?'

Agent: It is our policy not to take any reservations over the phone. You must go there first, O.K.?'

Traveller: 'But . . .'

The traveller could get no further with this agent, who appeared more anxious to get rid of him than to offer help. Four days later, immediately upon reaching city-B, he rushed over to the bureau's branch office; but this visit again turned out to be equally futile and frustrating. 'Sorry, all flights to city-C are now booked solid for the next five days', was the only answer he could obtain. In the end, the traveller managed to buy a ticket at the railway station for a three-day train trip to his final destination (Fukuda, 1986).

Parallels exist between the poor quality of Chinese goods today and that of Japanese goods at the end of the Second World War. The Japanese quality revolution and its amazing export success had given that island nation, with virtually no natural physical resources, the third highest GNP in the world by 1980. Japan supports over 115 million people (nearly twice the population of Britain), by exporting $75 billion (US) worth more goods than it imports. Both Japan's GNP growth rate and its investment rate are twice that of the United States (Pascale & Athos, 1982).

The success of Japan owes much to a complex national industry policy (Ouchi, 1984). But the thrust for quality goods and the role of the country's one million quality circles in this effort have been significant. The Japanese Union of Scientists and Engineers (JUSE), founded in the 1950s to promote quality control activities in industry, maintains that the Japanese saved over $50 billion (US) in the first sixteen years of their quality circle programmes, begun in 1962. Since 1978, the savings have been an estimated $5 billion (US) per annum. One Japanese company, Toyota, reported receiving 587,000 suggestions to improve its products in one year, mostly through quality circles, from its workforce of less than 40,000 people. In the potentially massive economy of China, with over a billion population, possible quality savings from quality circles and other quality programmes are enormous.

A subcommittee of the United States House of Representatives concluded its second detailed report on trade with Japan in two years with the following statement.

> It has become increasingly clear to us, and to many businessmen dealing with Japan, that our trade problems result less and less from Japanese import barriers and more and more from *domestic American structured problems of competitiveness and quality*. There are clearly lessons to be learnt from Japan.

Not surprisingly, some of China's Asian trading rivals such as Taiwan, Korea and Malaysia, have already learned the lessons and have well-developed quality circle programmes in place (Bank & Wilpert, 1983). A strategy focused on quality is still one of the best ways any country or company can respond to competition.

Both a strong domestic need for quality circles and the competitive example of other countries made the managers who arrived at the Commercial Cadre Institute of Beijing highly motivated to learn the principles, roles, techniques and theory of quality circles. The fifty management students came from a wide geographical region across China and ranged in age from 20 to 62, with an average age of 37. They represented a broad spectrum of industries, from agribusiness to the oil industry, from commercial institutions to retail trading, from transport to education, from purchasing groups to public sector administration, from marketing organizations to co-operative communes. Their positions also ranged from director and vice-director to frontline supervisors, from president and vice-president to foreman, from dean to lecturer. As most were management students, they viewed the training inputs from the perspectives of their own organizations and were eager to ask specific questions from their particular businesses and industries to strive to achieve a better 'fit' of the techniques and structures of quality circles with their business and organizational needs. We were impressed by the way the management students were able to learn from us what they needed to learn: to take it and to run with it.

There was also a cultural 'fit' that made them receptive to the quality circle message. The small-group focus and its work-group base were very compatible with both cultural norms and the spirit of collective responsibility. The consensus approach to decisionmaking promoted in quality circles, for example, was something they had sought to do all their lives. Tasks assigned to the small groups were taken seriously. Report-back plenary sessions were a matter of group pride in performance—the calligraphy was superb and the verbal report well-spoken.

Not only were the concepts compatible culturally, but the pedagogy used to communicate them was equally fitting. One-way lectures, case studies, group dynamics such as the classic 'Desert Survival', dialogue, slide lectures, etc, were all used. The managers enjoyed the new idea of case studies and turned their hand to working towards solutions to the problems they posed. They even wrote case studies. Their only fault was the failure to use quantitative data for decisionmaking. When they wrote their own cases, they left out the quantitative data that Western managers require. I would often forgo a full interpretation of the interactions, settling instead for résumés in English to keep the need to translate into English to a minimum and to keep the exchanges freewheeling. Having a skilful interpreter was key and I found I could speak quite naturally and think ahead while she rapidly interpreted my English.

In one of my first sessions I had explained the process for making micro-chips, concentrating on how the silicon chips are manufactured in a dust-free environment, ten thousand times freer of dust than European operating theatres. A single particle of dust could destroy the entire batch of chips, as well as ruin millions of pounds worth of equipment. Hence, employees take repeated air showers to free them from any dust particles and also wear protective clothing, rather like space suits. The rooms they work in have a series of air locks to keep the environment perfectly pure.

Two days later, a middle-aged manager at the back of the classroom near a window began to vigorously massage his head with both hands, throwing up dandruff in the sunlight. At first I ignored the disturbance and concentrated on the verbal exchanges at the front of the classroom. When the distracting action had carried on for over five minutes, I privately asked the interpreter what in the hell he was doing. 'He's preparing to make the micro-chip' came her swift and disarmingly witty reply.

Among themselves the Chinese management students argued fiercely for their points of view on issues, sometimes shouting in their enthusiasm. But, although issues were hotly debated, respect was shown for opposing views and somehow matters got resolved in consensus agreement. The dreaded 'loss of face' issue that dominates much of Chinese interpersonal relationships did not stop the cut-and-thrust of debate. There was not much debate among the managers about the principles, roles, techniques and theory of quality circles, these having evolved since the early 1960s, first in Japan and then globally. The core principles are widely respected and are normally part of a success criterion for the project. A quality circle is a small group of employees from the same work area who volunteer to meet regularly in paid time to identify, investigate, analyse and solve work-related problems. Voluntariness runs from the top to the bottom of a quality circle programme. Employees may be somewhat pressured by managers or by peers to join a quality circle, but they are not coerced into joining. No financial inducements are offered for participating in quality circles and no one is penalized for not taking part. Voluntariness is a *conditio sine qua non* of an effective and lasting programme.

The quality circles are also work-group-based, usually with the first line supervision as the leader. One of the primary aims of quality circles is to re-establish the essential role of frontline supervision. It is important that he assumes leadership of the circle and helps shape it through careful project selection and training. Over the last sixty years the role of first-line production supervisors has undergone extensive change. Previously, the supervisor exercised a good measure of control over the workforce and had a fairly straightforward relationship with his supervisors. Today the supervisor finds himself further removed from the decision making centres that directly affect shopfloor and departmental work. The supervisor has been viewed as a 'man in the middle' (Roethlisberger, 1945) who has to deal with the conflicting demands of management and workers, or what has been called a 'marginal man' occupying a position on the boundary between management and labour in a sort of organizational limbo (Wray, 1949). Much of the research that has been done on the superintendent is downward-looking, from his position in the organization, focusing on his relationship with subordinates and on the effects of his behaviour on workers' performance. An alternative perspective, that is, viewing the supervisory role looking upwards—his relationship with higher management—reveals further changes in the role, touching on his authority and the priorities that are set for him in terms of work objectives (Child, 1975). Against the background of these unsettling changes, quality circles can provide a simple, clear method of asserting the foreman's leadership at the grass-roots level. He is not only Chairman of the Circle, but he assumes a training role as well with regard to Circle members.

Training requirements are critical to the successful quality circle. First the group leader undergoes a training course in problem-solving techniques, which he then teaches to group members. Commonly-used techniques include Pareto analysis, a technique named after the nineteenth-century sociologist Vilfredo Pareto that often shows that about 80 per cent of costs can be attributed to only 20 per cent of the problems, and therefore helps quality circles to concentrate on the critical few problems rather than dissipating their energies on the many.

Other commonly-used techniques include brainstorming and cause-and-effect diagrams. A cause-and-effect (or fishbone) diagram is a technique used after brainstorming has identified a range of possible causes of a particular problem. The main categories under which causes are grouped are man-power, methods, materials and machines, and these categories can be broken down further into sub-causes. In Japan foremen over the past twenty years have continued to develop circle training until some of them are using university-level statistical techniques to solve problems. In the West the tendency is to keep it simple. Abstract theories or background topics are avoided and the training is limited to those techniques that can be immediately assimilated and used.

There are three main roles in a quality circle programme: the co-ordinator, the facilitator and the circle leader. This structure and role definition appealed to the Chinese managers. While the sponsor of a quality circle programme—the 'champion' who introduces it into the company because he believes in the idea and is prepared to promote it—can come from anywhere in the organization, the co-ordinator who volunteers to administer the programme should be a senior manager who is well-respected in the company and who is at the centre of the business. He should normally be a line manager rather than someone with a staff function. In a warehousing operation, he might be the traffic manager; in an engineering works he could be the production manager; in a retail operation he could be the marketing manager. His role includes the following activities:

— being a focal point;
— administrating the programme;
— dealing with communications;
— planning the future—making decisions about the programme;
— upholding the core principles.

The facilitator tends to be a middle manager and can either come from the line or staff side of the business. The role includes the following activities:

— making group self-sufficient
    — training
    — development
— having a *process* focus, not a 'task' focus'
— developing leaders
    — confidence
    — competence

— making it easy for others to
  — understand
  — support
  — 'buy in'
— oiling the wheels of the programme.

The quality circle leader's role encompasses the following activities:

— trainer of quality circle members;
— helps members feel comfortable in the meeting situation;
— ensures that there is no elitism among quality circle members and that they stay in touch with the work group;
— ensures that quality circles keep a problem-solving focus and stick to problems in the work group;
— makes it easy for others to co-operate with or join the quality circle.

  The theory behind quality circles goes back over twenty-five years to Douglas McGregor's seminal book, *The Human Side of Enterprise* (1960), and his enunciation of Theory X and Theory Y. Theory Y has been adopted as the theory underpinning quality circles, first by the Japanese and then by others. It is, in fact, true that quality circle members find their work in problem-solving activities a natural outgrowth of their job interest. Their motivation is intrinsic and their appetite for responsibility can be impressive to managers accustomed to mere compliance with directives. They also demonstrate a great capacity to solve organizational problems.

  IBM, with marketing operations in both Hong Kong and Beijing, is committed to quality circles at the corporate level and has had effective programmes world-wide since 1979. American research from IBM lists the benefits of a quality circle programme as:

— enhanced skill utilization;
— more effective communication;
— increased commitment to unit goals;
— team building;
— process understanding, and
— a greater acceptance of change.

In their own internal research, IBM USA found that the morale index, which included how employees rated the company, their managers, their salary and overall satisfaction, was 16 per cent more positive where they had quality circles than where they had no circles (76–60 per cent). Performance indicators, which include departmental innovation and efficiency and a commitment to producing high quality and understanding management's quality efforts, showed a similar spread. Where there were quality circles employees showed a 20 per cent higher positive rating than where there were no circles (66–46 per cent). On the topic of communications, which encompassed information from management, adequate information to do one's job, being kept well-informed by managers, the spread was again 17 per cent (58 per cent positive to 41 per cent positive).

In practical matters such as rework, IBM found that where there were quality circles the rework was 8.2 per cent, but where there were no circles it shot up to 12.9 per cent. On absenteeism, employees in departments that had quality circles showed a marked decrease (four times less)—0.447 hours per employee per month as against 1.99 hours per employee where there were no quality circles. The strength of this data lies in the fact that it was generated purely for internal purposes to see if quality circles were having an impact on the organization.

A major thrust of quality circles is their concern for data collection. Quality circle solutions to problems are based on fact and therefore involve thorough data collection. The factual nature of the circle's inquiry attempts to steer it clear of opinion and organizational politics. My usual classroom example for making a distinction between fact and opinion is to ask who is the greatest athlete of all time—eventually saying that there is no factual answer to the question, just opinion, however strongly held. In the West the names of Olympic athletes such as Jesse Owen or Carl Lewis are thrown up by the classes. The Chinese proffered gymnast Li Ning, who gained six medals in the 23rd Olympic Games at Los Angeles. In general, the Chinese managers lacked the general knowledge base taken for granted with a management audience.

We English-speaking lecturers are accustomed to scrawling on blackboards and flip-charts. We are amazed by the Chinese love of calligraphy. Words on a flip-chart are written in beautiful handwriting by a person who commands high esteem for this display of skill. Since the writing is pictorial, there are sometimes discussions among the students as to the appropriate Chinese character for the concept—a real concern for accuracy. Coloured chalk was used on blackboards in a decorative and ordered way that combined ascetic beauty with a need for structure. The sense of and need for order carried through to the structuring of lectures and the organizing of training materials. An almost military sense of order surfaced each morning at 10.00 a.m. as the management classes got together for a vigorous period of physical exercise. The love of order is built into the system. The Chinese set their programmes and dislike any changes in the timing of a seminar, its location or any of its features. There is a complicated negotiating process when the Chinese design their schedules (Terry, 1984).

Western zeal for bringing management techniques and technology to China should be tempered by awareness of a historical perspective. After all, the Chinese were ahead of Europeans in inventing the wheelbarrow by ten centuries, the crossbow by thirteen centuries, draught-animal harnesses by eight centuries, cast iron by twelve centuries, porcelain by thirteen centuries and mechanical clocks by six centuries (Needham, 1978). Mass production of iron axe blades, plough tips, belt buckles, and axle fittings by the stack-casting method still used today for precision parts such as gears, for example, took place in China as early as 800BC. A foundry excavated at Wenxian in Henan province, in the 1970s, held 500 sets of multiple moulds, many still usable, sixteen different designs each in thirty-six sizes from which could be made as many as eighty-four units per mould. Applied to the mass production of parts for farming equipment, it led to a vast increase in food production—and thus in population.

Long-term aid projects against this industrial background seemed inappropriate, demeaning and even useless. The temporary need the Chinese experience for inputs of management science such as quality circles and new technology from the West should be seen as simply that, a temporary need. The inborn sense of history a Chinese person possesses and cultivates throughout his life helps put such a transitory need in perspective. It is a serious mistake for a lecturer from the West to consider China a developing country in anything but income.

Chinese hosts, proud of their history, are keen to show lecturers from the West monuments of their remarkable past. On National Day my colleague Stan Cordell and I jetted 600 miles south-west of Beijing to the ancient capital of Xian, in Shaanxi province, to see the tomb of Emperor Shi Huang Di of the Qin Dynasty. When he died in 210 BC in Qi Yong, the Emperor had a terracotta army—about eight thousand life-size clay statues—buried with him. Rank upon rank of soldiers in battle formation, together with their horses, emerge from the excavation of the tomb. The management task of bringing master craftsmen from across China to create the terracotta army rivals the fierce beauty of the artefacts. The Emperor himself is considered to have been one of the greatest managers of all time for his effective use of central bureaucracy in uniting China 2,200 years ago (Fukuda, 1986).

From the sixth century until the first year of the twentieth century, the vast bureaucracy that ruled China drew its manpower from competitive, civil servant exams that tested a candidate's comprehensive knowledge of Confucian writings. This sprawling system of education was replaced by European models. Today formal schooling consists of six years of primary school and six years of middle school. For the very gifted (and lucky) students there is a four- or five-year university programme; but only 3 per cent of China's university-aged population attends an institution of higher learning. Since the early 1980s over a million university students have been at work trying to catch up on China's lost decade (1966–76) of the Cultural Revolution when intellectuals were considered the 'stinking ninth category' of citizens and many, including lecturers I worked with in Beijing, were sent to work on pig farms. Intellectuals and university people who spent years as peasant farmers as a way of expiating their 'guilt' for being pro-Western during the Cultural Revolution are now the men and women of the moment in China. The talents and abilities which a decade ago won them condemnation are now used to help create the new open China.

The Cultural Revolution is estimated to have ruined the lives of a hundred million Chinese with its fanaticism. (One autobiographical account of coming to manhood during that decade, 'Son of the Revolution' by Liang Heng and Judith Shapiro (1983), portrays the destructiveness of the event for Liang's own family.) Both the Cultural Revolution and the equally discredited 'Great Leap Forward', which attempted to merge China's agricultural co-operatives into large people's communes, plunged the nation into the economic chaos from which it is only now struggling to extricate itself. As oppressive as these two campaigns may have been for millions, the Chinese are not an oppressed people in the Third World sense of oppression. The iron bowl is a symbol of equality. (Seeing the driver of our car take his place around a common table with heads of universities, top politicians and foreign guests was a lesson in egalitarianism not lost on two lecturers from a snobbish class-ridden culture.) The emergence of Deng Xiaoping and his strategy of installing younger minds in positions of power, while opening up the country to the West, is being carefully watched by China's 650 million people under 30 years of age. Most are looking for educational opportunities, some basic freedoms and a quality of life that has eluded many of their parents.

Paulo Freire, the Brazilian educationalist, in his book, 'Pedagogy of the Oppressed' (1972), draws a powerful distinction between liberating education or problem-posing education and the traditional 'banking concept'. The 'banking concept' of education is focused on a two-stage action of the educator. First he prepares his lecture in his study or office or laboratory by thinking about the knowable object of his lesson. Then he expounds his knowledge to the students, expecting them not to know but to memorize the content of his lecture. In fact, the students do not practise any act of cognition, since the object towards which that act should be directed is the property of the teacher rather than a medium evoking the critical reflection of both teacher and students. 'Hence in the name of "preservation of culture and knowledge" we have a system which achieves neither true knowledge nor true culture', Freire concludes. By contrast, liberating education is not interested in the transfer of information but in acts of cognition. It promotes a learning situation, a dialogue between teacher and students in which they are joint owners of a process in which they both grow. 'Problem-posing education bases itself on creativity', says Freire, 'and stimulates true reflection and action upon reality, thereby responding to the vocation of men who are authentic only when engaged in inquiry and creative transformation'.

Anyone who visits China is a witness to the massive, creative transformation that is under way. An academic visitor, while working in the country, has a tremendous opportunity to make his contribution but must not fail to see the overall pattern that teachers and students are weaving in the carpet.

References

Bank, John & Wilpert, Bernard (1983). 'What's so special about Quality Circles?' Journal of General Management, 9: 21–37.

Child, John (1975). 'The Industrial Supervisor', in G. Esland *et al*. (eds) *People and Work*. Edinburgh, Holmes/McDougal.

Freire, Paulo (1972). *Pedagogy of the Oppressed*. Harmondsworth, Penguin Books.

Fukuda, K. J. (1986). 'Chinese Management: from the First Emperor to Deng Xiaoping'. *Leadership and Organisational Development Journal*, 7: 1–20.

Kingston, Maxine Hong (1981). *China Men*. London, Picador.

Liang Heng & Shapiro, Judith (1983). *Son of the Revolution*. London, Chatto & Windus.

McGregor, Douglas (1960). *The Human Side of Enterprise*. New York, McGraw-Hill.

Needham, Joseph (1978). *The Shorter Science and Civilisation in China*. Vol. 1 (abridged by Colin A. Ronan), Cambridge, CUP.

Ouchi, William (1984). *The M-form Society*. Reading, Addison-Wesley.

Robson, Mike (1982). *Quality Circle Member's Handbook*. Aldershot, Gower.

Roethlisberger, F. J. (1945). 'The Foreman: Master and Victim of Double talk'. *Harvard Business Review*, 23: 283–98.

Pascale, R. T. & Athos, A. G. (1982). *The Art of Japanese Management*. Harmondsworth, Penguin.

Terry, Edith (1984). *The Executive Guide to China*. Chichester, Wiley.

Wray, D. E. (1949). 'Marginal Men of Industry: The Foreman'. *American Journal of Sociology*, 54: 298–301.

Part III: Adapting the Labour Market

8 Labour Market Reform in Chinese Industry

Gordon White

Introduction

The strategy of economic reform ratified at the cardinal Third Plenum of the Chinese Communist Party's Central Committee in 1978 committed the Party to a comprehensive programme of sweeping changes in the previous system of economic planning and management in the urban-industrial sector. The reform agenda includes changes in labour policy, not merely because of perceived inadequacies in the previous administrative system of labour allocation, but because the economic reform programme was a comprehensive package, the progress of each of its components depending on the others. At the macro-level, movement towards the market in commodities and capital, it was felt, required similar movement towards a market in labour. At the micro-level, it did not make sense to give enterprise managers greater power over production, marketing, procurement and investment without a similar extension of power to handle labour power. Though this logic seems impeccable, there have been many problems—ideological, social, economic and political—which have blocked the path towards labour reform.

Not the least among these problems has been the ideological (and therefore political) sensitivity of the term 'labour market'. In the Marxian canon, a labour market, i.e. labour power as a commodity, is a major defining characteristic of the capitalist mode of production. To cover their political posterior, therefore, reform economists have until very recently been careful to avoid direct use of the term 'labour market' or 'labour power market', preferring rather to talk in more neutral terms of increasing labour 'flexibility' and 'circulation'. (The same squeamishness has prompted the use of the term 'waiting for employment' instead of 'unemployment'). Terminology aside, however, their practical policy proposals have clearly been aimed at changes in the direction of what I would understand as a 'labour market'. It has two important characteristics: (i) employment is entered into on the basis of an agreement between employer and employee, and terminated on the initiative of both or either party (subject to any contractual conditions). Although there is an irreduceable element of 'freedom' on both sides, the degree of 'voluntariness' and 'equality' in the relationship will depend on specific market conditions (*pace* neo-classical arguments, for example, about unemployment being 'voluntary', or the view of contemporary Chinese reform economists that labour contracts between an enterprise and its workers are inherently 'equal'). In this kind of system, labour allocation is a highly decentralized and atomistic process, and external barriers to labour mobility (for example, through direct state intervention) are assumed to be non-existent or marginal. (ii) There is an exchange of labour power for a certain amount of remuneration, usually but not exclusively in the form of a wage: labour power is sold as a commodity. The terms and conditions of the exchange (and the level of the wage) depend largely on the specific conditions of supply and demand in the labour market as a whole and its subsectors.

The latter criterion covers the *exchange* dimension of labour markets and draws our attention to recent wage reforms, notably the attempt to link wage levels with both individual and enterprise performance, thereby opening the way to greater use of the wage system as a price mechanism regulating labour movement. But the issue of wage reform is complex and is dealt with by another contributor to this volume (Henley), so I shall not attempt to deal with it here. The former criterion directs our attention to two interconnected questions: first, the degree to which labour can circulate on its own initiative through the economy as a whole; second, the job status of workers and staff within enterprises and the consequent power of managers to manage labour, whether hiring, firing or disposition with the enterprise. It is with these two questions that I shall be concerned in this paper. To the extent that the reforms increase the free circulation of labour in the economy and enhance the power of enterprise managers to hire and fire labour, then there has been a move towards a labour market in the sense of *circulation*. I shall confine my analysis to the urban economy (which conforms with Chinese reality since Chinese policy-workers have sought to draw a strict line between urban and rural labour systems through stringent and comprehensive controls over migration); within the urban economy, I shall concentrate on the dominant state sector which has been the main target of the reforms.

The Reform Analysis and Programme

(a) Diagnosis

Reform economists have pinpointed the interrelated problems of low levels of labour productivity, sluggish growth in labour productivity and heavy over-staffing in the state economy inherited from the Maoist era. The figures in Table 8.1, for example, suggest a glacial pace of improvement in labour productivity between 1965 and 1978.

Although these problems stem from a wide variety of causes, reformers have pointed to the negative influence of certain basic defects in established policies towards labour and employment. At the macro-level, they argue that, of all aspects of the previous system of centralized, administrative planning,

Table 8.1 Overall labour productivity of state-owned independent accounting industrial enterprises (at 1980 constant prices)

Year	Labour Productivity (Rmb/person/year)	Index (1952 = 100)
1949	3,016	72.1
1952	4,184	100.0
1957	6,362	152.1
1962	4,817	115.1
1965	8,979	214.6
1978	11,130	266.0
1979	11,838	282.9
1980	12,080	288.7
1981	11,863	283.5
1982	12,133	290.0
1983	13,049	311.9
1984	14,070	336.3

Source: State Statistical Bureau, 1985, p. 382

'the allocation of labour resources is by far the furthest from the market mechanism'. In accordance with the principle of 'unified employment and assignment', state labour bureaux at central and local levels had exercised a virtual monopoly over the allocation of urban labour, including both manual workers and technical-professional staff in both state and 'big collective' sectors (Zhao, 1980; Feng, 1981). The span of state control was too broad, argued the reformers, the machinery of administrative regulation too rigid and the system far too centralized, imposing (often inaccurate) plan priorities on individuals in their initial job placement. After job assignment, moreover, the individual found it hard to move from his or her original unit in the face of bureaucratic obstacles (inside and outside the enterprise) and other external controls, notably the system of residence permits (*hukou*) and ration coupons. At the micro-level, most workers and staff on the state payroll had lifetime tenure in their original units with job promotions or wage increments based heavily on seniority. Consequently, managers' power to dismiss workers and workers' motivations to move were both weak. This was the oft-decried 'iron rice-bowl' which reformers targeted as a major reason for poor productivity. Worse still, there was a tendency towards the hereditary transmission of jobs within state enterprises. Moreover, the 'regular' or 'fixed' workers in state enterprises, eating out of their iron bowls, had a privileged position in relation to other sectors of the urban workforce (mainly collective) because, apart from their relatively high and stable wages, they enjoyed an enviable array of welfare benefits not available elsewhere.

These reformist criticisms of the previous labour system are substantially correct (White, 1982: 620ff.). Why had this heavily-administered labour system emerged and to what extent did it contribute to the phenomena of low labour productivity and overstaffing? We can identify four major factors:

(i) *The politics of the socialist state*   From the mid-1950s on, the Chinese party-state has taken upon itself the task of finding jobs for the vast majority of urban job-seekers. In consequence, particularly in periods of a 'high tide' in employment pressures (such as the late 1970s and early 1980s), state labour bureaux have intensified problems of overstaffing in the state sector by forcing surplus urban labour power onto enterprises beyond their requirements. We can attribute this high degree of administrative intervention in part to the ideological commitment to full employment and to the inherent expansionist tendencies of a command state. But such an explanation would be inadequate since the degree of administrative regulation of labour in China is unusual among state socialist countries. One has also to look at societal pressures and historical circumstances. The Chinese state has been put under severe pressure by the chronic threat of open urban unemployment and the need to insulate the urban sector (through a 'low wage—high employment' strategy begun in 1957) from large-scale rural immigration. As the state has taken on the task of providing jobs, moreover, the urban population has come to expect it; an implicit political symbiosis has developed on which the state would find it difficult to renege. Since in the past the state sector has absorbed the majority of urban job seekers, the effects on average labour productivity in this sector have been negative.

(ii) *Urban surplus labour*   This has been and continues to be the main contextual constraint on policies aimed at raising labour productivity, as opposed to creating employment (for a Chinese analysis, see Zhao, 1982). Pressures in the cities in the late 1970s became very intense because of the results of an earlier baby boom and the backlog of jobless young urbanites returning from the countryside where they had been sent to 'settle down' during the Cultural Revolution decade (1966–76). Table 8.2 shows this bulge and the continuing urban employment pressures in the early 1980s.

Urban unemployment also reflects other earlier policy mistakes: the failure to take population-restraint policies seriously until the 1970s, a strategy of industrialization which favoured capital-intensive firms, and a strategy of ownership which failed adequately to encourage urban collective and private enterprise and created a dualism which increased pressures for jobs in the relatively privileged state sector.

(iii) *The 'Kornai effect'*   I have named this after the Hungarian reform economist who has identified the implications for labour utilization of a traditional central planning system, operating according to the logic of

Table 8.2 Persons entering employment in cities and towns (in millions, with figures rounded)

Item	1978	1979	1980	1981	1982	1983	1984
Total	5.44	9.03	9.00	8.20	6.65	6.28	7.22
1. *Major Sources*							
Labour-force in cities and towns	2.75	6.89	6.23	5.34	4.08	4.07	4.50
Rural labour-force	1.48	0.71	1.27	0.92	0.66	0.68	1.23
Graduates of tertiary education, secondary technical and workers' training schools	0.38	0.33	0.80	1.10	1.17	0.93	0.82
Others	0.83	1.10	0.70	0.86	0.74	0.60	0.67
2. *Assignment*							
State-owned units	3.92	5.68	5.72	5.21	4.10	3.74	4.16
Collective-owned units in cities and towns	1.52	3.18	2.78	2.67	2.22	1.71	1.97
Individual workers in cities and towns	—	0.17	0.50	0.32	0.33	0.84	1.09

Source: State Statistical Bureau, 1985:235

'resource constraints' and 'scarcity' (Kornai, 1980: Chap. 11), i.e. the tendency for enterprises to generate 'excess labour demand', seeking to enhance their ability to meet plan targets by building up hidden labour reserves and 'hoarding' labour. The main result is overstaffing, which Kornai calls 'unemployment on the job'.

To recapitulate briefly, the first and second factors create overstaffing through a combination of external political-economic pressures, the third by excess demand on the part of the enterprises themselves. Each factor in turn tends to keep labour bottled-up in the enterprise, reinforcing the 'iron rice-bowl' and reducing labour turnover and overall circulation.

(iv) *The mini 'welfare state'*   There are more basic characteristics of the Chinese socialist enterprise which account for low labour circulation and the continuation of the 'iron rice-bowl'. Most important has been the evolution of the enterprise as a 'mini welfare state' (Chinese analysts sometimes call it a 'small society', or even an extended 'family'). On the one hand, Chinese enterprises not only provide workers with a wage, but also with medical benefits, education, training, recreation, housing, social insurance and a pension; on the other hand, they appear to operate on the basis of implicit social contracts between management and workforce—a pattern of accommodation from which both sides benefit and from which each is loathe to break. These factors give state enterprises a stability and rigidity which is a major constraint on industrial reforms in general, and labour reforms in particular.

(b) *The reformist cure*

(i) *Policy goals*   In framing their labour policies, reform policy-makers and analysts have aimed to increase labour flexibility by reducing the administrative stranglehold of the state over labour allocation and granting managers greater power to manage labour by weakening the 'iron rice-bowl'. In the (hoped-for) new environment of 'socialist commodity production', at the macro-level these policies would enhance allocative efficiency in two senses—economic and socio-political. From an economic viewpoint, a more flexible system of labour allocation (whether or not it was a fully-fledged 'labour market') would be more successful in matching labour supply and societal needs, both quantitatively and qualitatively (i.e. allowing people not just to find any job, but the 'right' job). From a socio-political viewpoint, a more fluid system would be better able to match job openings and career structures with individual aspirations, thereby increasing work morale and labour productivity. Greater managerial powers over labour would allow enterprises to adapt more quickly to changing market conditions, would concentrate the workers' minds and would stimulate technical innovation and more cost-effective use of labour. Although the goals of full employment and job security were retained, they were changed from absolute to relative notions: i.e. a certain amount of 'waiting for employment' was not only unavoidable but functional to the nation's economic vitality (for example, Zhuang & Sun, 1983) on a 'labour reserve system'. Even if the state retained a commitment to arrange employment for job seekers and to that extent workers could expect a basic guarantee of job security, they could not expect to remain secure in the same job (on job security, see Xiao, 1983).

(ii) *Policy measures*   The measures proposed by reformers to increase labour mobility in the urban-industrial context can conveniently be grouped under three headings: a reduction in the role of the state, diversification of channels of labour allocation, and the establishment of a new employment system in state enterprises based on contracts. Let us discuss these in turn.

One of the main thrusts of the reform programme was to redefine and reduce direct state regulation of the labour-force. The principle of state planning was to remain dominant, i.e. state labour bureaux would continue to regulate the overall proportions of the national labour force, but would reduce their direct intervention in the detailed process of labour allocation. As part of this process of 'destatification', state responsibility for the 'unified allocation' of certain strategic groups was to be gradually reduced. In the past, these groups—notably graduates of tertiary educational institutions and technical high schools, demobilized army officers and soldiers—had been guaranteed jobs, and their disposition was planned and executed on a nation-wide basis by direct administrative action from the central labour bureau in Beijing. Moreover, the role of local labour bureaux, which had been responsible for finding jobs for virtually all urban job seekers in the past, was to change. They would continue to deal with overall planning of local labour requirements, but their role in the direct and detailed allocation of labour was to be taken over by other agencies, notably labour service companies and enterprises themselves.

There was thus to be a diversification of agencies involved in labour allocation. The reformist texts talked of a 'three-in-one combination' of direct allocation by state labour bureaux, decentralized allocation by labour service companies, 'talent exchange agencies' and enterprises, and self-employment by individuals and groups in co-operative or private businesses. The most important of the new agencies were the 'labour service companies' which began to emerge in 1979. Although most of these companies remained under state supervision, they enjoyed a certain autonomy, both as labour exchanges and as centres of job creation (by setting up their own independent enterprises). They were mainly involved in arranging jobs in the collective sector. In the state sector, while state labour bureaux still retained the power to set overall labour-force quotas, enterprise managers were to have greater power to choose which specific workers they wanted (and according to what criteria and by what method) within the state numerical quota. Eventually, the reformers argued, the supervisory role of labour bureaux should be gradually reduced until enterprises themselves could take most major decisions on hiring and firing their own staff and workers. If they needed more workers, managers should be allowed to advertise and deal with applicants directly. Successful enterprises should be able to attract labour from other enterprises by offering better wages and conditions. The third element of the new 'three-in-one combination' was the attempt to increase the choice available to individual workers and professional staff, particularly the latter (and especially after their initial job posting). Since experts were in short supply, managers were eager to prevent them leaving the enterprise; reformers deplored this and some went so far as to argue for 'free movement of qualified personnel and specialised cadres.' The aim of the official policy was more modest, with increased choice and personal mobility still seen merely as a 'complement' to the planned allocation of specialized labour.

The third main area of reform, which was launched in early 1983, was an effort to complement these system reforms by changes within the enterprise. The most important of these was the attempt to 'break the iron rice-bowl' of state workers by introducing the *labour contract system*. This reform aimed to increase the discretionary powers of managers over their workforce, in particular strengthening their ability to dismiss workers. In the past, virtually all state workers had enjoyed job security: henceforth, they would be employed on contracts of varying lengths, signed between themselves and their enterprise and enforceable through new labour legislation. At the end of the contract, if the worker's performance had been unsatisfactory or if the labour needs of the enterprise had altered in response to market fluctuations or technological change, the contract need not be renewed. In addition to increasing the flexibility of managerial controls over labour, this system would, it was hoped, improve labour productivity by increasing the motivation to work under the stimulus of job insecurity. The enterprises, labour service companies and local governments would each play a role in providing welfare benefits (which had formerly been the sole responsibility of the enterprise) and in retraining and redeploying redundant workers.

This package of labour reforms was begun in 1979 and its progress has very much followed the ups and downs of the overall reform process since then. In the next section I shall review the impact of these policies as of mid-1986 and assess the extent to which they have been successful in introducing a 'labour market' into China's urban-industrial economy.

The Progress of Chinese Labour Reforms

While there have been some changes in the role of the state in labour allocation, although non-state agencies of labour allocation have proliferated and there has been some limited progress towards establishing a labour contract system in the state sector, these cannot be interpreted as a decisive shift from administrative allocation of labour to a labour market. Nor have they led to a dramatic increase in labour mobility or labour productivity in the state sector or the urban economy more generally. In short, from a reformer's point of view, progress in implementing new labour policies has been frustratingly slow and results disappointing.

If we deal with the case of state agencies, the degree of administrative control over labour planning and allocation by means of directive methods remains high, most notably in the state sector, but also in the wider urban economy. State labour bureaux at various levels still dominate the process of labour allocation, although a good deal of their previous responsibility for the details has been devolved to other institutions, notably labour service companies and enterprises. Attempts to abolish the system of 'unified allocation' of strategic groups (notably college graduates) have encountered a good deal of opposition and have made limited headway. An experimental reform at Beijing University, for example, caused a public disturbance among graduating students in 1984. But various experimental compromise solutions are being tested at present, such as an arrangement whereby graduates are placed in jobs for three years according to 'unified allocation', after which time they are free to find their own jobs elsewhere.

Although the emergence of labour service companies in cities across the nation has diversified channels of labour allocation, increasing the flexibility of the labour system and its capacity to handle detail, these institutions do not represent a radical break with the principle of directive labour allocation.

Most of these companies remain appendages of state institutions of various kinds (including labour bureaux, government departments, enterprises, schools, etc.);they have functioned essentially to create new jobs rather than increase labour mobility and their operational methods tend to extend the principle and practice of 'unified allocation' into the non-state sector of the urban economy.

At the level of the enterprise, however, there have been some changes of significance, though falling far short of reformist goals. While enterprises are still bound by official numerical quotas for their existing and new workforce, managers now have much greater power to choose individual workers rather than merely to accept a batch dispatched by the local labour bureau as before. In some sectors, moreover, such as construction and transportation, managers have even wider powers (for example, to take on workers outside the plan) and managers in the collective sector in general have a much freer hand than their state counterparts. Indeed, the greater freedom of the collectives and the fact that of late some have performed as well as and better than state enterprises has opened up opportunities for individuals to move jobs independently. Municipal labour bureau officials in Beijing, for example, told me the attraction of prosperous collectives was drawing workers away from state enterprises (White, 1985: 16). There has also been more halting progress towards increasing the circulation of specialized/professional labour. New institutions have been established to handle movement between enterprises, sectors and regions. These go under a variety of names: in Beijing, for example, they are called 'talent exchange agencies'. Mobility in some sectors seems to have increased significantly. Members of the Beijing Chinese Academy of Social Sciences, for example, complain that a lot of their younger staff had left recently, partly because their wages are low and partly because they think that 'if you stay at the academy, you are a worm; if you go out, you are a dragon'. Others were being enticed from the capital by the prospect of becoming bigger fish in the provinces.

Yet progress at the level of the enterprise has also been frustrating for the reformers. Although managers have increased their powers over the hiring of labour, it is still extremely difficult for them to fire workers except for serious misdemeanours. Progress towards implementing the labour contract system has also been slow. Between 1983 and 1986, the new policy did not get beyond the experimental stage. Moreover, it was only applied to a portion of *new* state workers, leaving the established workforce unaffected. Although officials of the Ministry of Labour and Personnel can point to a steady increase in the number of 'contract workers', as of mid-1986, they are still a very small proportion of the state labour-force. Moreover, the numbers cited (3.5 million by mid-1986) may be misleading on several counts: some are in collective, not state enterprises; some are not 'labour contract system workers' in the intended sense of the reforms, but temporary workers merely hired for a limited period or a specific task: they also tend to be concentrated in certain sectors, notably mining, chemicals and construction. Clearly, the task of redefining the employment status of the state workforce has only just begun; the 'iron rice-bowl' is still intact.

Constraints on Labour Reform Policy

There are many factors to explain why the real impact of labour reforms has so far fallen short of reformers' intentions. Some of the problems lie in the nature of the policies themselves. In the case of the attempt to introduce a labour contract system, for example, the official policy was very ambiguous, allowing lower administrative agencies and enterprises a great deal of room for manoeuvre in interpreting the policy as they saw fit. Moreover, the implications of the new policy were not adequately thought through. A wide range of practical problems emerged during 1983–6 which appear either not to have been foreseen or not prepared for: the question of the applicability of the labour contract system to different types of enterprise or production process; the potential damage to the solidarity and morale of enterprise workforces; managerial reluctance to take on the extra administrative burden that the new system created; detailed questions of terms and conditions of work for contract workers and adequate provision for their welfare, retraining and re-employment if they are laid off at the end of a contract. Most crucial was the fact that, to be successful, the labour contract policy required complementary (and quite sweeping) changes in other areas of policy: education and training, social welfare provision, labour insurance, housing and law. A clearer conception of 'policy linkages' was required, followed by co-ordinated action on all these fronts. Except in a few exemplary cities, this does not appear to be the case.

Other factors that have blunted the impact of labour reforms are to be found in the policy on environment. The ideological framework, as we saw at the outset, made it difficult for reformers to come up with a convincing 'socialist' rationale for the establishment of a labour market. To their political opponents (notably residual Maoists) and to many of the state workforce, innovations such as the labour contract system were steps in the direction of 'capitalist wage labour'. There were also disagreements within the reform camp between more conservative and more radical views: for instance, some reform economists were sceptical of the value of the labour contract system and saw it as a threat to the 'socialist nature' of state enterprises.

The factor of bureaucratic inertia, of institutional resistance from a political-administrative apparatus whose power is being undermined, is also important. There is evidence to suggest that state labour agencies are reluctant to devolve any more than relatively marginal power to lower-level units and enterprises. The principle of official reform, proclaimed by central and local labour bureaux, is still to 'control the big things and decentralize the small'. In spite of some degree of administrative decentralization to local governments, the MLP still appears to rule the roost in a highly centralized system of administrative labour planning and allocation. In spite of greater powers to state enterprises in recruiting labour, they must still answer to local labour bureaux on personnel questions, often against their own best interests. Labour bureaux and their appendages, the labour service companies, still take on the responsibility for finding jobs for the vast majority of urban job seekers. The principle and practice of comprehensive administrative regulation of labour is still firmly in place. Once such a complex network has been established and consolidated over more than two decades, it is very difficult to shift.

Lest we slip too easily into a 'bureaucratic vested interest' type of explanation, one major qualification should be noted. The official commitment to full employment since the revolution has created a strong political relationship, an implicit social contract, between the Chinese state and its urban constituents. A kind of institutionalized patron-client relationship has been established wherein the state assumes the role of provider and the urban population come to depend on the state and to expect its largess. There is thus a mass constituency to retain state labour controls that coincides with and feeds the institutional self-interests of state labour agencies. If this relationship is threatened, if the state is seen to renege on its commitment to full employment, its legitimacy suffers and there is a danger of mass discontent and protest. Policy-makers are keenly aware of this danger and talk of the need to proceed cautiously with labour reforms, in fear of disturbing 'social peace'.

This pressure on state labour agencies is kept intense by the continued problem of urban surplus labour, the looming menace of rural–urban labour migration and the consequent fear of unemployment among urban dwellers. The continued dualistic structure of the urban economy, moreover, means that urban job seekers still tend to aspire to jobs in the privileged state sector and are loath to settle for second best in the collective or private sectors. Thus, even in those areas where local labour officials may have agreed with the need for reforms to increase labour mobility and raise labour productivity, these were pushed down the scale of priorities by the overriding primacy of creating jobs. The policy goals of greater labour productivity and more employment are, in the short term at least, incompatible, and the political situation has dictated that the latter take precedence.

If we focus on labour reforms which affect industrial relations within the enterprise, the obstacles to change have also been formidable. If the society at large is characterized by an implicit 'social contract' over full employment, the Chinese enterprise itself has a micro-version, based on an established patron–client relationship between managers and workers. Managerial indulgence has purchased worker co-operation in the process of meeting plans, both sides embedded in an institution which has provided security and relatively privileged status. While many managers would like the boat to go faster, they are also afraid of rocking it. This is particularly visible, for example, in the effort to implement the labour contract system: many managers have been cautious and sceptical, worried about its effects on the unity and morale of their workers; many workers, on the other hand, were downright hostile and made their position known in the usual informal ways in which disagreement and defiance is communicated in an authoritarian system such as China. We are entering here the informal realm of politics within the enterprise—politics, as it were, with a small 'p'—as opposed to the formal, public realm of big 'p' Politics.

Future Prospects for a Labour Market in Chinese Industry

To summarize, labour reforms thus far have not been successful in creating anything resembling a labour market in the state sector: state workers, to adapt the economists' term, are 'sticky outwards'. Circulation within the state sector and movement into the collective and individual sectors is still far below the reformers' expectations. Outside the state sector, however, the job status of workers and the flow of labour is much closer to the notion of the labour market. In the 'small collective' sector, workers do not tend to enjoy 'fixed' jobs, their income and tenure depend on the profitability of the firm, and they are more likely to move to better jobs elsewhere in the state or non-state sector. The Chinese urban labour scene, therefore, is still dualistic.

Overshadowing this is the dualism of the rural–urban divide. Rural surplus labour is estimated by Chinese economists at about one-third of total rural labour. Using 1982 figures, for example, the total agricultural labour calculated as necessary to cultivate available land was 157.51 million, total rural labour power was 332.78 million—of which 57.88 million were working outside agriculture—leaving a hypothetical surplus of 117.38 million, or 35.3 per cent (Feng, in White, 1985: 3). Although these are hypothetical calculations, reflecting widespread underemployment and not unemployment, the new rural responsibility systems have already accelerated the process of extruding labour from agriculture. This labour must be absorbed into the non-agricultural economy. Increasing numbers of peasants are being allowed into the larger cities on temporary contractual employment; while some Chinese analysts argue for a greater flow, so far official policy has been to restrict acess to the cities. The main strategy is to absorb rural surplus labour into 'township and town industries', usually in the vicinity of the peasants' home villages. This massive flow of labour power is under far less regulation than in the urban sector and much more closely resembles a real labour market. There is also evidence of rapidly increasing inter-regional labour mobility, both within and between provinces. The scale of this movement is difficult to quantify as yet, but examples abound. Many of the growing number of maids in private households in Beijing, for example, are recruited on temporary contracts from the poor province of Anhui. While, in the northern province of Shanxi in mid-1985, this author visited a rural shoe factory, many of whose workers came from the central province of Jiangsu on one-year contracts. Not only are the administrative constraints on this kind of movement much less than before, but the practice now receives official encouragement and may be expected to increase in future.

What are the prospects for establishing a labour system approximating a 'market' in the state sector? Clearly, another round of labour reform has begun (in mid-1986) and the term 'labour market' is gaining currency and acceptability. Past experience suggests that progress will continue to be slow. The continued threat of urban unemployment (heightened by the prospect of greater rural immigration), and the dualistic structure of the urban economy (which is eroding very slowly) still make the prospect of a 'fixed' state job very attractive. In an opinion poll taken in 1986, for example, 77.3 per cent of urban residents surveyed replied that 'in choosing a job, stability is more important than prospects for raises'. These factors will not change rapidly. Success in labour reforms, moreover, depends on success in other areas of reform, notably enterprise management, the wage system, housing policy, education, and so on.

The way in which Chinese state enterprises have evolved into 'small societies' is also a major constraint on changing the labour system. This solidarity is a facet of the 'organization oriented' enterprise of which the large Japanese firm is a prime example (for this notion, see Dore, 1973 and Shirk, 1981). Indeed, for the short and medium term at least, the evolution of the Chinese socialist labour system may be comparable in major ways to its Japanese capitalist counterpart. This may not be to the taste of many Chinese reformers, who regard this kind of enterprise solidarity as an impediment to efficiency and the dualism of the urban economy as a structural distortion. However, the Japanese version has been rather successful; should we expect anything less of the Chinese?

References

Dore, Ronald P. (1973). *British Factory–Japanese Factory, the Origins of National Diversity in Industrial Relations*. Berkeley, University of California Press.

Feng, Lanrui (1981). 'On factors affecting China's employment'. *Renmin Ribao* ('People's Daily'), 16 November, in *SWB:FE*, No. 6888.

Godfrey, Martin (1985). *Global Unemployment: The New Challenge to Economic Theory*. Brighton, Harvester Press.

Kornai, Janos (1980). *Economics of Shortage*. Vol. A, North-Holland.

Liu, Shugui (1986). 'Is unemployment a social phenomenon peculiar to the capitalist system?' *Gongren Ribao* ('Workers Daily'), 18 August, in *SWB:FE*, No. 8354.

Shirk, S. L. (1981). 'Recent Chinese labour policies and the transformation of industrial organisation in China'. *China Quarterly*, No. 88 (December): 575–93.

State Statistical Bureau (1985). *Statistical Yearbook of China 1985*. Beijing and Hong Kong.

White, Gordon (1982). 'Urban employment and labour allocation policies in post-Mao China'. *World Development*, **10**, No. 8: 613–32.

White, Gordon (1985). *Labour Allocation and Employment Policy in Contemporary*

China (transcripts of a research trip, June 1985). Brighton, Institute of Development Studies.

Xiao, Liang (1983). 'Replacing the "lifetime system" with the contract system—a probe into reform of the workforce utilisation system'. *Shijie Jingji Daobao* ('World Economic Herald'), Shanghai, 23 May, in *CREA*, No. 383, 19 September 1983.

Zhao, Lukuan (1980). 'Several problems of labour and employment in our country'. *Renmin Ribao* ('People's Daily'), 19 August, in *FBIS*, 4 September.

Zhao, Lukuan (1982). 'On China's employment problem under conditions of relative over-supply of labour'. *Renmin Ribao* ('People's Daily'), 2 March, in *FBIS*, 11 March 1982.

Zhuang, Qidong & Sun, Keliang (1983). 'Probing into the question of implementing the labour reserve system'. *Renmin Ribao* ('People's Daily'), 23 February in *CREA*, No. 322.

9 The Development of Work Incentives in Chinese Industrial Enterprises — Material Versus Non-Material Incentives

John S. Henley and Nyaw Mee-Kau

Introduction

Labour is one of the key factors in the process of industrial growth in any economy. Whether China will achieve its objectives of modernizing its industry by the year 2000 under its current 'Four Modernizations' Programme is heavily dependent on the resourcefulness and skills of workers in the industrial sector. The Communist Party devotes a lot of its efforts to indoctrinating Chinese workers but there is little empirical evidence as to what motivates workers.

This paper discusses the factors affecting the work motivation of Chinese workers in state-owned enterprises and the problems encountered in current wage reforms. The first section of the paper examines and analyses oscillations in policy as regards the varying emphasis put on non-material incentives (moral incentives) at different periods since 1949.

In the second section, the wage system and latest wage reforms are examined, in particular, the problems of changing the existing wage structure. The range of techniques and systems of non-material incentives currently in use is considered in the third section. Workers' participation in the management of the enterprise via the Workers' Congress has been historically central to Chinese Communist doctrine. The effectiveness of this forum for eliciting the consent and motivation of the work-force towards high productivity is assessed.

Section four will present the results of a small survey of work motivation in twelve Chinese industrial enterprises carried out during a study tour of five major industrial cities in the summer of 1984.

Policy Oscillation Over Material Versus Non-material Incentives

Ideology has played a major role in the reconstruction of the Chinese economy since the civil war ended in 1949. Ideological considerations have also shaped the course chosen in developing and modernizing industry. A notable feature of policy changes has been radical shifts from a primarily calculative and pragmatic ethos to one of intense political fervour and emphasis on moral rectitude in everything followed by a return to pragmatism. Oscillations in policy orientation have also been reflected in the relative emphasis placed on material and non-material incentives in the work place.

The Chinese Communist Party (CCP) has for a long time pursued a policy of combining both material and non-material incentives (or 'moral encouragement') to stimulate productivity towards growth. Material incentives have been developed according to the socialist principle of 'from each according to his ability and to each according to his work'. In practice this means payment of a basic wage according to national scales plus an incentive bonus, developed at plant level. Moral encouragement has relied on a variety of different campaigns designed to strengthen the political and ideological education of workers so that they recognize their moral obligations to work hard for the benefit of the nation since, under socialism, they are 'the masters of the house'.

The recent history of China can be divided into the following periods: economic rehabilitation (1949–52), First Five-Year Plan (1953–7), the Great Leap Forward (1958–60), economic recovery (1961–5), the Cultural Revolution (1966–76) and the Post-Mao Period after 1977. In general, material incentives were emphasized during periods of political moderation and industrial growth while moral incentives were stressed during periods of political extremism and low growth (see Table 9.1).

The economic rehabilitation period following peace in 1949 was a transitional period characterized by experimentation, pragmatism and diversity. During this period, the leadership's overriding concern was to consolidate its political power. Enterprises with clear connections with Chiang Kai Shek and the Kuomintang regime were nationalized while other enterprises were allowed to remain partially private. Impressive economic progress was achieved during this period. Cadres from the old liberated areas as well as new workers who joined the labour-force after 1949 were paid with goods in kind while other office and factory workers were paid a mixture of commodities and wages. This partial rationing system sometimes referred to as the 'supply system' was a practice borrowed from the pre-liberation days when commodities were in short supply and money values were highly unstable.

There were no clear-cut incentive policies prevailing during the economic rehabilitation period. Although political indoctrination was pervasive as part of the campaign to institutionalize the new regime, it did not impinge directly on factory workers beyond general exhortations to work to rebuild the nation. Financial incentives, however, were of some importance for, according to an official estimate, industrial workers paid on piece-rate systems accounted for 35.5 per cent of all production workers.

The First Five-Year Plan (1953–7) was also a period of substantial industrial growth, though not without problems of industrial management. The management system was in large part copied from the Stalinist Soviet model which, of course, included political campaigns and ideological indoc-

Table 9.1 Development periods, policy orientations and economic growth, 1949–1983

Periods	Policy Orientations	Annual GNP Growth-Rates*	Annual Industrial Growth-Rates*
		%	%
Economic Rehabilitation (1949–1952) (1949–1952)	moderation/pragmatism	22.1	35.6
First Five-Year Plan (1953–1957)	moderation/pragmatism	6.7	9.3
Great Leap Forward (1958–1961)	extremism	–6.6	–18.2
Economic Recovery (1961–1965)	moderation/pragmatism	8.1	15.1
Cultural Revolution (1966–1976)	extremism	–2.5** 6.1†	–11.0** 7.2† 9.3
Post-Mao Periods (1977–1983)	moderation/pragmatism	10.7	9.3

Source: Computed from State Statistics Bureau, *Glorious 35 Years, 1949–1984*, Beijing, China Statistics Publication, Beijing, 1984 (in Chinese).

* compound annual growth-rates.
**1966–8.
†1969–76.

trination but was orientated towards material benefits for model workers. Industrial morale was reported to be high during this period and structural problems were not so obvious when basic levels of plant utilization had only just begun to recover their normal levels. According to Yu:

> At that time people did not care too much about their own gains and losses and much work got done quite easily. The political atmosphere then ('the revolution had just won a nation-wide victory and people were still ecstatic') and the people's enthusiasm covered up to a certain degree the defects of the economic structure. [Yu 1985: 32].

Material incentives were also increasing in coverage so that by 1954 industrial workers on piece-rate bonus systems accounted for over 40 per cent of the total industrial labour-force. There was also a fairly significant wage differential in the complicated wage system during the period. We will examine this in the next section. In general, 'egalitarianism', which was later blamed for the lack of initiative among workers and staff during the Cultural Revolution, was not apparent in official policy pronouncements. After the expulsion of Russian advisers and Mao's proclaimed Great Leap Forward (1958–60), Chinese wage policy entered a period dominated by 'leftist' ideas. The primacy of moral encouragement was asserted over material incentives. Mao believed that rapid transformation of China to communism could best be achieved by creating a new type of selfless and pure communist man. An intensive nation-wide campaign was therefore launched, aimed at eliminating class distinctions, in particular the distinctions between manager and worker, and between mental and physical labour. Party theorists proclaimed 'poverty is revolutionary while wealth is revisionist', and commanded 'smash bourgeois rights'.

The coverage of bonus payments to industrial workers was reduced and managers and technical staff were excluded from receiving a bonus (Li, 1985: 107). The Soviet-inspired work quota system and piece-rate system were eventually abolished in 1958 (*Encyclopedia*, Vol. 1: 553); they were replaced by a semi-wage, semi-rationing system in a number of enterprises (Feng & Zhao, 1984: 596). Official criticism of the principle of distribution of wages according to work created a situation where 'it made no difference whether one worked or not or did more work or less'. Industrial output fell dramatically and as a consequence there was a sharp drop in the purchasing power of wages.

Liu Shaoqi assumed responsibility for reconstructing the economy when Mao sidestepped into the 'second line' in 1961, after the collapse of the Great Leap Forward. Liu initiated an economic recovery programme which was characterized by ideological moderation, the restoration of the bonus system, and a host of other measures to revitalize industry. Political campaigns were sharply reduced. According to Xiang (1982: 110), in 1963, only 19.9 per cent of workers and staff were paid piece-work wages while, by 1965, a comprehensive bonus system was available for most workers. There was renewed industrial progress during the recovery period, 1962–5. Annual industrial growth was estimated to be 15.1 per cent.

In spite of rapid industrial growth under Liu's leadership, China reverted to ideological extremism in 1966 when Mao emerged from the 'second line' to launch the Great Cultural Revolution (1966–76) and Liu was purged. Politics was again in command. During this ten-year period, the principle of 'to each according to his work' was once again criticized for containing capitalist elements. For example, it was widely suggested by leftists that 'the bigger the differences in the payment for labour, the more capitalism there is' and that 'equal allocation of work points is more communist'. As a result of the official stigma attached to material incentives, bonus and piece-rate systems were sharply reduced or simply abolished. Egalitarianism was now the guiding principle of policy so that funds which had previously been used for above-norm piece-work wages or bonus were evenly distributed every month as a supplementary wage. There was little difference in income, no matter how hard or how well individuals worked, or even whether they worked at all. According to Xiang (1982: 112), the consequence was absolute egalitarianism whereby 'the advanced gained nothing, the backward lost nothing and the initiative of the masses was seriously dampened'. This observation reflects the general consensus among recent Chinese assessments of wage and incentive policies during the Cultural Revolution, namely that the 'Gang of Four' and their associates believed that the 'spirit is all-powerful' and that intensive political education was therefore the most socially efficient way of stimulating industrial production. Chinese experience suggests that modern production methods require more than just enthusiastic workers. Without professional engineers, scientists and managers purged during the Cultural Revolution as capalistic elements, workers' efforts are unlikely on their own to be sufficient to produce economic progress.

After waivering for two years following the death of Mao and the downfall of the 'Gang of Four' in 1976, the Chinese Communist Party finally resolved to carry out economic reforms at the crucial Third Plenary Session of the CCP in December 1978 under the leadership of Deng Xiaoping. The socialist principle of 'to each according to his work' was reinstated and piece-rate and bonus systems were revived so that, by 1979, about 90 per cent of workers and staff had received a bonus. All workers and staff in state-owned enterprises are now paid some form of output incentive or bonus in addition to their basic wage. Since 1978, there have been no political campaigns at enterprise level although political work (moral encouragement) is still stressed in official documents and conferences and through the media.

The brief history of changes in industrial policy affecting wage incentives presented above suggests that ideological moderation implies official encouragement of the extensive use of material incentives at enterprise level. By contrast, periods of political extremism have been associated with egalitarianism and a belief that problems of industrial efficiency were amenable to political solution. As is now well recognized by Chinese leaders, excessive emphasis on egalitarianism undermines the technical and managerial leadership of the enterprise to such an extent that any enthusiasm and energy released from ordinary workers by moral incentives cannot compensate for the absence of competent leadership. Equally, the individualism fostered by material incentives tends to undermine the solidaristic collective orientation encouraged by political education and moral incentives. The problem for any socialist society is to establish the appropriate balance between the processes of competition and co-operation in the work-place consonant with wider political and economic objectives.

Since 1979, the industrial productivity policy of the CCP, as in earlier prosperous periods, has involved combining both material incentives and moral incentives to mobilize the labour-force. While ideology cannot easily be dispensed with in a socialist country, when it is pushed to the extent of severely undermining authority structures within the enterprise, it results in the paralysis of decisionmaking and a sharp decline in productivity. In China, 'only a few workers are willing to make greater contributions to society without bothering about remuneration', as one cadre candidly admitted in a letter to *Gongren Ribao* ('Workers' Daily') in 1982. Recognizing the importance of remuneration to workers and staff in the new economic environment, the CCP has placed great emphasis on wage and bonus reform as part of the current economic reform programmes. Distributional concerns and debate about worker's solidarity seem to have been assigned a low priority.

According to the 'Decision of the Central Committee of the CCP on Reform of the Economic Structure' (hereafter referred to as the 1984 Decision Document):

> In the enterprises, the difference between the wages of various trades and jobs should be widened, so as to apply fully the principle of rewarding the diligent and good and punishing the lazy and bad and of giving more pay for more work and less pay for less work as well as to fully reflect the difference between mental and manual, complex and simple, skilled and unskilled, and heavy and light work. In particular, it is necessary to change the present remuneration for mental work which is relatively low. [p. 13].

The Wage System and Wage Reform

In China, the principal forms of material incentives include basic wages (time-work or piece-work), subsidized commodities, bonuses, and welfare benefits such as privileged access to public housing. We shall focus on the wage system and the current wage reforms.

The industrial wage system in China is highly complicated. The current system, which was partially copied from the Soviet system practised in the 1930s, was established through the wage reforms of 1956 and 1963. Wage scales vary among different branches of industry, trades, enterprises, types of work and regions. At present, there are literally hundreds of wage scales and more than one thousand wage grades (Feng & Zhao, 1984: 607). For simplicity, the Chinese industrial wage system can be roughly broken down into three sub-systems: (1) the system of wage brackets for workers; (2) the post or job-type wage system; and (3) the system of wage brackets for cadres.

Under system (1), industrial workers are allocated to grades which are differentiated according to variations in the level of skill required of the job-holder. At present the majority of workers, such as those employed in the machinery and the chemical industry, are paid according to an eight-grade wage system, while a few industries adhere to a seven-grade system. For example, workers in the machinery and electronics industry in Jilin Province (in north-east China) are paid on an eight-grade structure with a differential of 17.8 per cent between each grade.

From Table 9.2 it can be seen that the standard monthly wage for unskilled labour (grade 1) is set at ¥33 (approximately US$10.60), whereas a highly-skilled worker (grade 8) receives ¥99.5 per month. As the wage grade coefficient and the standard monthly wage vary between each industrial sector as well as between enterprises of the same sector in different geographical regions, wage payments for ostensibly similar jobs requiring identical levels of skill may be different. Thus, workers in heavy industry are generally paid better than their counterparts in light industry, even though the content of their jobs is the same in every respect.

Under system (2), industrial workers are paid according to the job-type they hold in the enterprise. The system is usually adopted in those industries or enterprises where skills are less complicated, job differences small and the division of labour highly developed. Production workers in the textile or chemical industries are typically paid according to job-type (Jiang & Shen, 1985: 335).

Under the third system, remuneration for cadres (factory directors, other managers and technical staff) is governed by the system of wage brackets which was first implemented in 1956. The system was simplified and consolidated in 1963. Under the system, China is divided into seven regions, and within each region an industry is assigned to one of four categories according to its importance. For example, steel production as a heavy industry is usually classified as 'category one'. The categories are further subdivided according to size and scale. Because of the variety of combinations possible, of regional location, plant size and scale, wage grades may vary between enterprises. At present the minimum number of grades for cadres is seventeen with a maximum of twenty-three (*Encyclopedia*, Vol. 1, 1984: 59). Within the enterprise, the wage scale for a particular post may cover several grades which overlap with each other.

The variation in the Chinese system of wage brackets and posts reflects the principle of 'to each according to his work'. The motivational interpretation of this principle was given by Lenin who argued that wages were the primary means of stimulating workers to labour diligently until their social conscious-

Table 9.2 Grade-patterns of machinery workers in Jilin Province (year unspecified)

Wage Grade	1	2	3	4	5	6	7	8
Standard Monthly Wage (in yuan)	33	39	46	54	64	74	85	99,5
Wage Grade Coefficient	1.000	1.178	1.388	1.635	1.926	2.269	2.560	3.960

Source: Li (1985: 119)

ness had progressed to a higher, communist stage. Apart from the large number of wage scales and grades, China has in the past officially adhered to a 'rational low-wage policy', where wage increases were infrequent, occuring at intervals of several years. For practical purposes, a real wage increase requires promotion to a higher grade. With a low-wage policy, China has been able to increase capital accumulation and investment in heavy industrial development programmes, but recent experience suggests a trade-off between material incentives, investment rates and efficiency of plant utilization and a trend towards greater concern for the latter with improvement in incentives as a major policy instrument.

From the 1956 wage reforms until 1976, the following wage adjustments were made:

1. Managers' and other cadres' wages were reduced by between 3 per cent and 10 per cent in 1957 because of concern by the Party leadership over the high pay of top-ranking officials in the Soviet Union.
2. Industrial workers' wages were increased by around 30 per cent overall in 1959, whereas the increase for cadres was only 10 per cent.
3. In 1963 there was a wage increase that ranged from 5 to 40 per cent, generally favouring workers and lower-ranking cadres.
4. In 1971, industrial workers employed before 1957 or 1966 were upgraded by one grade (Li, 1985: 107–9).

The first wage increase after the Cultural Revolution came in 1977. Low-paid and long-established workers' wages were increased by 40 per cent. Since then, there has been a series of other grade adjustments and wage increases. Nevertheless, despite recent wage increases, average industrial wages remain relatively low for, historically, the growth-rate of real wages has been very modest (0.3 per cent per annum between 1953 and 1978). During periods of ideological extremism average industrial wages even declined (see Table 9.3).

A number of problems have been found with the wage system and current wage reforms are now targeted at these. The chief problem has been identified as the overwhelmingly egalitarian nature of the wage system. For example, wages and bonuses of workers and staff were unrelated to the performance of the enterprise and were paid irrespective of how well or how poorly the enterprise was managed. The way in which an individual performed also made little difference to the level of pay. This practice, now officially derided as 'eating from the same big pot', still operates in many state-owned enterprises. It is argued that egalitarianism has gone too far and has seriously reduced the initiative and motivation of good workers. As the 1984 Decision Document admits:

> The [egalitarianism] has resulted in . . . the practice of 'eating from the same big pot' prevailing in the relations of the enterprises of the state and in those of the workers and staff members to their enterprises. The

Table 9.3 Wages of workers and staff in state-owned enterprises, 1953–1983

Year/Periods	Average Wage Level (Yuan)	Average Growth-Rates (%)	
		Money Wage	Real Wage (1952 = 100)
I. First Five-Year Plan, 1953–1957:		7.4	5.4
1953	496		
1957	637		
II. Second Five-Year Plan, 1958–1962:		−1.5	−5.4
1958	550		
1962	592		
III. 1963–1965 (part of Economic Recovery Period)		3.3	7.2
1963	641		
1965	652		
IV. Third Five-Year Plan, 1966–1970:		−1.4	−1.2
1966	636		
1970	609		
V. Fourth Five-Year Plan, 1971–1975:		0.1	−0.1
1971	597		
1975	613		
VI. Fifth Five-Year Plan, 1976–1980:		5.5	2.9
1976	605		
1980	803		
VII. After 1980, 1981–1983:		6.0	1.6
1981	812		
1982	836		
1983	865		

Growth-rates of average wage: 1953–1978: 1.04% (0.3%)
1979–1983: 5.3% (1.7%)
(real growth-rates in brackets)

Source: Computed from *Glorious 35 Years, 1949–1984*, compiled by State Statistics Bureau, China Statistics Publication, Beijing, 1984 (in Chinese), p. 166.

enthusiasm, initiative and creativeness of enterprises and workers and staff members have, as a result, been seriously dampened and the socialist economy is bereft of much of the vitality it should possess. [p. 5]

A second major criticism has been that wage grades are often complicated and difficult to justify using economic criteria. For example, the system of setting wage norms according to the relative importance and administrative affiliation of the enterprise produces arbitrary distinctions. Thus wage norms in heavy industry are generally set higher than those in light industry, yet much of so-called light industrial work is heavy in practice and is also of strategic and economic importance. In addition, the rewards for managerial and technical work compared with manual work are meagre indeed. According to data published in 1979, university graduates of 1959 were being paid around 25 per cent less than workers who entered the labour-force in 1951 with only junior high school certificates (both groups were of the same age). There have also been cases reported where workers have been reluctant to be promoted to cadres, or have asked to remain on manual wage scales (Zhao & Pan, 1984: 163).

A third complaint, voiced at enterprise level in particular, has been that there is over-centralization of wage management and enterprises have no autonomy in setting wage rates. Increases in rates were controlled centrally, regardless of local conditions. In spite of centralization, many enterprises have no work norms or measures for assessing productivity. Some enterprises have also resorted to improper ways of funding bonus payments (Feng & Zhao, 1984: 160).

Recognition of the limitations and arbitrariness of the wage system as outlined above has forced Party leaders to promote a series of wage reforms. Indeed, wage reform is now an integral part of the more general economic reform programme officially announced in the 1984 Decision Document, and the latter draws on the experience of a number of experiments carried out since 1978. The guiding principle of the current wage reform, 'to each according to his work' is laid down in the 1984 Decision Document (p. 24). Deng, the architect and prime mover behind the reform programme, has explicitly elaborated the principle; it,

Calls for distribution according to the quantity and quality of an individual's work . . . a person's grade on the pay scale is determined mainly by his performance on the job, his technical level and his actual contribution. [Deng, 1984: 117].

The most salient feature of the current Chinese economic reform programme compared with past reforms is that enterprises are now being given more autonomy in the decisionmaking process which, among other things, includes decisionmaking power over wages and rewards (Henley & Nyaw, 1986; and 1984 *Decision Document*). This is a significant departure from the two major wage reforms of 1956 and 1963. Although there are wide variations in wage reform programmes among different experimental enterprises, they all aim 'to better link wages and bonuses with the improved enterprise performance' (1984 Decision Document). A brief description of some of the more important pilot experiments seems warranted:

1. Many enterprises adopted the floating wage system. Under this system part (usually less than 50 per cent) of a worker's standard wage and bonus (sometimes including part of the profit at the disposal of the enterprise) becomes a 'floating wage' which is then paid to workers on the basis of their performance. This seems to be a very popular wage reform to date.
2. Some enterprises have introduced a 'floating' promotion system financed from part of the wage and bonus fund. This has enabled enterprises to promote a greater number of the more capable workers and technical staff than was possible under the rigid wage increase system normally operating.
3. Other enterprises have adopted what is termed the 'structural wage system'. Under this system wages are broken down into four parts: a base wage, a seniority wage, a position wage and a flexible wage. The base wage is supposed to ensure that a worker's basic needs are met so that, although the basic wage remains relatively stable over time, it may be adjusted according to the inflation rate if it is deemed necessary. The seniority wage is based on years of working experience but is subject to performance appraisal. The post wage is a responsibility payment to cadres, technical staff or highly-skilled workers. Finally, the flexible wage is based on a measure of the enterprise's performance and of the contribution of individual workers. In general, it consists of a floating wage, bonus and subsidized benefits.

The Bonus

The bonus has a long history as an important component of the Chinese wage system. The current reform programme aims to restore the bonus element in an industrial worker's wages to something like its original significance. In the past, state-owned enterprises were restricted to paying no more than two months' basic wages as an annual bonus. Since the replacement of 'profit delivery' by taxes in October 1984, enterprises now pay a contracted tax rather than handing over any surplus (or loss) to the state ('the contracted responsibility system'). In connection with this reform, enterprises can now 'decide on the amount of bonuses for their workers and staff members according to the results of enterprise operation while the state only collects an appropriate amount of tax on the above-norm bonus from enterprises' (1984 *Decision Document*: 23). With the new ruling, bonus limits were lifted so that tax only became payable on bonuses of over four months' basic wages. According to a statement by Vice-Premier Tian (1986: 10), most industrial enterprises paid four months' bonus in 1985. On the other hand, based on the contracted responsibility system, 'enterprises which have failed to fulfil their quotas and paid less taxes and earned less profits must reduce or stop bonuses, or even withhold portions of their employees' wages.' (Jin, 1984: 4). This would seem to suggest that there is still some way to go before enterprise bonus levels reflect real profits or efficiency.

The success or failure of the wage reform in China is likely to have a far-reaching effect on the economy. At present, the wage level in China is still very low. Monthly pay for a skilled worker at grade eight is slightly over ¥100 (US$32). Deng anticipates that, as production expands, there will be more promotions to higher grades and increases in standard wages of each grade (Deng, 1984: 117). However, because of the low base wage and the ambitious development programme of the state, China is likely to remain a low-wage economy for a fairly long time. Another problem facing wage reformers is how to widen differentials for higher-level technical and managerial manpower to reflect more accurately supply-and-demand conditions in the labour market. In addition, imbalances in differentials between skilled trades that do not reflect marginal productivity have yet to be resolved. What is not in doubt is the intention of the Chinese leadership (see 1984 Decision Document: 23).

Another critical issue in wage reform is the linkage between wages and prices. Because of the irrationality of official prices that do not reflect relative scarcity, the profit performance of enterprises is blurred (Henley & Nyaw, 1986). How to link wages with the economic performance of the enterprise remains an unsolved problem and further experiments have been abandoned pending wider reform of prices generally (Tian, 1986: 10). From a worker's point of view, the key issue is maintenance of his real wage in the face of changes in hitherto state-controlled commodity prices nearer to true market values.

The lifting of bonus limits is a bold and significant development. Enterprise management now have the ability to reward the good and diligent and punish the lax and unproductive. This ought to enhance the motivation of workers and technical staff, but in order to have any effect income differences must increase. The social and political implications of these changes should not be underestimated. Although the Chinese leaders hope that the gaps 'will encourage the advanced and push those who lag behind' (Jin, 1984: 26), this has yet to be proved. No doubt they are also aware that the ranks of the Red Guard during the Cultural Revolution were swelled by a disproportionate number of temporary and contract workers from state enterprises. Many of their victims were the better-paid and educated permanent workers and cadres now enthusiastically embracing the reform programme.

Non-material Stimuli and Democratic Management

The Chinese Communist Party's ideology has traditionally stressed that all types of material incentive should be used hand-in-hand with moral encouragement ('non-material stimuli'). Although the superiority of non-material incentives has never been questioned, the extent to which they have been used has varied during different periods, as discussed earlier. In many ways, moral incentives have acted as a symbol of the extent to which the leadership believes economic problems are amenable to political solution. The seven principal types of moral encouragement campaigns used in China are summarized in the list below. These emulation drives generally aim at increasing economic efficiencies, such as output volumes, product improvement, energy saving, cost reduction and profitability.

Forms of emulation campaigns

1. *Advanced worker*   An award to those workers who have achieved good performance, judged by administrative units and trade unions at regular intervals.

2. *Model worker*   An award to those workers who achieve outstanding performance in their work in production, technological development, etc., judged by a democratic selection process including representatives from staff and workers. Model worker campaigns operate at different levels: national, provincial, municipal or country level, in descending order of prestige.

3. *Emulating, learning from, catching up with, helping and overtaking the advanced units*   First introduced in the 1960s, these were implemented in various departments, enterprises, factory workshops and sections for both cadres and workers. Objectives are to raise the initiative of cadres and workers; judging is criterial: the 'five goods' for cadres are good ideological work, good planning execution, good enterprise management, good welfare management, and good attitudes of workers. The 'five goods' for workers are good political thought, good implementation of work, good discipline, good learning and good team work.

4. *Small Target (or 'hundred point') emulation*   This is a form of emulation campaign within the enterprise: the collective leadership of the enterprise divides the overall technological and economic targets into smaller targets for workshops, sections and individuals. This emulation is judged or appraised periodically and, because enterprises award one hundred points for full implementation of targets, it is also called the 'hundred point' emulation.

5. *Emulation among workers of the same type of work*   Campaigns are aimed at workers in different or similar industries but who do the same type of work and need some sort of problem-solving ability. The focus is on sharing problems and solutions.

6. *Inter-factory emulation*   This was first started in the 1950s for factories in the same line of business. Emulation is based on physical or value targets such as production, energy saving, product quality and reduction of costs; for factories in different industries, emulation criteria are based on labour efficiency, profit, return to capital funds, etc.

7. *All-Excellent Industrial Project*   This is awarded to good-quality projects where plans are fully implemented within a given time period, labour productivity surpasses the target set by the state and material consumption is less than budgeted, with no accidents (*Encyclopedia of China's Industrial Management*, Vol. 1, 1984: 542–3).

The Party and factory administration play a central role in emulation campaigns. The Communist Youth League and 'mass organizations' at the enterprise level such as trade unions and women's groups are also actively involved in launching emulation drives. Winners of emulation campaigns are awarded or designated 'advanced' factory unit or worker. Other titular honours such as 'model worker', 'labour hero', 'outstanding worker' or 'Red Standard bearer' are presented if workers meet certain stringent criteria stipulated by the appraisal committee comprising of the Party, factory administration and mass organizations. In practice, most of the moral incentives are also accompanied by monetary awards or benefits in kind such as access to better housing, sponsored trips, and so on. The Party has a long tradition and experience of organizing ideological and political work. The main purpose of ideological indoctrination is twofold: (1) to heighten the political consciousness of workers, and (2) to instill a sense of responsibility as 'masters of the house'. The Party considers that ideological-political work is critical in ensuring that production plans and other tasks at the enterprise are fully implemented. This was reaffirmed in the 'Programme for Ideological and Political Work Among Workers and Staff Members in State-owned Enterprises for Trial Implementation' adopted by the CCP in July 1983.

As a strategy for enhancing managerial control of the labour process, moral encouragement programmes parallel schemes to enhance intrinsic work incentives and internalize motivation advocated by American social psychologists such as Mayo, Herzberg, Maslow and MacGregor. At certain times, the Chinese Communist Party has sought to elevate moral encouragement to a pre-eminent position within the structure of controls of the labour process, particularly during the Great Leap Forward (1958–60) and the Cultural Revolution's early phase (1966–8).

There is considerable debate about how effective moral encouragement is. Clearly, to a political party steeped in revolutionary tradition, moral campaigns have an important symbolic status and serve to remind present generations of the heroic sacrifices of past national heroes. However, when ideological work has been pushed to extremes at the expense of material incentives industrial discipline has suffered. Today's leadership would seem to accept that there is a limit to the way in which moral encouragement can be used as a mechanism to spur and improve work performance. During the reconstruction period in the 1950s, the need for self-sacrifice was self-evident given the widespread destruction of the economy. In the 1980s, it is also self-evident that industrial modernization and reform is a complex process which cannot be managed merely by political means.

Another strand in the system of management of the labour process is the system of organizational democracy (Adizes & Borgese, 1975; and Crouch & Heller, 1983). Workers' participation in management, among other functions, is intended to elicit the consent and motivation of the work-force. It is in this sense, as part of the apparatus of moral encouragement, that we now consider the practice of democratic management in China.

China adopted the 'triumvirate' or triple alliance system in 1949 which offered a limited form of worker participation in management. However, the system was not very successful owing to, among other things, the lack of democratic spirit (Henley & Nyaw, 1986). The triumvirate system was abolished in 1952 and was replaced by the Stalinist 'one-man management' system during the First Five-Year Plan (1952–6). The Stalinist system proved to be a problem for Chinese leaders concerned about the autocratic aspects of the system. While theoretically there was worker's participation in management, Lenin's principle of 'democratic centralism' seemed to decline in importance over time. More importantly, it ran counter to the Yan'an way of doing things which emphasized human solidarity and the importance of seeking a consensus. The system was divorced from the 'mass line' which demanded participation from below and the blending of local initiative in management. It was also divorced from the principle of 'concentrated leadership and divided operations' of the Yan'an model as practised during the pre-liberation days (see Selden, 1971; and Brugger, 1981).

Thus, at the Eighth Party Congress held in August 1956, it was announced that the 'one-man management' system would be replaced by a system whereby the factory director took responsibility for production under the leadership of the enterprise Party committee. In addition, the workers' congress system under the leadership of the Party committee was promulgated to encourage workers' participation in management through making proposals to management. However, it had no executive authority since it had no powers to make decisions binding on the factory director.

During the Cultural Revolution, workers' congresses, trade unions and enterprise Party committees all disappeared. When the Cultural Revolution officially ended in 1976, they were reinstated in their former roles. There was some initial confusion about the exact status of the workers' congress until the publication of the 1984 *Decision Document*. In June 1981, the Central Committee issued an apparently important document on workers' congresses entitled 'Provisional Regulations Concerning Congresses of Workers and Staff Members in State-Owned Industrial Enterprises'. According to this document the workers' congress was to become an 'organ of power' of the

Table 9.4 Staff and workers' participation in management (unit: number)

| Year | Workers' Congresses Established | | Democratically-Elected Workers' Congress | | |
	Total	% of Enterprise Trade Unions	1st Degree Election* No.	2nd Degree Election** No.	3rd Degree Election[+] No.
1980	36,208	9.63	965	11,186	33,225
1981	101,130	24.59	8,993	14,834	29,465
1982	191,693	44.20	15,320	23,505	52,337
1983	229,043	51.20	27,972	33,676	49,412

Source: Zhongguo Shehui Tongji Ziliao (China's Social Statistical Data), Beijing, State Statistical Bureau, 1985, p. 301 (in Chinese).
* 1st degree democratic election refers to the election of factory directors (managers)
** 2nd degree election refers to the election of workshop directors and deputies
[+] 3rd degree election refers to the election of workshop section chiefs or group heads

enterprise and this gave rise to some speculation that China was about to embark on a more active form of worker participation than had occured in the past. However, this never seemed particularly likely given that one of the first major policy declarations by Deng, in July 1978, stressed the importance of developing a proper responsibility system in which managerial authority prevailed over the purely political.

Among other things, the workers' congress to date has the power to examine and adopt resolutions on production and budget plans prepared by the director, to decide welfare funds for workers and staff, to discuss and pass resolutions relating to wage adjustment and workers' training, and to elect factory directors subject to approval by higher authority. The delegates of the workers' congress generally also include workshop directors, section chiefs and group heads who may or may not be elected by workers. In general, workers should constitute not less than 60 per cent of the total number of representatives. The number of workers' congresses established has increased very rapidly since 1980, as has the election of factory directors, workshop directors and section chiefs of enterprises, including collective enterprises (see Table 9.4). The table indicates that the practice of electing different levels of management is spreading but, as might be expected, it is less common the more senior the official involved.

The revival of the workers' congress represents a step towards organizational democracy which gives some additional rights to workers; in particular, it requires top management to report on their activities on a regular basis. Nevertheless, the factory director has the authority to return a resolution to the workers' congress for reconsideration. Should this fail, the dispute may be referred to a higher authority in the state apparatus who will make the final ruling.

It would seem that the revived workers' congress represents a consultative forum that imposes limited obligations on top management. Like most representative bodies in capitalist economies, congresses tend to be dominated by more skilled workers and supervisors. When not in session, decisions of the congress are handled by standing committees that draw on specialists with knowledge of the problems concerned. There seems to be no uniform pattern as to whether the trade union or the Party services these committees. However, since the Party Secretary is the final arbiter in disputes with management, his influence tends to be pervasive. Despite this, the development of the workers' congress system does offer some scope for meaningful participation beyond the mere 'formalism' of the past. Whether this will increase the motivation of workers and staff and hence lead to better work performance or merely offer another career route for ambitious Party members remains to be seen.

Empirical Evidence of Work Motivation

It is notoriously difficult for outside researchers to examine empirically the factors influencing work motivation in socialist command economies since any conclusion of such research is likely to be interpreted as an evaluation of communist ideology in practice. The authors could not resist the opportunity during a study tour of some twelve industrial enterprises ranging from iron and steel companies to textile factories in five large cities (Beijing, Chengdu, Chungking, Wuhan and Shanghai) in 1984, to hand out a simple questionnaire for workers and cadres to fill in, separately and independently, without consulting others. The questionnaire consisted of twenty motivational factors and respondents were asked to rank the importance of each factor from 1 (least important) to 10 (more important).

Something over a hundred questionnaires were handed out, with the assistance of our host factory director or Party Secretary. There were

Table 9.5 Factor influences of work motivation in China*

Factors	Workers			Cadres		
	Mean Score	SD**	Rank	Mean Score	SD*	Rank
Working environment	8.14	2.00	5	8.13	1.70	9
Personal fulfilment	7.36	2.37	10	8.18	1.93	2
Recognition	6.79	2.10	15	6.58	2.24	13
Relationship with peers	7.43	1.87	9	7.83	1.81	7
Relationship with supervisors	7.57	2.17	7	7.96	1.72	5
Development of individual potential	7.36	3.23	10	8.14	1.71	3
Interest of work	7.86	1.66	6	7.95	1.56	6
Increase in basic wages	9.07	1.39	1	7.77	2.16	8
Certificate of 'merit' and 'model workers'	6.86	2.80	14	5.04	2.66	18
Bonus	8.71	1.49	2	6.55	2.27	14
Responsibility and challenge of work	7.36	2.62	10	8.31	1.56	1
Provision of better housing	7.58	2.28	7	7.38	1.94	11
Freedom of choice of work	6.71	3.17	16	6.12	2.58	16
Promotion	5.64	3.43	20	6.37	2.40	15
Travel and holiday	6.64	2.95	17	5.29	2.45	17
Duration of working time	6.21	3.09	19	4.70	2.31	19
Opportunities for study and retraining	7.14	2.91	13	7.71	1.93	9
Spouse working in same city	6.64	4.16	17	7.34	3.01	12
Job security	8.43	2.28	3	7.44	2.40	10
Working for the 'Four Modernizations'	8.21	2.75	4	8.18	2.56	2

* Scale of importance: from 1 (very low) to 10 (very high)
** SD refers to the standard deviation from mean
Sample of workers = 25, cadres = 77

thirty-eight returned questionnaires from workers and eighty-six from cadres. Fifteen questionnaires from workers and nine from cadres were rejected respectively, mostly because the returned questionnaires were incomplete. The empirical results are shown in Table 9.5.

The statistical results suggest that Chinese workers today place great emphasis on material incentives such as wage increases and bonuses. These items were ranked first and second in terms of mean scores. Non-material stimuli such as recognition or a 'model worker' award have low rankings. By contrast, cadres put more emphasis on the importance of non-material incentives such as 'working for the Four Modernizations', 'responsibility and challenge of work', 'recognition and development of individual potential'. These were ranked the four most important factors in influencing work motivation. Material incentives such as wage increases and bonuses ranked eighth and twelfth respectively.

The above responses of workers are similar to the findings of a survey by Chinese psychologists Xu and Lin (1980) on the psychological dynamics of the Chinese worker's ideology in two unspecified cities. Apart from 'working to the Four Modernizations', wage and bonus ranked high as motivational factors in the survey of workers' motivation. Although Xu & Lin's survey can be faulted because most of the questions they asked were highly ideological in flavour, it does tend to confirm our belief that material incentives are as essential to Chinese workers as they are to other workers managing on low wages. Cadres know from their training that money wage rates are uniformly low in China even for senior managers. They probably recognize that such material rewards as are available are paid in kind in the form of various privileges as much as they are paid in cash.

Conclusion

The Chinese authorities clearly have high expectations of reformed state enterprises. By enlarging the decisionmaking power of enterprises, they hope they have created a climate conducive to increasing the initiative and productivity of management and workers. At the level of the individual the outcomes are more obscure but clearly hinge on the appropriateness of the blend of material and non-material incentives. Our brief review of incentive policies past and present, and our excursion into casual empiricism would seem to suggest that Chinese workers are no different from other nationalities and cultures. The dictatorship of economic need is as potent as elsewhere and egalitarianism on an empty stomach undermines industrial discipline and productivity. Equally, the current wage reforms which aim to widen wage differentials according to merit, skill or productivity as well as the lifting of bonus limits are likely to be applauded by the beneficiaries. The wider distributional consequences are not so clear.

Since October 1986, all employees of state enterprises have been subject to the contracted responsibility system whereby they risk dismissal if they fail to satisfy their contract. Even more radical, state enterprises will be able to go bankrupt. In such circumstances, the whole concept of moral encouragement takes on a new meaning. In the past, there have been times when over-reliance on non-material incentives has proved to be self-defeating and ultimately demoralizing. It remains to be seen whether the current strong emphasis on material incentives and economic efficiency will provoke a backlash in the defenders of communist ideology such as the party conservatives backing the drive against 'bourgeois liberalism' in early 1987 aided and abetted by those who lose out from the new policies, such as the poorly-educated and unskilled urban underclass. Pronouncements on future wage reforms will provide important indicators as to the likely direction of development of the Chinese political economy.

References

Adizes, I. & Borgese, E. H. (eds) (1975). *Self-Management: New Dimensions to Democracy*. Santa Barbara, A.B.C. Clio Press, Inc.

Beijing Municipality Economic Planning Commission (1985). *Wage Reform and Structural Wage System*. Beijing (in Chinese).

Brugger, William (1981). *China: Liberation and Transformation, 1942–1962*. London, Croom-Helm.

Chen, C. Y. (1984). *Fundamentals of Thoughts and Political Education Work in Enterprises*. Beijing, Enterprise Management Press (in Chinese).

Chuan, Zhehua, *et al*. (1982). 'Democratic Management Enhances More Vitality to the Industrial Enterprises'. *Shehui Kexue* ('Social Science', Shanghai), No. 2 (in Chinese).

Crouch, Colin & Heller, F. A. (eds) (1983). *International Yearbook of Organizational Democracy, Vol. I (Organizational Democracy and Political Processes)*. Wiley.

Deng Xiaoping (1984). *Selected Works of Deng Xiaoping*. Beijing, Foreign Language Press.

Encyclopedia of China's Industrial Management 1984. Beijing, Enterprise Management Press, Vols. 1 and 2 (in Chinese).

Feng, Lanrui & Zhao, Lukuan (1984). 'Urban Employment and Wages', in *China's Socialist Modernization*. Yu Guangyuan (ed.), Foreign Languages Press, Beijing.

Han, Xiulan (1983). 'Democratic Management in China's State-owned Industrial Enterprises'. *New Asia Academic Bulletin*, 5 (in Chinese).

Harper, Paul (1971). 'Workers' Participation in Management in Communist China'. *Studies in Comparative Communism*, July–October, pp. 111–40.

Henley, John S. & Nyaw, M. K. (1986). 'The Developments in Managerial Decision Making in Chinese Industrial Enterprises', in Stewart Clegg and Gordon Redding (eds), *The Enterprise and Management in East Asia*. Centre of Asian Studies, University of Hong Kong.

Jiang, Yiwei & Shen, Hungshen (1985). Industrial Enterprise Management. Beijing, Economic Management Press (in Chinese).

Jin, Qi (1984). 'New Bonus System Lifts Limits. *Beijing Review*, 27, No. 26, 25 June.

Li, Guoying (1985). *Shehui, Zhuyi Gougzi Gailun* (Fundamentals of Socialist Wage Structure'). Rev. edn, Jinlin People's Press (in Chinese).

Ma, Hong (1983). *New Strategy for China's Economy*. New World Press, Beijing, China.

Ng, Sek Hong (1984). 'One Brand of Workplace Democracy: The Workers' Congress in the Chinese Enterprises'. *Journal of Industrial Relations*, March: 56–75.

Riskin, Carl (1973). 'Maoism and Motivation: Work Incentives in China'. *Bulletin of Concerned Asian Scholars*, July: 10–24.

Selden, Mark (1971). *The Yenan Way in Revolutionary China*. Cambridge, Harvard University Press.

State Economic Planning Commission (1984). *Ideological and Political Work in Industrial Enterprises*. Beijing, Economic Science Publication (in Chinese).

Tian, Jiyun (1986). 'On the Present Economic Situation and Restructuring the Economy'. (A speech made by Vice-Premier Tian Jiyun on 6 January, at a meeting of cadres from central organizations). *Beijing Review*, 29, Nos. 6 & 7, 10 February.

Tung, Rosalie L. (1981). 'Patterns of Motivation in Chinese Industrial Enterprises'. *Academy of Management Review*, 6, No. 3: 481–9.

Wang, Tung (1985). *Gongye Qiye Laodong Guanli* 'Labour Management of Industrial Enterprises'). Liaoning People's Press (in Chinese).

Xiang, Qiyuan (1982). 'Economic Development and Income Distribution', in *China's Search for Economic Growth*, Xu Dixin *et al*. Beijing, New World Press.

Xu, Liencang & Lin, Wenchuan (1980). 'A Psychological Study of the Workers' Ideological Dynamics'. *Kuanming Daily*, 22. August.

Yu, Guangyuan (1985). 'Reform During Socialist Construction in Terms of World and Chinese History'. *Social Sciences in China*, 3: 23–38.

Zhao, Lukuan & Pan, Jinyun (1984). *Labour Economics and Labour Management*. Beijing Press, Beijing (in Chinese).

10 The Workers' Congress in Chinese Enterprises

Ng Sek Hong and Russell D. Lansbury

Introduction

Chinese policies on enterprise-level management have undergone a full cycle of changes during the past three decades. It is argued that, since Liberation, China has oscillated between 'centralised suffocation and decentralised anarchy' (Brugger, 1983). When the Communist Party gained power in 1949 it embarked on a programme of heavy industrialization within a socialist institutional framework. The First Five-Year Plan, 1953–7, which was launched with Soviet economic aid, was essentially a replica of the so-called Stalinist development strategy which emphasized heavy industry using capital-intensive techniques of production. While this strategy brought China considerable economic growth, it neglected small industries and agriculture and resulted in a structural imbalance in the economy. Realization of the Soviet model's strategic weakness and its inappropriateness to China's needs later paved the way for the 'Great Leap Forward' of 1958–60. The management system introduced at the enterprise level during the First Five-Year Plan was a Soviet-style one which contained a well-defined hierarchy with elaborate procedures and regulations covering all aspects of operation.

The Great Leap Forward marked the beginning of the 'Maoist' approach to development in which agricultural and rural policies were emphasized, small industries promoted, labour-intensive methods adopted and ideological incentives encouraged. In urban areas the Great Leap Forward was characterized by extensive administrative decentralization and the establishment of numerous small-scale enterprises employing mainly local resources and indigenous techniques of production. The campaign marked an attempt by the Chinese to grapple with the problem of appropriate technology to spread technological knowledge to the masses. Yet the Great Leap Forward produced many excesses and wastages—including the mobilization of sixty million people to build 'backyard steel furnaces' which later proved to be wasteful of resources. It took three consecutive years of bad agricultural harvests to force the Government to give up the Great Leap Forward.

China's problems were further compounded by the upheaval which accompanied the Cultural Revolution in 1966. According to the new line that was espoused by the 'radicals', management and their technical staff were no longer in control of production but were there simply to assist workers to manage the enterprise. Revolutionary committees were established in each factory and management could act only with their approval. Yet, despite its excesses, the Cultural Revolution did highlight the existence of a vast reservoir of useful technical experience among workers that could be tapped for productive use. Although moderate economic growth occurred during this period, with 'politics in command', there was nevertheless widespread misallocation of resources and fragmentation of the economy. Furthermore, the breakdown in industrial discipline gradually led to a reaction and the reimposition of hierarchical authority structures. In 1970 the All-China Federation of Trade Unions, suspended since 1968 at the height of the anti-Lui purge, was allowed to reopen its offices, and union officials were gradually released from their subservience to the revolutionary committees.

After the death of Mao in 1976 and the arrest of the Gang of Four, there came another change in the direction of policy towards economic growth. Deng Xiaoping became Vice-Chairman and pursued a new economic policy which stressed the importance of managerial authority, technical training and material incentives as a means of raising productivity among the work-force. Deng enunciated the 'Four Modernizations', which called for comprehensive improvements in industry, agriculture, national defence and science and technology. He also emphasized the need for centralized administration, authority based on technical competence and the importance of the organization of production. Trade unions were revived, albeit as an instrument of the state, to protect and improve the welfare of the workers.

The Role of the Worker's Congress in the Enterprise

The workers' congress in China has been renewed and revitalized since the beginning of the 1980s, as the principal form of democratic management in the context of the current modernization process. In 1981, the Central Committee of the Chinese Communist Party and the State Council promulgated the Provisional Regulations concerning Congresses of Workers and Staff Members in State-owned Industrial Enterprises. This was reaffirmed by the Twelfth Central Committee of the Party at its Third Plenary Session, which exalted enterprise autonomy and worker participation as being among the guiding principles for steering China's nation-wide efforts at urban economic reforms. Its decision declared, *inter alia*, that in the enterprise:

> While the director assumes full responsibility, we must improve the system of congresses of workers and staff members and other systems of democratic management, give play to the authority and role of the trade union organisations and workers' and staff members' deputies in examining and discussing major decisions to be taken by the enterprises, supervising administrative leadership and safeguarding the legitimate rights and inter-

ests of the workers and staff members. [Decision of Central Committee, 1984].

Democratic management and its linkage to economic development are not a unique experience specific to contemporary China. Monat has observed

a general drive, noticeable in many developing countries, towards a closer association of workers and their trade unions with national economic development at various levels. Southern Asian governments, for instance, which are trying to develop workers' participation, often do so with the declared objective of enlisting workers' support for national development through improved industrial relations. [Monat, 1985:21]

Nevertheless, the Chinese endeavour represents one of the more concerted and structured approaches to the notion of participative management in the context of a vast and developing economy. After its revival, following the Cultural Revolution, and its enhanced propagation since the late 1970s and early 1980s, the institution of the workers' congress has evolved through a variety of experiences. Yet relatively little analysis has been made of the development and effectiveness of the workers' congress in Chinese enterprises (Lansbury et al., 1984).

Before the Cultural Revolution, the workers' congress was an adjunct to the 'factory management committee' and comprised part of the dual structure of work-place democracy in the Chinese enterprises. With a history dating back to the days of Chinese Communist Party insurgencies during the 1920s, the workers' congress complemented the factory management committee. It constituted an ancillary arrangement of 'democratic management' in support of the notion of 'director's accountability under the leadership of the party's branch secretary'. During the 1950s, however, the Three and Five 'Anti' Movements, which were politically inspired to combat 'bureaucratism' and 'economism' in the enterprise, sharply curtailed the role of the factory management committees. Before the Cultural Revolution, the principal task of the workers' congress was limited to merely reviewing the performance and advancing criticism of the enterprise management. Nevertheless, the workers' congress did persist through the 1950s and 1960s, despite the decline of the factory management committee. It received the endorsement of the Chinese Communist Party, for instance, at its Eighth National Congress in 1956, as instituted under the leadership of the Party branch secretary. A central directive was subsequently issued exhorting every enterprise to practise this approach to worker participation, and the institutional status of the workers' congress was further consolidated in 1961.

The Cultural Revolution which beset China during the 1960s and early 1970s seriously disrupted the functioning of the economy, and production in most enterprises fell into disarray. The twin machinery of the factory management committee and workers' congress was suspended throughout the country, and enterprise management fell under the *de facto* control of the revolutionary committee.

After the disastrous interlude of the Cultural Revolution, the state appeared anxious to revive work-place democracy under a unitary system in order to buttress enterprise autonomy. In place of the dual structure preceding the Cultural Revolution, the workers' congress was subsequently reactivated, but not the factory management committee. In 1978, Deng Xiaoping declared before a national conference of trade unions that 'democratic management should be put into effect and the system of workers' congresses should be established and perfected in all enterprises.' (Ng, 1983: 59). In 1981, the Central Committee of the Party and the State Council promulgated the *Provisional Regulations* mentioned above. By June 1982, more than one hundred thousand enterprises and government organizations within China were declared to have established congresses of workers and staff. This followed the democratic election of factory directors on an experimental basis which began in a number of provinces, autonomous regions and municipalities in 1980.

Recent Developments—The Role of The Workers' Congress

By far the most innovative aspect of the revitalized 'workers' congress' system is its new power to elect the factory or enterprise management (*Provisional Regulations* 1981, Article 5, Clause 5). In 1982, the *Beijing Review* reported that '29,400 grass-roots units have democratically elected group and section leaders, 14,800 units have elected workshop heads and deputy heads and 8,900 elected factory directors and deputy directors, managers and deputy managers and other administrative personnel.' Nevertheless, the electoral arrangement was practised largely on an experimental basis and systems varied considerably in procedural details between the enterprises. In 1985, the All-China Federation of Trade Unions at the Second Session of its Tenth Executive Committee noted the following variations in the practice of the electoral rules:

> In those enterprises owned by the whole people, directors and managers should be chosen either through democratic elections in accordance with the arrangements of the higher organ of the enterprises or the combination of appointment by leaders at the next higher level and recommendation by workers. In collectively-owned ones, leaders are elected directly by workers. [Gong, 1985a: 3].

There have been various reports, many of which are expressed in euphoric terms, concerning the degree of democratic and production efficacy achieved under this new approach. The following excerpt of case reports in Wuhan illustrates the tone of 'official' reports on the subject:

> The day we came to the Wuhan No. 3 Printing and Dyeing Mill, an election for the factory director was taking place. At a meeting organised

by the presidium of the workers' congress of the factory, several candidates
spoke on how they would manage the factory if they were elected . . .
A young worker said to us, 'The leadership has put no restrictions on the
election. No candidate has been nominated from above. As masters of the
enterprise, we are free to choose whoever we think is qualified for the job.'
So far, workers in more than 100 enterprises in Wuhan have democratically elected their own directors or managers. The elections have been
conducted under the leadership of the workers' congresses of these enterprises . . .
Yuan Jipeng, 35, was elected director of the Wuhan Washing Machine
Factory. He has relied on workers to run the enterprise. As a result, the
factory's economic results have improved markedly and the profits in 1984
more than tripled those in 1983.
A trade unionist of the Wuhan Electronics Bureau said that the democratic
election of factory directors had elevated the status of trade unions.
Today, when the workers have any problems in mind, they would talk
with trade union cadres, believing that they truly represent the interests of
the workers. [Chinese Trade Unions, 1985: 5]

An important corollary implied by the systematic propagation of the workers'
congress as the principal organ of democratic management is the enhancement of the trade union structure and activities. This is particularly significant at the grass-roots level of the individual enterprise where the union
committee deputizes for the congress when the latter is in recess. The
All-China Federation of Trade Unions has exhorted its grass-roots units (i.e.
the enterprise trade unions) to establish and perfect the system of workers'
congresses and promote democratic management in enterprises. Enterprise
trade unions are required to not only 'enthusiastically support the implementation of the system of the director assuming full responsibility, guarantee his
exercise of command over production, management and administration', but
must also 'guarantee the workers' right to participate in democratic management and safeguard their status as masters of the enterprise.'
On a visit to the Shanghai Municipal Trade Union Council in 1985, for
instance, one of the authors (Ng Sek Hong) was told that a new office, the
Director of Democratic Management, was recently created at the Sixth
Plenary Session of its Seventh Congress. The Director's portfolio included,
inter alia, the design of a comprehensive programme of worker education to
promote grass-roots participation of union members in the process of work-
place 'industrial democracy'. A tripartite institutional relationship is implicit
in so far as the functioning of the workers' congress system depends upon the
joint efforts of the party committee, the trade union and factory management
under the recently popularized model of 'factory manager responsi-
bility/workers' congress decision'. During another visit to China, early in
1986, the same author was informed by the Guangzhou Municipal Trade
Union Council that, in this city, fifty-three test-case enterprises had recently

been designated to experiment with the merger of the workers' congress representative committee and the trade union representative committee.

The means by which trade unions operate within the enterprise, *vis-à-vis* the workers' congress, in mobilizing the work-force, is illustrated in the following account of the Fuzhou Pencil Factory which has been promoted as a model example by the Minister of Light Industry:

> When asked about their reforms, the factory's Party and management leaders all commented that the trade union had played an important role, . . . Huang Baozhu, 38, is its trade union chairwoman. She originally headed the production department . . . In the course of reform, Huang integrated mass work with economic work. She did everything to safeguard the workers' legitimate rights and material interests . . . Huang presided over 11 workers' congress meetings and organised the representatives of workers and staff members to discuss the regulations conscientiously one by one, and made necessary revision and supplements . . .
>
> In early 1983, the plan for reforming the system of applying for reimbursement for medical expenses was submitted by the factory director to the workers' congress for discussion and approval. Huang said that, as a matter closely connected with the workers' interest, this should be handled with great care . . .
>
> The trade union also changed the method used in emulation drives by organically integrating them with bonus distribution . . . Huang voluntarily took on the job of examining the factory's bonus distribution plan and handling its readjustment . . . . [Zou & Chen, 1985: 7].

The Workers' Congress and 'Institutional Harmonization'

In its augmented form, the workers' congress is intended to help transform the structure of power and control in the enterprise. The gradual transfer of power from the Party committee to the factory executive (i.e. enterprise directors and middle-level cadres) is consistent with the overall state strategy of fostering enterprise autonomy under the approach of 'market socialism'. Now that the workers' congress is capable of removing, validating or electing the management in the enterprise, it is clear that the factory director will find it necessary to seek legitimation of his role and position from the congress. Consent from the work-force thus provides the mandate for the director's leadership position. Worker participation, combined with electoral pressure on the enterprise director to be responsive to grass-roots demands, is designed to stimulate initiative, flexibility and sensitivity to external as well as intra-organizational exigencies. Economic decentralization, enterprise autonomy, democratic management and the system of factory director responsibility and workers' congress are thus all interrelated aspects of the nation-wide approach to economic reform and modernization.

In a sense, the retirement of the Party to a 'backstage' advisory role leaves a considerable degree of ambivalence, if not a power vaccuum, within the enterprise. The competence of the workers' congress in serving as the functional equivalent of the Party in the work-place is not without its problems. These are due to both the lay nature of membership in the congress and the democratic nature of the system. The plenary assembly of the congress, which elects the enterprise leadership, is comprised of deputies who are themselves elected from and by the workers in the enterprise. Thus, enterprise directors may find themselves vulnerable to the popular yet potentially wasteful demands of the masses. Furthermore, the work-force can be susceptible to manipulation by the management. In summary:

This is the tenuous relationship between 'the demands of the working masses' that industrial democracy encourages and 'the ability of the political leaders to deliver the goods'. When tilted out of balance, inflated 'rank and file' expectations can pose a serious impediment to the stability of the governmental framework of 'democratic centralism' and party hegemony [Ng, 1983: 73].

The state's cognizance of a propensity towards syndicalism in the work-place, as well as the concern of a (fundamentally) command economy to institute 'necessary supervision and control over the director after the enterprise is given greater autonomy', helps explain the desire of the trade union movement to monitor, if not control, the workers' congress. Trade unionism within China takes the form of mass organization of workers under the leadership of the All-China Federation of Trade Unions (ACFTU). As in other socialist countries, the ACFTU is also a quasi-official agency which acts as the state's transmission belt. In designing and nurturing the establishment of the workers' congress, the stage planners have sought to substitute the Party with the trade union institution, albeit in a more subtle manner, to 'police' democracy, ensure discipline and monitor enterprise management in the work-place. The trade unions thus perform a quasi-official 'guardian' role, whereby they act as the standard-bearer of both 'democratic centralism' and 'market socialism'.

The trade union branch within the enterprise is the structural corollary to the workers' congress, representing a continuation of the pre-Cultural Revolution arrangement of a dual system of industrial democracy in the work-place. When the congress takes recess between its two half-yearly plenary sessions, it is deputized and given administrative support by the enterprise trade union. The rationale for making the trade union committee the executive organ of the congress is both administrative and technical, in that the full-time union officials can offer their professional expertise and advice to the lay workers' delegates on the congress. The dual arrangement is also ideologically consistent with the orthodox stance of socialist unions to foster the democratic participation of the industrial proletariat. The *raison-d'être* for the involvement of the trade union organizations in the economic and democratic reforms of the Chinese enterprises has been explained by a senior official of the All-China Federation of Trade Unions (ACFTU) in the following terms:

> At present, trade unions will do the following three things: One, they should organise the workers and staff members to study and discuss the Party's decision and drive home the nature of the great undertaking, its objectives and contents as well as general and specific policies . . .
> Two, in connection with invigorating enterprises, the central task of the reform, trade unions should help perfect the workers' congress system, strengthen worker participation in management so that their democratic rights are fully guaranteed . . . They should help enterprises to institute the economic responsibility system and see that the socialist principle of distribution—to each according to his work—is fully implemented . . . Three, while taking part in the economic reforms, trade union organisations will have to make reforms in their own work . . . [Gong, 1985b: 3].

The third issue cited above highlights an internal reorientation problem endemic in the organizational structure of the Chinese trade union, precipitated by its role in fostering and directing the evolution of the workers' congress. To fulfill this task, the ACFTU is required to undertake extensive

> investigations and study, exploring new ways that will make organisational set-up, specific activities, working methods and the work style of the leadership all fit squarely into the present reform program so as to make trade unions play a much more active role in the political, economic and social activities of the state and in invigorating grass-roots enterprises, thus creating a new situation in the trade union work, characteristic of the Chinese working class. [Gong, 1985b: 3–4].

The Trade Union Role in The Workers' Congress

The requirement that the trade unions deputize for the workers' congress in the wake of economic reforms and democratization of the enterprise poses some far-reaching challenges to the Chinese labour movement, which has only been recently resurrected from the political freeze of the Cultural Revolution.

The new 'integration' strategy reinforces the importance of the 'grassroots' organization and the influence of the otherwise centrally administered union bureaucracy in the enterprise, where its presence used to be a feeble one. The union has also become more visible within the enterprise now that it deputizes for the workers' congress during its recess. Such processes enable the union to enjoy the prerogative of the congress over plant-wide management, with a mandate derived from its 'agency' role for the congress. Such arrangements, albeit of a hybrid nature, may provide the trade union organization with a practical means of realizing grass-roots participation in the enterprise. Moreover, the congress-cum-union arrangements help to avert competition between the congress and the union at the enterprise level. Indeed, where attempts have been made to create a system of parallel yet separate systems of worker representation within the socialist countries of Eastern Europe, conflict and competition have followed.

Nevertheless, the merging of the role of the union and the congress at the enterprise level raises the issue of the viability of such an 'interlocking' system. While there may be functions specific to the union and the congress, these functions are always mutually compatible. There is a limit to the extent to which the union can fully substitute for the workers' council or congress. As Sturmthal has remarked in regard to workers' councils:

> The councils, though representing management, favour higher wage rates; the unions, though officially the spokesman of the employees, advocate restraint . . . In the process of wage determination the councils and the unions may thus appear as opponents, with the council most often closer to the employees and their interests than the unions . . . The councils are, therefore, likely to be closer to the union rank and file than the unions themselves, and closer even than the local union branches. [Sturmthal, 1964: 171–2].

It is also problematic whether this type of combined machinery is conducive to the bona fide articulation of workers' occupational rights and interests. Evidently, a socialist country cannot free itself entirely from the problem of labour protests and their authentic representation, particularly when it attempts to move towards a system of industrial pluralism. China has not been immune from the spontaneous and sporadic eruption of industrial upheavals (Hearn, 1977: 163). Before the reorganization following the Cultural Revolution, the trade unions in China could have exonerated themselves from the embarrassment of such cross-pressures, especially since they were so weakly represented at the work-place level. Now, however, the Chinese unions are required to play the contradictory roles of 'adversary' and 'transmission belt' for enterprise management. With the regeneration of grass-roots union organization in the production unit, through the extended system of the workers' congress, union branches can no longer evade their 'shop steward' role and must vigorously pursue any shop-floor grievances raised by members. Any challenges to managerial decision, inspired by their members' job interests and demands, are likely to place the union in a confrontation with the workers' congress. Ironically, however, it is the workers' congress for which the union now deputizes.

In Search of a Democratic or Technocratic Management?

It has thus become important for the trade unions to streamline their integration with and accommodation to the functioning of the workers' congress. This is vital now that the Party has vacated its role in favour of the workers' congress at the enterprise level. The paramount issue facing the trade unions, therefore, is how to monitor, support and deputize for the workers' congress without usurping its role.

Since the workers' congress has been given the task of democratically electing and appraising the enterprise directors, an important issue for both the congress and its trade union proxy is how to define their attitudes towards the management. This is clearly potential for conflict between the elected nature of factory management and the state's pragmatic concern for technocratic expertise in organizing production activities. The latter theme was explicit in the 1984 Decision of the Party's Central Committee:

> The Central Committee has pointed out on many occasions that in our drive for socialist modernisation we must respect knowledge and talented people. We must combat all ideas and practices that belittle science and technology, the cultivation of intellectual resources and the role of intellectuals . . . The Central Committee calls for completion of the reshuffling of leadership in enterprises, especially key enterprises, before the end of 1985. In addition, plans should be drawn up and effective measures taken to train fairly soon a large number of directors (managers) who can successfully organise and direct enterprise production and operations, . . . This contingent should consist of qualified personnel in all trades and occupations for the whole chain of enterprise management. [Decision of Central Committee, 1984: 33].

Conceivably, the electoral arrangements in the enterprise can subvert these criteria and threaten to displace technically able, experienced but less popular cadres with those of mediocre qualities who obtain electoral support. This contradiction is mirrored in the state's recognition of 'the imperative to guard against the tendency to stress unduly management by the masses, while ignoring management by specialised personnel.' (Beijing Radio, 1972). This attests to the state's dilemma in its attempt to democratize factory management by way of plant-wide elections via the congress while retaining the highest level of expertise among its enterprise managers.

Similar problems of conflicting demands between democracy and technical expertise beset Yugoslavia which, since the 1950s, has replaced state-appointed factory directors with those elected by the workers' councils. The Yugoslav response to the dilemma of professional versus democratically-elected managers has led to the codification of elaborate and stringent regulations on managers' qualifications which effectively circumscribe the actual choice of candidates. However, such measures can restrict the genuine application of principles of industrial democracy and worker control in the enterprise. Thus, in Yugoslavia, despite the existence of workers' councils, differences persist between the workers and management authorities. These parallel the attitudes of labour and management which have been so frequently noted by sociologists in capitalist countries (Banks, 1974: 44).

Within China, the balance between managerial prerogatives and workers' participation in management of the enterprise has been a continuing source of concern.

Not only does technocratic management have to be reconciled with industrial democracy, but its implications may also impede the operation of the central 'command economy', particularly in regard to the hitherto centralized system of manpower allocation by the state. The liberalized economic policy, with its concern for labour productivity and functional specialization, has inspired the reformist call for fundamental and far-reaching reconstruction of the state's manpower policy at both the macro and enterprise levels. In this regard, it has been argued that:

> To make the best possible use of people's talents, the state should make overall arrangements, but the enterprise should be free to select its worker and staff members, and each person should also enjoy some freedom to choose his or her job. [Xue, 1981: 216]

As mentioned previously, the urgency of such reforms in recruitment strategy is acknowledged in regard to scientists, technicians and other specialists. In place of the previously unsatisfactory situation whereby 'labour and personnel departments have often assumed a bureaucratic attitude and have arranged jobs for people without regard for their capabilities', the new manpower approach now advocates that 'the state should give them the right to choose their jobs under certain conditions.' (Ibid., 1981: 217). It is also deemed desirable that 'examinations should be given . . . and their performances reviewed at regular intervals so that some may be promoted or transferred to more important jobs.' (Ibid., 1981: 255).

The permissiveness now granted to the experimental enterprises on the hiring, firing, transfer, promotion and demotion of employees, if extended to other production and economic units, would be likely to introduce and institutionalize a voluntary 'labour market' at both the national and regional levels. The effective operation of this type of labour market within the framework of a planned command economy would present a new challenge to the State Bureau of Labour. Moreover, the new abilities of the pilot enterprises to censure individual workers by demotion, dismissal, transfer and other disciplinary sanctions are likely to create new labour grievances and aggravate role conflicts for the workers' congress and its trade union 'proxy'. The situation is made more complex in that the congress is not only the representative organization of the rank-and-file but also the ultimate source of managerial responsibility. The dilemma implied by the present process of liberalizing the labour market has been summarized by Shirk as follows:

> Because much of the industrial modernisation in China has proceeded under State administration, without a labour market, and in lifetime employment enterprises, workers expect the State, represented by their companies, to guarantee their security . . . Although policy-makers have

urged as part of the effort to make enterprises more rational and efficient that incompetent workers be dismissed, the factory authority who are supposed to implement this policy find it unthinkable . . . [Shirk, 1981: 592–3].

Adding to the chaos are the inequitable effects arising from the failure to structure and regularize the myriad of incentive payments. These have been introduced into enterprises under the recent 'self-management' campaign in order to stimulate labour productivity. The distribution of bonuses has become increasingly non-discriminant in that they are not geared consistently to performance or any other criteria. Instead of reinforcing the efficacy of a 'payment by result' approach, the incentive schemes have tended to create a system of 'effort according to the amount of reward' (Jingji Guanli, 1981: 71–3). As Shirk notes:

they have unwittingly precipitated dichotomisation within the work-force between those who are 'efficiency-oriented' (such as the technical cadres and skilled workers) and those who are 'organisation-oriented' (like the political-administrative cadres, unskilled workers, cultural revolution generation workers etc.), since the latter might find such effort-reward schemes threatening or ideologically alien. [Shirk, 1981: 591].

Conclusions

Any debate concerning the wisdom and direction of current economic and managerial reforms inside China cannot be divorced from the political imperative to preserve a degree of 'democratic centralism' which can keep both 'bureaucratic' and 'syndicalist' tendencies in check, as seen in the replacement of Hu Yaobang as Party Secretary. The dual theme of 'democratization' and 'decentralization', which emphasizes the independence and self-determination of the enterprise, epitomizes the institution of the workers' congress. Strategically, the workers' congress seeks to formalize the desired demarcation between economic and political functions within the production unit of the enterprise. The overall leadership of the Party committee has now retreated back-stage, but still exercises control via 'political and ideological work to ensure implementation of Party principles and policies'. The unitary authority of the Chinese state thus remains sacrosanct. There is no loose coalition of equal and pluralistic power centres which differentiate the Party, the enterprise and the labour movement. In so far as China continues to be a command economy which 'entails central planning, administrative allocation and State ownership of enterprise', workers' participation has to be interpreted as more of a political than a managerial issue which is 'functional to the extent it can play a role of control and supervision over the enterprise leadership.' (Ruble, 1979: 235). The state remains suspicious of 'grass-roots' industrial democracy *per se* and guards against the devolution of central power, lest the popular demands of the masses prove an impediment to 'democratic centralism' and 'Party hegemony'. Such considerations may effectively constrain China's current efforts to remove elements of bureaucratism by simplifying administrative procedures in state enterprises and rationalizing their organizational structure. In this context, the All-China Federation of Trade Unions and its grass-roots organizations at the enterprise level will continue to play a key institutional role in 'holding the ring' and will determine the future viability of the Chinese approach to democratic management.

References

Banks, J. A. (1974). *Trade Unionism*, London, Collier-Macmillan. Beijing Radio Broadcast, October 1972, cited by Christopher Howe (1973), 'Labour Organisations and Incentives in Industry: Before and After the Cultural Revolution' in Schram, S. (ed.), *Authority, Participation and Cultural Change in China*. Cambridge, Cambridge University Press.

Beijing Review (1982). **25**, pt. 1, No. 26: 6.

Brugger, W. O. (1983). 'Industrial Management in China: Summary of a First-Hand Investigation', delivered to a Conference on *Chinese Modernisation: The Latest Phase*. Australian National University, Canberra, February.

Chinese Trade Unions (1985). No. 1: 5.

Decision of the Central Committee of the Communist Party of China on Reform of the Economic Structure (1984). Beijing, Foreign Languages Press, Chap. 7: 25.

Gong Yan (1985a). 'Bring into Full Play the Role of Trade Union Organisations in Economic Reform'. *Chinese Trade Unions*, No. 2: 3.

Gong Yan (1985b). 'Economic Reforms and Trade Unions: An Interview with Luo Gan, Vice Chairman of the All-China Federation of Trade Unions'. *Chinese Trade Unions*. No. 1:3.

Hearn, J. M. (1977). 'W(h)ither the Trade Unions in China?'. *Journal of Industrial Relations*, **19**:163ff.

Jingji Guanli (1981), No. 6:71–3.

Lansbury, R. D., Ng Sek Hong & McKern, R. B. (1984). 'Management at the Enterprise Level in China'. *Industrial Relations Journal*, **15**:56–64.

Monat, J. (1985). 'A Review of International Experience in the Field of Workers' Participation'. *Asian Labour*, **33**:21ff.

Ng Sek Hong (1983). 'One Brand of Workplace Democracy: The Workers' Congress in Chinese Enterprise'. *The Journal of Industrial Relations*, **25**:59ff.

Ruble, B. A. (1979). 'Dual Functioning Trade Unions in the USSR'. *British Journal of Industrial Relations*, **17**:235ff.

Shirk, S. L. (1981). 'Recent Chinese Labour Policies and the Transformation of Industrial Organisation in China'. *China Quarterly*, No. 88, December: 592–3.

Sturmthal, A. (1964). *Workers' Councils: A Study of Workplace Organisation on Both Sides of the Iron Curtain*. Cambridge, Mass., Harvard University Press.

Xue Muquiao (1981). *China's Socialist Economy*. Beijing, Foreign Languages Press.

Zou Lizhang & Chen Huifa (1985). 'Taking the Initiative in Enterprise Reform'. *Chinese Trade Unions*, No. 1:7.

Part IV: Widening the Debate

11 Problems in the Reform of Ownership Relations in China

Liu Guoguang
Translated by Andrew Watson

Introduction

The reform of the economic system currently under way in China includes reform of two related aspects: one is reform of the mechanisms of economic activity and the other is reform of relations of ownership. Reform of the mechanisms of economic activity is aimed at solving problems in the relationship between centralization and dispersion, between planning and the market, and between invigoration at the micro-level and macro-control. It aims to transform past mechanisms which had excessive concentration of decision-making power, spurned the role of the market, and involved direct state management of microeconomic activity into mechanisms which combine concentration and dispersion, planning and the market, and macro-control and micro-invigoration. This reform of the mechanisms of economic activity must affect existing relations of ownership. In the past, many economists in China mainly emphasized research into the reform of the mechanisms of economic activity and looked upon relations of ownership, especially socialist ownership by the whole people as realized through the system of state ownership, as a fixed premise. Practice in economic reform over the past few years has demonstrated that changes in the mechanisms of economic activity, including changes in the structure of decisionmaking power, strengthening the market mechanism, and adjusting relationships of economic benefit, invariably involved not only changes in the forms of management but also changes in asset relationships. The adjustment and improvement of relations of ownership is a necessary condition for the reform of the mechanisms of economic activity. Only if the two are undertaken together can reform be successful (see Liu, 1986).

Before economic reform began, in 1979, the system of ownership of the means of production in China basically consisted of two forms of public ownership existing side-by-side, that is ownership by the whole people and collective ownership. This system was, for the most part, formed in 1956 when the socialist transformation of the system of ownership was basically completed. It was greatly influenced by the traditional Soviet model but later, under the impact of 'left' thinking, it also developed its own abnormalities. Its main characteristic was to emphasize that the larger the scale and the more public the system of ownership, the better it was. It only paid attention to developing the economy under the ownership of the whole people. It neglected and weakened the collectively-owned economy, and spurned and eradicated the individual economy. There was a great hurry to combine units and to move to higher levels of organization in order to achieve a 'transition in poverty'. Small collectives were combined into big ones, and big collectives were promoted to state management. In the countryside, the people's communes combined economic and governmental functions. In the towns, the collective economy became, in reality, enterprises under local state control. Furthermore, in the state-run enterprises themselves there was no division of responsibility between levels of administrative control and of economic management so that they became even more subordinate to the agencies of state administration. In terms of managerial methods, units under each type of system of ownership all tended to become similar to the state-run economy. This trend towards a unified, single system of economic form and economic management prevented the development of economic forms outside the state-owned economy. It meant that we could not mobilize all types of initiative, and it led to increasing rigidity in mechanisms of economic activity. This was a major factor in the setbacks suffered in China's economic development in the past (see Decision of the Central Committee, 1984).

The trend towards a single form for the system of ownership and the mode of management did not correspond to the real economic situation in China nor to the needs of development. In the first place, it neglected the fact that the level of development of the forces of production was not very high and that the level of development in various economic departments, trades and regions was extremely uneven. Currently, China has both modernized, large-scale production and backward, small-scale production. It has mechanized and automatic operation, and large amounts of manual labour. Even the forces of production are not developing solely in the direction of large-scale concentration but have many different trends, some heading towards concentration and some towards greater dispersion. The existence of many different levels of the forces of production requires a corresponding multiplicity of forms of the system of ownership and of modes of management. It is also necessary to note that China is a large country with a large population. The pressures on employment are very great. There is a great diversity of demands for construction and for the people's livelihood. The state's resources are limited and, if the state-run economy had to do everything, it could not solve all of these problems. It is necessary to mobilize all forces, including the state, the collective and the individual. We can only meet the needs of modernized construction by economic development through many kinds of forms.

New Ownership Reforms

Over the past few years, reform in the relations of ownership has begun in the countryside. The appearance of the household responsibility system using contracts related to output smashed the old model of the collective economy which was based on collective labour distribution in common and unified management. It has gradually led to the formation of a new model of the socialist co-operative economy which corresponds to the rural forces of production. In a situation where the system of public ownership of land and of the basic means of production is maintained, the family has become the basic unit of production management. As a result, the rural co-operative economy has been enriched with new content in the form of household management. At present the great majority of contracting and specialized households in the countryside use household management for the basic production processes of crop growing, animal rearing and processing. They are developing many different forms of co-operation and association for services required before and after production which lie outside these basic processes, such as irrigation, plant protection, material supplies, product sales, storage, transport, market and technical information, and some basic land management. In this way they have gradually established a new direction for the co-operative economy which interrelates specialization, the socialization of production and the production of commodities. Following on the establishment of the household responsibility system using contracts related to output, the combination of governmental and economic functions which had persisted for over twenty years has also been reformed. Village government has been re-established to take over the task of government administration. In this way, rural collective ownership no longer has the character of state ownership.

Recently, we have also explored ways of changing the management of the collectively-owned economy in non-rural areas so that it ceases to be run like the economy under the ownership of the whole people and its collective nature is restored. For example, collectively-owned enterprises (co-operative factories) in urban areas under the management system of the Second Ministry of Light Industry used to be economically subordinate to their controlling department, handing over profits and having their losses made good. Now, measures are being adopted to give them independence and to give them responsibility for their own profits and losses. Rural marketing and supply co-operatives, which had in practice already been brought under state ownership, are also gradually being changed so that they are no longer managed by officials but by the people instead. The co-operative character of the basic-level marketing and supply co-operatives is gradually being restored by sorting out their shares, by increasing the number of peasant shareholders and by democratically electing their executive and supervisory committees. Nevertheless, since these collectives developed for many years in conditions where there was no division between the enterprise and the administering government agency, most of their capital funds are not owned by their employees and they still hand over profits to the many administrative agencies which control them. Furthermore, because many of the problems associated with the separation of government and economic organizations in the countryside have not yet been solved, many rural and township enterprises are still owned by the township government and have little autonomy. As a result, it is still necessary to do a lot of work before official management can really become management by the people and before they truly have autonomous management and responsibility for their own profits and losses.

Over the past few years, the individual economy run by labourers in the towns and the countryside has rapidly recovered and developed. By September 1985 the numbers of individual industrial and commercial enterprises throughout the country had developed to include over eleven million households and over sixteen million people. Of these, the number in urban areas has risen to some 2.6 million households and 3.6 million people, which is around twenty-four times greater than the 150,000 people involved in 1978. These figures also include a very small number of private enterprises which have developed from among the larger household undertakings and which have a lot of capital funds, employ a large amount of labour and are capitalist in nature. This non-socialist economy operates in conditions where the system of public ownership has absolute dominance. The situation is therefore fundamentally different from that of the 1950s when the question of whether socialism or capitalism was the victor in the economy was still not decided. In such a large country as China, with a population of one billion, permitting a small, non-socialist economy predominantly consisting of individual management to exist with certain limits has positive significance for the development of the socialist economy. As for the very small number of private concerns which are in fact capitalist in nature, these may continue to operate on an experimental basis provided they do not adversely affect the dominance of the system of public ownership and help to enliven the economy and develop the forces of production. In order to limit their negative aspects, however, we must strengthen supervision and regulation of them by means of taxation and industrial and commercial administration. At the same time, on the basis of summing up our practical experience, we must seek ways of inducing these private concerns to become co-operatives or to accept the state as a shareholder.

In recent years a new development in the changes to the structure of the system of ownership in China has been the widespread appearance of new types of economic associations or groups of enterprises which cross the boundaries between different systems of ownership or between regions and departments. The nature of enterprise ownership is becoming more and more mixed. Ownership by the whole people, ownership by collectives and ownership by individuals is no longer so sharply divided and separate as in the past. There is not only association among state-owned units and among collectively owned units but also association between state and collective, between state and individual, between collective and individual, and among individuals. By 1984 there were some one thousand industrial enterprises operating under a combination of ownership systems. These accounted for 0.2 per cent of all industrial enterprises (430,000). They employed 370,000 people, some 0.3 per cent of total wage employees in the national economy (118.9 million), and their output value was ¥8.6 billion, some 1.2 per cent of the total value of industrial output (¥703 billion). As the commodity economy develops, this mixed ownership economy will grow further. It plays a positive role in breaking down the boundaries which used to exist between departments and regions and in promoting the separation of ownership and managerial authority. At the same time, through state participation in other forms of economic association and the formation of enterprises controlled by the state, the position and role of the economy under the ownership of the whole people in the entire economy will be further strengthened.

Diversifying The Structure of Ownership

A great variety of forms have evolved in the diversification of the structure of the system of ownership. This has given rise to two problems. The first of these is that there is unequal competition. Many preferential policies have been adopted to foster the development of the collective economy, the individual economy and joint equity ventures with foreign investment. Meanwhile, measures to enliven state-owned enterprises, especially large and medium-sized enterprises, have developed relatively slowly. As a result, the technologically backward is able to put pressure on the advanced, and small enterprises undermine large enterprises. This has led to irregularities in the distribution of income so that state enterprises get less than collectives and collectives get less than individual and foreign capital enterprises. Such phenomena are not the inevitable accompaniment to the introduction of a variety of forms of ownership and management. They arise from the incompleteness of reform measures. The cure for the state-run enterprises' inability to compete with other economic elements lies in reform of the management of state enterprises and an increase in their vitality. Irrational prices have given the other economic elements, especially individual and private concerns, the opportunity to use large price differentials to earn large circulating profits. The solution lies in the reform of prices. The solution to the problem of unequal competition between different economic elements requires a comprehensive adjustment of tax, credit and other economic policies.

The second problem created by the diversification of ownership is the need to determine what proportion each system of ownership should occupy in the economy so that the dominance of the systems of public ownership is guaranteed while, at the same time, the other systems have enough scope to be vigorous and all the potential in the economy is realized.

Table 11.1 The proportions of ownership in the economy (%)

	Gross Value of Industrial Output	Total Social Commodity Sales
Public Ownership	73.6	45.6
Collective Ownership	25.0	39.7
Individual Ownership	0.2	9.6
Others*	1.2	n.a.
Joint Operation**	n.a.	0.2
Peasant Sales to Non-rural Residents		5.0

*Includes industries managed jointly by the state and collectives, by the state and private individuals, by collectives and private individuals, by joint equity ventures with foreigners, by foreign investment, by collectives, industrialists and businessmen, and so forth.

**Jointly operated commerce includes co-operation between different economic forms and between Chinese and foreigners.

Currently state ownership still accounts for the largest proportion of the entire economy and the non-publicly owned proportion remains very small. Taking account of the fact that the publicly-owned economy, especially the state-owned economy, still forms the overwhelming proportion, we need not be in too much of a hurry to determine the rational proportions for each type of ownership. In our policies and measures we should give the non-state owned economy equal status with the state-owned economy and test the efficiency and vitality of each in equal competition. We should allow a process of market evalution to sort out the good from the bad in order to determine the size limits of the different ownership systems in an unhurried way. Those which, through market competition, are shown to be effective should be allowed to continue to develop. Those which can only be propped up by relying on state support can only be helped for a short while. They cannot be sheltered for ever. These methods are not a threat to the state-owned economy, which at present occupies such a dominant position. On the contrary, they provide strong motives and pressures for it to accelerate reform and improve efficiency. In this way, we can ensure the superiority of the state-owned economy in the economy as a whole.

The State-owned System

We must also consider the issue of the reform of the state-owned system itself. The state-owned economy is the leading component of the entire economy. In the working mechanisms of the socialist economy, it constitutes the foundation at the micro-level for macroeconomic management. The reform of the working mechanisms of the economy has not weakened the role of macro-regulation but has strengthened its position and significance. Whether a system of macroeconomic regulation and control is effective, however, is not merely determined by whether the national economic plan corresponds to reality, whether macroeconomic management is scientific and rational, or whether economic policies and measures are appropriate. To a large extent it is also determined by whether microeconomic units are responsive to measures for macro-regulation and control, that is, whether the foundation required for macro-management exists at the micro-level. The internal content of the relations of ownership determines the direction of enterprise economic activity and enterprise responsiveness to changes in economic parameters (the latter being the major means of macroeconomic management after the transition from direct to indirect controls).

Since the beginning of economic reform in China, we have done a lot to transfer authority and control over profits to state-run enterprises and we have increased their rights and motivation. We have, however, neglected to strengthen enterprise responsibility for bearing their own financial risks and the pressures upon them from outside. At present, state-run enterprises only have responsibility for profits and they do not have to be responsible for any losses they make. When they have financial difficulties they can obtain support in a variety of ways, including bargaining with their superior administrative agency, having the tax upon them reduced or waived, getting a larger subsidy, borrowing funds or adjusting prices. In this way they pass on the burden to the state and society. In a situation where the social relationship between the state and the enterprise is a paternalistic one like this it is very difficult to expect enterprises in their management and decision-making to respond sensitively to indirect macroeconomic controls. For these reasons, if we want to build a firm foundation at the micro-level for the reform of macroeconomic management, it is necessary to make changes in the internal content of the system of state ownership itself.

Changing the internal content of the system of state ownership is of immediate practical significance. Since the end of 1984, there has been an expansion of total demand in the Chinese economy. This is quite different from the expansion induced by investment alone, as was the case previously. This time the expansion of consumption has also played a major role in stimulating the economy. The inflation of the consumption fund has created a dramatic expansion of market demand which has made enterprises move into top gear to increase production and investment. This has accelerated the expansion of investment and economic overheating. The expansion of the consumption fund is directly related to the blurring of internal financial and ownership relations in the state-owned enterprises. After the enterprises gained more autonomy, they developed their own economic interests and pursuits. Their objectives and motives became distinct from the general objectives of the state and society. In this situation, without changes in the internal content of the relations of state ownership there is no force within enterprises to represent state interests and no mechanism to ensure the integrity and growth of state assets. Enterprises thus inevitably tend to pursue their own short-term interests and the consumption interests of their employees, and it is difficult to give consideration to the long-term development of enterprises and the long-term interests of society.

Given the position of state ownership in the economy and its current situation, internal reform should become one of the key points in the reform of the entire relations of ownership. The difficulties for the reform of the state-owned economy do not lie in the large number of small-scale enterprises suited to decentralized operation (in 1984, of the total of 437,200 industrial enterprises, 430,800, or 98.5 per cent, were small-scale enterprises). Economic reform in several socialist countries has shown that the contracting, leasing and selling of appropriate small-scale state-owned enterprises to labourers' collectives or to individual management is effective and beneficial both for overall economic activity and for the management of the enterprises themselves. In China, leasing and contracting has been adopted for many such enterprises. The contractor has independent managerial authority and bears responsibility for profits and losses. In most cases this has brought good economic results. Nevertheless, leasing and contracting to individuals has also led to some bad effects, especially in terms of distribution. The differentials between the incomes of some contractors and those of ordinary workers have become too wide. In some places it has been pointed out that experience in the leasing and contracting of rural and township enterprises shows that collective contracting and leasing whereby the enterprise is contracted or leased to its leading group has better economic results than leasing or contracting to individuals. The implementation of the contract is more guaranteed and the division of income is fairer. In sum, it is best to make bold use of contracting and leasing for appropriate small-scale enterprises, especially those suited to decentralized management and those in the tertiary sector relying mainly on labour. This realizes the separation of ownership rights and management authority. It is beneficial for enlivening the economy, strengthening the division of labour and co-operation between different economic elements, and encouraging appropriate competition.

The really difficult issue in the reform of the state-owned economy lies in the large and medium-sized enterprises which, although not great in number, account for a very large proportion of output value. In 1984, there were 6,400 such enterprises, which formed only 1.5 per cent of all industrial enterprises but accounted for 45 per cent of total industrial output value. We are still exploring ways of properly handling the separation of ownership rights and management authority for these enterprises so that, without changing state ownership rights, we reform the system of management and expand their managerial autonomy. In recent years we have changed the system of state enterprises handing over their profits to the state into a system of taxation. Apart from collecting an income tax at a unified tax rate, we also levy an 'adjustment tax' which is fixed proportionately to the after-tax profits of each enterprise. The original purpose of this method was to ensure the state's financial revenue and to protect the original assets and interests of the enterprise. Since its introduction, however, it has given rise to the shortcoming of punishing the successful. Large and medium-sized enterprises which are well-run bear a larger burden by having to pay over a greater amount. They have no resources left for research and development. In other cases, we have introduced experiments in contracted management at a small number of large and medium-sized enterprises such as the Capital Iron and Steel Company and the Number Two Vehicle Plant. These enterprises use a system of total contracting in return for the handing-over of profit in graduated stages. Where enterprise profits are growing rapidly, enterprises are thereby able to retain a lot more profit for their own technical transformation. But this system is not easy to introduce in enterprises where the profit is increasing only slowly or else declining. It is therefore still necessary to study the best way of handling the relationship between the enterprise and the state. We must distinguish between different situations and find different solutions.

Embryonic Forms

In recent years, the appearance of various embryonic forms of share economy as a means of amassing capital funds together with experiments in a small number of enterprises to allow employees to buy shares in the enterprise have awakened people to the possibility that a shareholder economy might become a major economic form in the structure of ownership. In particular, this might be a major means of reforming enterprises under the system of ownership by the whole people. In general terms, the adoption of a shareholder economy in China can be seen to have the following advantages:

1. The relations of ownership become more concrete and the previous situation where enterprises under the ownership of the whole people were owned by all but no one had responsibility for enterprise assets is changed.
2. Mutual constraints are established between the owners of an enterprise, the managers and the producers, so that enterprise managerial behaviour is rationalized.
3. Idle capital funds existing in society can be brought together, promoting the horizontal flow of capital funds and the formation of a price for them. This helps to restrain the inflation in investment, and improves the allocation of social resources.
4. The purchase of shares in the enterprise by its employees can make them more concerned about improving the management of production.

Strictly speaking, the share system is merely the external form of the relations of ownership. The internal content of the system of ownership in a share economy will be quite different, depending on whether the major shares are in the hands of the state, of groups, or of individuals. If the orientation in the introduction of shares for state-owned enterprises is mainly towards the individual ownership of shares, this will fundamentally negate the general aim of ensuring the dominance of public ownership. Furthermore, given the low level of individual incomes, it is at present impossible for the assets of state-run enterprises to the value of several hundred billion yuan to be converted into shares bought by individuals. Even if it did become possible in future, it could give rise to a social strata of people living off profits as shares become concentrated in the hands of a small minority. This does not match China's socialist nature and, therefore, such proposals are not desirable.

Another suggestion is that the orientation of shareholding in state-owned enterprises should be towards the ownership of shares mainly by groups of enterprises. There is a lot of potential for enterprises to buy shares, and this is increasing following the extension of profit retention within enterprises. If, however, assets currently under state ownership are transformed into assets owned by enterprise groups, including mutual investment between enterprises, this will give rise to the question of whether the payment for labour and authority over assets of new enterprise employees should equal those of the original employees. If they are the same, this is really no different from ownership by the whole people. If there is discrimination, this will lead to divisions between groups within the enterprise. This would not only hinder the rational circulation of labour but would also exclude the horizontal circulation of capital funds. Some of the joint labourers would become masters who have ownership authority over the means of production and others would become hired workers. Shareholding based on ownership by groups of enterprises is therefore also not desirable.

Conclusion

For these reasons, the orientation of shareholding in state-owned enterprises should still be towards the ownership of shares chiefly by the state so that the state legally maintains the ownership of most of the means of production. The state as shareholder will participate in the major enterprise decisions through its representatives on the board of directors. This will protect the interests of the state as owner of the assets but will not lead to intervention in the actual running of the enterprise which will be the responsibility of the enterprise managers. The latter will pay compensation in return for the right to make use of the means of production of the enterprise. The problem is that the state is not an abstract thing. What kind of agency should hold the shares on behalf of the state and carry out the functions of the owner of capital funds? Should it be a specialist administrative department? Or a comprehensive functional department? Or a financial agency run as an enterprise? This question must be decided in a way which guards against administrative interference in enterprise management and also fully protects the state's interests as the owner of the assets. It requires further investigation.

In classical Marxist writings, the shareholder system in the capitalist economy is described as a premise for the establishment of socialist public ownership. In the third volume of *Capital* (Marx, n.d.: 493), share companies are seen by Marx as social capital in contrast to private capital and as social enterprises in contrast to private enterprises. They are a further development of private asset-holding within the framework of the capitalist mode of production itself. Nevertheless, a warning can be taken from the fact that examples in the international socialist movement of the introduction of a share system in enterprises under the socialist system of ownership by the whole people have not yet been entirely successful. It seems that such a new problem in the practice of socialism cannot be solved by sticking to convention and blind rejection, nor by rash and indiscriminate action. It is necessary to carry out profound investigation and analysis of the positive role it could play, the negative effects that could arise, and the objective and subjective conditions required for the establishment of a share system. Only in this way can a realizable programme be put forward.

References

C.P.C. (1984). *Decision of the Central Committee of the Communist Party of China on the Reform of the Economic Structure*. Beijing.

Liu, Guoguang (1986). 'Changes in ownership forms: problems and possibilities'. *Beijing Review*, **29**, No. 19, 12 May: 17–22.

Marx, Karl (n.d.). *Capital*, Vol. 3, in *Complete Works of Marx*. Vol. 25, Beijing, p. 493.

12 Capitalist Efficiency Without Capitalist Exploitation — Some Indications from Shenzhen

Leslie Sklair

Introduction

The decisions of the Third Plenum of the Eleventh Central Committee of the Chinese Communist Party in December 1978 began a process of transformation that has had, and is continuing to have, profound effects on the whole of the Chinese economy and society. By signalling the removal of close central controls on most of the rural economy and much of the urban economy through the introduction of a variety of 'responsibility systems' which have devolved decisionmaking to the direct rural producer and to enterprise management in more and more urban enterprises, the Chinese leadership has permitted, and even encouraged, an unprecedented level of discussion and debate on the very nature of socialism in China. Chinese socialism is increasingly being conceptualized in terms of its relationship to the global capitalist forms from which it must learn and borrow if 'socialist moderniza-tion' is to be achieved, according to authoritative Chinese sources. Ma Hong, the President of the Chinese Academy of Social Sciences (CASS), echoes the official line when he describes the Chinese economy as a 'commodity economy under the socialist system', and argues that, in order to develop, it must take advantage of advanced foreign technology and be prepared to exploit the international division of labour (Ma, 1985). Such ideas, which would have been anathema (on the level of rhetoric if not entirely on the level of practice) even a dozen years ago when the Maoist road to development and its peculiar interpretation by the Gang of Four still held sway, may be taken as official state policy today.

Under the general slogan of 'socialist modernization', a fundamental trans-formation of the Chinese economy and society is under way, which deliber-ately sets out to negate much of the past history of the PRC—not only the familiar periods of 'radical excesses' like the Great Leap Forward and the Cultural Revolution—and to affirm that a new and radically reformed version of socialism is in the process of formation. There are three central features of this fundamental transformation of the Chinese economy and society to which I wish to draw special attention here. These three central features are:

1. the relationships between the socialist planned economy and the capitalist commodity economy;
2. the precise role of foreign investment, trade, technology, and other forms of external capitalist penetration; and
3. the effects of these on the life-styles and attitudes of the Chinese people.

All three relate backwards to the traditional Soviet-inspired conceptions of socialist-communist society that have provided an often unwelcome model for non-Soviet communists (in China and elsewhere) since 1917. They also all relate immediately to what Bahro (1978) has termed 'actually existing socialism' and a more sober assessment of where China now stands. Finally, these three central features relate to the future, to the contours of a society in transition in which new standards of social and economic behaviour will prevail, and new opportunities for personal and collective fulfilment will be available. What distinguishes all this from what has happened before in the short history of the PRC is not the fact that an apparently root-and-branch revision of policy has occurred relatively quickly—the years since 1949 have witnessed several bewilderingly swift changes of policy—but the nature of the changes now taking place. One can hardly disagree with the view expressed in the *Guangming Daily*, commenting on a Central Committee 'Decision' of late 1984, that the reforms exemplify 'the greatest Marxist theoretical courage in discarding certain static views on the understanding of socialism formed over a long period in the past which do not correspond to actual circumstances' (Jia, 1985: 3).

The question I pose here is *not* whether this 'theoretical courage' leaves any recognizably *socialist* content to the Chinese economy and society, for I hold that those who see the Chinese reforms as 'socialism versus capitalism' will inevitably end up locked into simplistic conclusions dictated by such a simplistic formula. My question, rather, is whether the attempt to promote socialist modernization through capitalist efficiency, that is, learning from and borrowing certain capitalist methods of production, management and social organization, can successfully filter out or neutralize precisely those elements of capitalist exploitation which are the difference between capitalism and socialism. There are really two questions here, namely, is it possible in principle? and are the Chinese actually doing it in practice? In order to begin to answer the second question, I shall refer specifically to the case of the Shenzhen Special Economic Zone, the site of the most intensive penetration of capitalist practices in China.

Planned Socialism and Commodity Capitalism

In any transition from one mode of production to another, elements of the old and the new co-mingle. 'Pure' modes of production exist only in abstraction—as Marx was the first to point out: in any actual social formation we are seeking to distinguish dominant from subordinate economic, political and ideological formations. Bettelheim puts the point forcefully when he argues that a transitional phase is constituted by a lack of conformity between newly dominant social relations and forces of production. 'The new social relations do not yet dominate by their own strength', he says, 'conditions for expanded reproduction of these social relations are not yet given' (1975:23). Under these conditions what he terms 'mediations' are necessary, the prime example of which is the New Economic Policy of the Soviet Union in the 1920s. The China of the post-1978 Reforms may also be conceptualized in these terms.

In recent years the problematic nature of such phenomena, at least in the perceptions of those trying to study societies that have not achieved an advanced state of industrialization, has increased greatly. An enormous literature has grown up around the idea of 'the articulation of modes of production' (Wolpe, 1980: Introduction), though the bulk of this concerns societies in transformation around capitalism, not socialism. This is partly due to the widespread view that the idea of a 'socialist mode of production' is a contradiction in terms, and that socialism is itself a transition, namely the stage of transition between capitalism and communism. Although this view does have some merit, I find it unduly restrictive and, in relation to comtemporary China, bordering on utopianism. If communism is that stage in human affairs when scarcity is abolished and the social product is derived from each according to ability and distributed to each according to need then, as Chinese commentators have frankly acknowledged for some years, communism is not on the agenda in China. On the other hand, socialism, as a mode of production geared to raise the material well-being of the whole population through the domination of a planned collective over a commodity market economy, is very much on the agenda in China.

A theory of mediations in the transition to socialism in the Chinese economy and society must begin by conceptualizing the dominant and the subsidiary mode(s) of production and how they articulate. The dominant mode of production in China, whether we call it *socialist* or not, is one in which the accumulation of capital occurs through the collective economy rather than private enterprise, though this does not exclude the possibility that some capital accumulation does take place through private enterprise. Where the state or other collective entities owns the means of production, or if not all the means of production, at least the 'commanding heights of the economy', then it may even operate through market mechanisms and, indeed, might gain great benefits from doing so. However, the hegemony of the collective over the private, the plan over the market, must prevail, if the socialist mode of production is to survive and flourish. The contradiction that is built into the very core of the theory of mediations in the transition to socialism is that the evidence from virtually all socialist societies suggests that rapid progress in the development of the forces of production is at least unlikely, and at most impossible, where there are comprehensive restrictions on the rural producers and urban enterprises and where the free market is severely curtailed. This empirical reality lures us dangerously to the brink of the conceptual contradiction that the progress of socialism depends upon the restoration (or creation) of capitalism. Under real communism there would be no problem, because scarcity would be abolished and plenty would exist for all. The problem of the transition to socialism, of course, is precisely the problem of how to turn scarcity into plenty in a way that protects the interests of the masses.

Extending the economic opportunities of rural producers and urban enterprises does not, of course, necessarily entail the restoration of capitalism. This may, however, be an effect of such policies and practices, and a theory of mediations can only work if it has the capacity to grapple with such effects (or counter-effects) in the concrete reality of the articulation of modes of production in the transition to socialism. This would imply a method of categorizing the economy, both in its rural and urban sectors, and a method of identifying the key characteristics of the collective economy, and the non-collective or even anti-collective mediations on whose protection or restoration the progress of the collective economy is considered to depend.

Reflections very much like these have led the Chinese to reconsider the nature of the socialism that is being created in China. The whole question of commodity production and the role of the market, as they operate within the socialist mode of production (see Hsu, 1985), reverberates at both a theoretical and a substantive level. Theoretically, there is a definite impression of cognitive risk-taking by Chinese intellectuals in the debates around Marxist conceptions of the economy and society (modes of production and social formations) that have taken place since 1978. Following the lead of the political centre, Chinese intellectuals in the social sciences are increasingly arguing that one key difference between socialism (at least in China) and capitalism is *efficiency*, often encapsulated in the notions that higher production is far less important than greater productivity, and that an obsession with quantity has led to the neglect of quality. This is, of course, not an entirely new theme in the PRC. Chen Yun, a leading economist and planner in the 1950s and early 1960s and recalled in 1978 to play a key role in working out the reforms, had waged a long struggle for these views all through the Maoist period. For example, in a long campaign against over-ambitious steel targets he had constantly urged lower levels of production and higher levels of quality (Lardy & Lieberthal, 1983: Introduction and Chap. 14). Chen's belated reappearance in the highest echelons of the Chinese planning hierarchy and the publication of his papers from the 1950s and early 1960s are, according to Lardy and Lieberthal, a clear indication that the Maoist mobilization approach to economics and social change has finally been discredited, and that Chen's careful, balanced approach to the economy that laid more emphasis on the production of consumer goods, was firmly in the ascendant. It is also important to note that Chen was a strong proponent of:

1. central control of finance and production in the commanding heights of the economy (heavy industry, extractive industries, infrastructure), coexisting with genuine decentralization and enterprise-level decisionmaking for the rest of industry, as long as it was efficient;
2. what are now known as the responsibility systems in the countryside; and
3. a greater share of state resources for agriculture, as contrasted with the Maoist strategy of leaving the task of rural capital accumulation largely in the hands of the communes.

These were all policies that Chen pushed, particularly before and during the Great Leap Forward, with relatively little success. They are now more or less official policy, enshrined in the new Seventh Five-Year Plan (1986–90), and it can be said that, by the mid-1980s Chen and his supporters (based in CASS and other economic and planning research and policy institutions) had won both the arguments and the political victory.

It is in this context that the current Chinese interest in what capitalist practices have to offer must be comprehended. There is a sense in which the Chinese leadership is seriously comparing the socialist system with the capitalist system, but the nature of the comparison itself is eclectic rather than systematic. The socialist planned economy is conceived as an organic whole while the commodity character and market mechanisms of capitalism are conceived piecemeal as economic levers, which, when used in a rational fashion, may render any economy more efficient. These 'piecemeal economic levers' are the 'mediations' in the transition to socialism. Citing Lenin's views that the lessons of bourgeois economic progress have to be learned before they can be transcended and that much of the economic triumph of capitalism is, in fact, due to the historic efforts of the labouring masses, many Chinese commentators are beginning to argue for the virtual 'value neutrality' of technical knowledge that has been so widely rejected by Western social scientists. This is clearly indicated in a paper in the journal *Social Sciences* in which the writer boldly asserts: 'Technology and labor management knowledge by themselves do not have any class or ideological character' (Bao, 1985: 155). The creation of the Chinese Enterprise Management Association (CEMA) in 1979 and the establishment of a training scheme with the collaboration of the EEC in 1983 to produce MBA-equivalents (see Warner, 1985), are institutional confirmations that, for the time being at least, the perennial struggle between 'the reds' and 'the experts' has been resolved in favour of 'the experts'. Few will regret the defeat of the hegemony of 'the reds' over technical expertise that the Gang of Four had encouraged, but no doubt there remain many inside (and outside) China who still take Mao's balanced dialectic of 'red and expert' seriously. It was not so much a stark all-or-nothing choice between 'politics in command' and 'economics in command', argued Mao, but more a realization that the 'relationship between redness and expertness, politics and work is the unity of two opposites' (cited in Brugger, 1977: 230). The syllabus of the CEMA-EEC MBA Programme does not attempt to unite these two opposites in any way.

This is not to say, however, that the Chinese conception of economic management is simply a copy of Western management theory and practice. Firstly, there are several competing Western theories and practices and few organizational principles are universally accepted; and secondly, the Chinese themselves do have a long tradition of political and military administration whose efficacy is massively confirmed by the fact that China today is one (albeit vast and variegated) sovereign state. One has only to look at a map of Europe, Africa or the rest of Asia, or study the proliferating membership of the United Nations, to appreciate the magnitude of this achievement. The exaggeration of an economics professor at the Beijing Economics Institute can, therefore, be forgiven when he claims that 'The World is Studying Ancient China's Management Ideas' (Yang, 1985), and he does make the interesting point that in management studies the initiative has swung away from individualistic styles of control (characteristic of the United States) to teamwork-based systems (characteristic of Japan and, presumably, more compatible with Chinese socialism). Yang notes that two PRC scholars had recently published a book on *Sun Yi's Art of War and Enterprise Management* to pull some of these ideas together!

These techniques, tools, mechanisms, methods, or whatever, of production and administration, then, are *not* seen as anything intrinsic to capitalism, but as purely technical and utilitarian means that can be applied to the achievement of chosen ends. In the socialist planned economy, the collectively chosen ends are social justice, human self-realization, and a society based on the formula of 'from each according to ability, to each according to work'. Under the capitalist system the ends are chosen by the small class that owns and controls the means of production, driven by the profit motive, where the anarchy of the market ensures massive social inefficiency. While it is obvious that there are areas in which capitalist enterprises have attained much greater efficiency than enterprises in socialist economies, this is not taken to imply that the capitalist system is in any way superior to the socialist system. All capitalist and all socialist societies have commodity economies (for example, they all continue to use money in economic transactions), but it is precisely the fixation of capitalism with the commodity form and the relations of production based on private property that ensures the eventual triumph of socialism as an economic and social system. In words reminiscent of Lenin on imperialism, Xu and Yang (1985) stirringly announce that 'Socialism is the Highest and Final Phase of the Commodity Economy'. This is so because only socialist planning, by replacing the anarchy of capitalist commodity production, will be able to produce a truly rational and scarcity-free society.

Behind all the dogma and rhetoric there is a most serious intent, and the seeds of an analysis that demands to be recognized by a crisis-ridden capitalism. In order to focus on this more directly, I shall now move on to discuss how these relationships between planned socialism and commodity capitalism have started to work out in practice in the context of foreign investment and, particularly, in the case of the Shenzhen Special Economic Zone.

Foreign Investment

Although China was never entirely autarchic between 1949 and 1978—even during the decade of the Cultural Revolution some substantial foreign trade deals (import of turnkey chemical fertilizer plants, for example) took place—the volume and character of external economic relations have been transformed in recent years. While the balance between imports and exports has produced both trade deficits and surpluses in individual years since 1978, the total volume of foreign trade (imports plus exports) much more than doubled between 1978 and 1986, a growth-rate substantially greater than that of national income. Much of the rise in both exports and imports (and increasingly in the imported components and materials that go into goods for export) is due to the foreign investment that has flooded into the country since the 'open-door' policy was inaugurated in 1978 as a key constituent of the reforms.

The 'open-door' policy was enshrined in the Sixth Five-Year Plan (1981–5)—exceptional not only for its content but also for the fact that it was the first to be published since the First Five-Year Plan (1953–7). In the preamble to Chapter 19 on 'Economic Relations and Trade with Foreign Countries', the Plan asserts that:

> on the basis of self-reliance we will continue the policy of opening to the outside world and substantially develop our trade, economic and technical exchange with other countries based on the principle of equality and mutual benefit. We will make the best use of available foreign funds and import advanced technology suitable for China to promote its economic construction.

In addition to the new freedoms that the reforms progressively gave to enterprises, provinces, and even individuals, to engage in foreign trade, a small number of Special Economic Zones (SEZs) were set up as an experiment, quite clearly to give the Chinese authorities some idea of what might happen if foreign capitalists were given the opportunity to invest in industrial, agricultural, commercial and infrastructural enterprises in a relatively unfettered fashion.

The first SEZs were established in South China, mainly to take advantage of the proximity to Hong Kong and the traditional links with Overseas Chinese originating from the area. Indeed, family and locality ties have played a part in the foreign investment that has already taken place. The most important of the first four zones is at Shenzhen, taking up the whole of the

China–Hong Kong border. This is a huge area of over 300 sq. kms and is more sensibly looked at as a series of interconnecting zones, each to some extent specialized in industry, commerce, oil, tourism, recreation, and so on. The population of the zone has grown rapidly, mainly by internal migration from the rest of China, and it now stands at more than a quarter of a million.

The other three zones are much smaller and much more recognizably economic zones of the type common in Asia and other parts of the world. They are at Zhuhai, adjoining Macao; Shantou (Swatow), on the east coast of Guangdong province; and Xiamen (Amoy), on the Fujian coast, a little further to the north. Shenzhen has attracted a great deal of investment and attention, and it has already been identified as a key site of China's drive towards modernization (Wong & Chu, 1985) or development (Sklair, 1985). It is, therefore, entirely appropriate to ask how the relationship between socialist planning and commodity capitalism, and the search for efficiency without exploitation, have proceeded in Shenzhen.

Most of the foreign investment in Shenzhen is on a joint venture basis, though not normally equity joint venture. The most common arrangement is for the foreign investor (preponderantly overseas Chinese from Hong Kong or elsewhere in South-East Asia, but with a sprinkling from the United States, Japan and Europe) to provide the technology and the management and sometimes specialized services and components, while the Chinese partner (who might be a state enterprise or agency, or collective enterprise) provides land, labour and buildings. Such joint ventures are clearly neither straightforward state enterprises nor are they straightforward capitalist enterprises. They have, in fact, been labelled 'state capitalism under a socialist system' (Bao, 1985: 153), in recognition of their dual nature. This label signals the risk inherent in direct foreign investment, and the expectation that the increase in efficiency both within the enterprise and through the effects on the rest of the economy, will outweigh the negative consequences of capitalist exploitation.

The first part of this equation is clear enough. The Chinese authorities have publicly and repeatedly in the last few years acknowledged the backward state of the vast majority of their industry and infrastructure. The impression is rife that practically any technology and techniques from the capitalist countries would be an improvement, and the occasional attempts of some firms to dump obsolete technology on the Chinese have not much changed this.

The question of exploitation, on the other hand, presents considerably more difficulty. As Brugger notes, in a volume of essays most appropriately entitled *Chinese Marxism in Flux: 1978–1984*, there were more than six hundred articles on alienation published in China between 1978 and 1983, and this outpouring of analysis and opinion was only stopped by the authorities when the question of alienation under socialism was raised (Brugger, 1985: Introduction). The connection between alienation and exploitation in Marxist theory is, of course, very close. Although there are many subtle distinctions to be made between various Marxist interpretations of alienation (Meszaros, 1970), there is general consensus on the position that the private ownership of the means of production produces surplus value through the exploitation of the working class and from this exploitative relationship alienation in its various forms is said to characterize the capitalist system. The socialist-communist position has usually consisted in the argument that state ownership or ownership 'by the whole people' of the means of production by definition abolishes exploitation and with it alienation in socialist societies. While the logic of this argument may be impeccable, various critics of 'orthodox Marxism' from the left and the right have been profoundly dissatisfied with its truth content, and this has led to a truly huge volume of writing on the 'class nature of the state', the bureaucracy as a 'new class', and so on.

The introduction of direct foreign investment does clearly change the situation somewhat. While there may be a case for arguing that the urban workers in a state-owned factory, or the rural workers on a collectively-owned field in a socialist society are not exploited in the way that the workers in privately-owned enterprise in a capitalist society are, the case of the worker in a privately-owned enterprise in a socialist society, even where the enterprise is a joint venture with a state partner, does present obvious difficulties for the conventional socialist view of exploitation.

In the case of fdi, as in the case of the expansion of free enterprise in the countryside that has similarly resulted from the reforms of 1978, the leading motif has undoubtedly been pragmatism. As I have already noted, investment by foreign capitalists in China has been authoritatively characterized as 'state capitalism under a socialist system' and this is said to involve 'a certain amount of exploitation', but of the Chinese state as much as the Chinese workers. Although the foreign capitalists do extract profits—a net loss to the state—the greater productivity and technology used more than compensates for this loss. The Chinese workers in such joint and other foreign enterprises are 'not at all the same as workers employed in a capitalist society', but the differences appear to boil back down to the pre-existing socialist character of Chinese society (Bao, 1985). Greg McCarthy puts his finger on the problem in his insightful analysis of the role of the Chinese state in the transition to socialism when he argues that the nature of surplus extraction in China (in domestic or foreign-owned enterprise) remains untheorized (McCarthy in Brugger, 1985: Chap. 5).

While the volume and impact of foreign investment in China as a whole has increased enormously in recent years, it is still relatively insignificant over the country as a whole. Of the few *places* where it has had a more substantial and visible effect, Shenzhen is arguably the most important, and it is, therefore, unsurprising that the question of the role of fdi in a socialist society has been frequently raised in relation to the SEZ. From the very establishment of the Special Economic Zones, it must be said, Chinese writers acknowledged that exploitation, in the form of exported surplus value, was an inevitable consequence of foreign investment. Reflecting the general view of capitalist investment as a secondary or supplementary feature of the economy in parallel with the view that the open-door policy was decidedly secondary to self-reliance in the economy as a whole, Chinese commentators have had to perform something of a balancing act. On the one hand, the impression of constant growth in and upgrading of the foreign investment component in the SEZs has to be maintained, while on the other hand, the fundamental rationale for the whole experiment, namely to develop the socialist planned economy, cannot be forgotten. The first of these two objectives is clearly easier to achieve than the second. Numbers of contracts signed with foreign investors, capital investment sums 'committed' and 'in use', and the growth of production, are regularly reported. The contribution all these make to the development of the socialist planned economy is, of course, not quite so clear-cut. Although jobs and the earning of foreign currency were important initial objectives of the Special Economic Zones, they have been progressively downgraded (probably because enclave foreign investment rarely provides either a multitude of cost-effective jobs or much net foreign earnings for the host government) in favour of the provision of modern technology and management methods. Indeed, one writer argues specifically that whereas capitalists seek to make money out of fdi, the Chinese do it for the sake of technology and management skills (Wang, 1985).

Nevertheless, the scale and impact of foreign investment in Shenzhen has stimulated new catergorizations of the economy in the zone. Xu (1985) usefully quantifies production in Shenzhen and Shekou (the separately administered industrial zone to the west of Shenzhen) by sector. He distinguishes the share of total output of (a) the state capitalist sector, for state and foreign-owned joint enterprises; (b) foreign wholly-owned enterprises; and (c) collective enterprises, foreign investors with non-state partners; as follows:

Zone/Sector	State Capitalist	Foreign	Collective
	%	%	%
Shenzhen	50	30	20
Shekou	81.4	18.6	0.01

This, Xu argues, gives the Special Zones a dual character, and management structure must reflect this. In brief, state capitalism under the socialist planned economy must reflect aspects of both capitalist and socialist organization, and all the signs to the present indicate that the capitalist elements are mainly concentrated at the micro-level of enterprise management, while the socialist elements are mainly concentrated at the macro-level of the aggregate of enterprises and the industrial-commercial structure of the zone as a whole.

For example, radical changes have been taking place in the system of hiring and firing workers and this appears to have gone further in Shenzhen than elsewhere. Since 1982, a labour contract between employer and worker, mediated by the Labour Services Bureau of the Zone (Sklair, 1985: 857–93), has replaced the 'iron rice-bowl' that guaranteed workers more or less lifetime employment in the enterprise. These, and several other of the post-1978 reforms of enterprise management, well described by Lockett and Littler (1983), mostly introducing what could loosely be termed 'Western-capitalist' features, have become intrinsic components of the industrial-commercial landscape of enterprises in Shekou and Shenzhen. One partial exception to this trend—notwithstanding the abortive experiments to introduce 'worker's participation' into the capitalist factory in the West—has been the spread of cadre elections in the factories of the SEZ. Here, workers directly elect their managers but the slate of candidates is prepared by the Supervisory Department (directed by the Party leadership) in the factory. This mechanism, therefore, does represent a minimal socialist check to the revered capitalist principle of 'management's (absolute) right to manage', but the function of the electoral hurdle is probably as much to legitimize the management in the state capitalist factory as it is to challenge what management does. Certainly, the system has been utilized to get rid of ineffectual managers (Fang, 1985).

The role of the trade unions effectively fills the silence left by the unasked questions about exploitation in the Chinese workplace, inside and outside Shenzhen. A report in the Beijing *Worker's Daily* (in JPRS-CEA-85-020: 149–51) explains that the hundred joint ventures set up in the SEZs in the 1980s required thousands of workers, many of whom were quite inexperienced in the ways of factory life. Therefore, it was necessary in Shenzhen for the city-wide trade union to establish eighty-two grass-roots unions to resolve the contradiction between capital and labour, namely by explaining to the workers how important it is for China that foreign investors have a reliable work-force. This is entirely true, since the main reason for any foreign investor to source production in a low-wage country is a favourable balance between productivity and costs. Given the generally (though not absolutely) non-adversarial character of Chinese trade unions, it comes as no surprise to learn that managers from Hong Kong working in Shenzhen prefer to have unions to help them sort out their problems.

I have been careful, in the course of this discussion, to avoid any subjective interpretation of exploitation. It would not be difficult to argue that the conscientious and able worker in a foreign-owned or joint-venture factory in Shenzhen is better paid, has better conditions, and perhaps even higher job satisfaction than workers elsewhere in China. If this could be established then it would follow that such a worker could not be more exploited, subjectively, than the worker outside Shenzhen. But, for Marxists, exploitation is not primarily about subjective feelings and this is why the argument that Shenzhen represents state capitalism within a socialist planned economy is so important for the Chinese analysis of foreign investment in general, and special economic zones in particular. The assumption is that the state, by controlling the macro-economic environment for the benefit of all the people, more than compensates for the modicum of exploitation, at the enterprise rather than at the individual level, that foreign investment inevitably produces. This assumption effectively closes off the debate about the economic character of exploitation by putting such a premium on the potential benefits of economic efficiency. It is only in the context of the capitalist influence on life-styles that we can begin to unpack this relationship.

Capitalist Efficiency and Socialist Life-styles

By the end of 1980, when the first fruits, both ripe and rotten, were falling from the economic reform tree, Deng Xiaoping and other top Party people began to speak out about the need to create a 'socialist spiritual civilisation' to combat the rising tide of 'spiritual pollution' (Gold, 1984). In a campaign that has gone on more or less intensely since then, we can identify the main social and ideological defences that the Chinese Communist Party was to muster against the corrosive effects of capitalist-Western influences. We may analyse the battle against spiritual pollution on two levels and for two main groups, namely against economic malpractice and bourgeois life-style, as practised by cadres and the masses, particularly youth.

It is now common knowledge, and widely discussed in the Chinese mass media, that corruption is rife in certain sections of the Chinese economy. There have been some well-publicized major scandals in recent years, prime amongst which was the case of the large group of cadres in Hainan Island who had embezzled substantial amounts of money from an illegal import business (see 'Ta Kung Pao' (Hong Kong), 8–14 August 1985), and enough cases of relatively minor malpractices often connected with black markets in scarce raw materials, consumer and producer goods, to prove the point that in this respect at least China is becoming more like most other countries in the Third World. This is not to suggest that such practices were entirely absent before 1978—there is ample evidence of small-scale urban and rural bribery and corruption (Chen & Ridley, 1969; and Frolic, 1980)—but that the character of economic malpractice had changed in both scope and extent. For example, in March 1982, a Guangdong newspaper detailed the problem under the title 'Fully recognise the seriousness of the corrupting influence of capitalist ideology in the economy' (in JPRS 80773, *Economic Affairs* 230, 11 May 1982: 21–4). The paper equates economic crime with capitalist corruption in four respects. Firstly, with the spread of foreign capitalist influence, especially in the south, economic crime has spread everywhere. Secondly, whereas in the 1960s, a bribe of ¥1,000 represented a major offence, now the sums involved run into hundreds of thousands. Thirdly, it is the cadres who are providing a 'protective umbrella' for the criminals where they are not actually the criminals themselves. Fourthly, the ideology that 'everything depends on money . . . plays a disintegrating role in our socialist system'.

(ibid.: 23). All of these effects are directly related to the opportunities presented by the economic reforms, specifically the open-door policy. The Special Economic Zones are said to create particular and severe problems and the point is made that successfully attacking economic crimes, far from inhibiting growth and foreign investment, will ensure continued progress.

There is clearly a strong sense of ambivalence in the Chinese treatment of foreign investors that makes it very difficult to distinguish between sharp practice and outright corruption. In an attempt to outflank the exploitative nature of capitalist business enterprise, many bodies in Shenzhen, both local authority and commercial, appear to have been over-zealous in ensuring that foreign investors evaded no local charges or obligations. The story of sanitary fees collected from Shenzhen foreign investors by no less than five separate agencies (reported in JPRS–CEA–85–091: 74) is typical. This is not necessarily currupt practice, but the implication is that much of what is collected goes into the pockets of the cadres.

Although cadres have the greatest opportunities for such illegal activities, the rise in economic crime among ordinary people has also been noted. Much of this concerns the smuggling of goods from Shenzhen, increasingly a duty-free area, into the rest of China. This has been a problem in Shenzhen since the early 1980s. It was reported in 1982 that fifty Army cadres had been drafted into the zone to deal with such economic crimes, and the claim that smuggling was 'basically under control' (SWB/FE/7232/BII/1–3: 1983) must be taken with a large pinch of salt. These problems, and the sheer magnitude of the task of handling a reported fifteen million border crossings per year in and out of Shenzhen, have forced the authorities to implement a 'two-line administration' pledged to an eventual free flow of goods and people between Hong Kong and Shenzhen, creating one large zone by 1997, and a strictly controlled and fenced border to the north, between Shenzhen and the rest of China (Inland). The point of this second line is to prevent illegal activities between the zone and inland, while facilitating legal trade and transfers. The very success of Shenzhen in attracting state and non-state collective and individual business from the rest of China and the multitude of interconnections that have been established, clearly makes the two-line administration very difficult to implement successfully.

The other main form of public economic malpractice is the currency black market. It is almost impossible for the foreigner to spead renminbi in Shenzhen. The authorities issued Foreign Exchange Certificates and a new Special Economic Currency is under consideration, but Hong Kong dollars are preferred by far for most transactions. The major Western credit cards are also accepted in an increasing number of establishments. Small-time illegal money changers operate relatively openly, and a recent report of the arrcst of a gang of twenty-one foreign-currency profiteers, caught with HK$139,000 and ¥145,000 on their persons stressed that twenty of them were from outside the SEZ (JPRS–CEA–85–042: 166).

Economic crime, among cadres and the general public, then, is a feature of

Shenzhen life, but there is no indication that it has reached anything like massive proportions. Though one would be unwise to ignore it entirely, it is unlikely that its manifestations have had serious effects on the economy of the zone as a whole. The Chinese government appears willing and able to seek out and punish the worst cases of economic crime, even where they involve cadres high up in the Party and state apparatus. Although regularly breached, the tenets of communist public ethics are still more honoured in their observance, in so far as economic behaviour is concerned.

The identification of spiritual pollution outside the economic sphere is at once more difficult to pin down and, potentially, much more threatening to the survival of Chinese communism. Here it is necessary to separate the cadres, especially those who are Party members, from the masses, rather more systematically for reasons of history and practice. There is a long and well-documented tradition of cadre socialization in China, in which the communist virtues and the conditions for the formation of a new communist personality are laid down by the top Party leaders. Liu's *How to be a Good Communist*—which was circulated in many millions of copies in Chinese and in translation before being reviled during the Cultural Revolution—and, of course, Mao's *Little Red Book*, give the main lines of the reconstruction of men and women thought to be necessary to ensure the victory of communism in China.

The central theme that runs through these statements of principle and practice is that the personal interests of a Party member must be unconditionally subordinated to the interests of the Party and, through the Party, to the people. It is notable that this call to subordinate individual to collective interests is still at the heart of Chinese communist ethics, and that 'individualism' is still considered to be the prime bourgeois deviation. A detailed study of the question of individualism within the Party (Wang, 1982) identifies ten manifestations of it as follows.

1. low Party concept where members seek personal goals;
2. counterposing individual interests to those of the Party;
3. conceit, complacency, and opinionated attitudes;
4. seeking favours and being moody;
5. using Party position for self and family advancement;
6. factionalism and favouritism;
7. departmentalism (an enlarged form of individualism);
8. attitude of playing-it-safe;
9. selfishness that can lead to corruption; and
10. being infatuated with the capitalist life-style.

The upshot of all these failings in a Party member, Wang argues, is the acceptance of the philosophy of life of the exploiting classes. It will be recalled that during the trial of the Gang of Four the Gang were accused of some of these moral shortcomings. Madame Mao was supposed to have enjoyed wearing fashionable foreign clothes and watching foreign pornographic movies in private, for example, but these were vices to which only the elite had access. Since the early 1980s, more and more Chinese, probably most in the largest cities and everyone in Shenzhen, have access to foreign goods, ideas and values. Capitalist life-styles are no longer over the horizon but, as it were, on the doorstep.

This creates serious dilemmas for cadres and Party members who are responsible for pushing forward the economic reforms, and these are most serious for those who have regular dealings with foreign capitalists. Cadres in Shenzhen, under the twin microscopes of the Hong Kong media and the leadership in the Party centre in Beijing, who have kept a close watch on developments in the SEZs, have clearly found it difficult at times to read the signals. An interesting story circulating in Hong Kong in 1984 illustrates this nicely. Deng, on an unpublicized visit, had come to Shenzhen to see for himself whether the reports of rampant spiritual pollution were true. Liang Xiang, the suave and sophisticated mayor of Shenzhen at the time, not wishing to give the wrong impression, replaced his normal business suit with a 'Mao-tunic' to meet Deng who was, apparently, reassured that spiritual pollution was under control in the zone. The success of the Shekou Industrial Zone provides yet another example. Yuan Geng, the leading cadre of SkIZ, and widely credited with being the originator of the 'Shekou model', asserts that the secret of Shekou's success is the mutual trust that has been built between the zone administration and foreign investors. Yuan's slogan, 'time is money, efficiency is life', may encourage good business practices and put foreign investors at their ease, but it could also create confusions when set against the recurrent official attacks on the 'everything depends on money' ideology.

For the ordinary people in China this might even appear as a dialectical contradiction. How this contradiction is to be correctly handled is clear enough from the official rationale of the individual consequences of the post-1978 reforms, first in the countryside and now in the urban setting. This is, more or less: 'time is money, efficiency is life'. Those who use their time most efficiently will get rich more quickly, with the blessing of the Government. As two Chinese philosophers have recently said: 'The rich of today come from the people . . . There is nothing dishonourable or immoral about them' (Shen & Jiang, 1985). The antithesis is that spiritual pollution, capitalist attitudes, the actual creation of capitalist exploitation, and eventually the re-establishment of exploiting classes in China, are all potential effects of the rapid growth of prosperity in some areas and among some groups. The synthesis, proposed by Party theoreticians, is that under capitalism the purpose of the unequal distribution of income and wealth is to solidify the power of the capitalist class to continue their exploitation of the subordinate classes. 'Get rich quick' in capitalist societies leads to class polarization. Under socialism, however, unequal distribution serves to bring along the poorer sectors of society, it serves to motivate the less well-off, and to demonstrate that through hard work and intelligence, anyone can do better. Socialist state planning and the communist virtues will ensure a minimum of exploitation (even for those working for capitalists in Special Economic Zones), and will protect the weak, namely those unable to work, or those whose limited access to resources inhibits their earning power. There is less certainty, however, over the question of the practical implications of the correct handling of the contradiction outside of the direct economic sphere.

A glimpse into this important topic is provided by two articles by Yu Guangyuan, a Vice-President of the Chinese Academy of Social Sciences. The first, 'Socialist Viewpoint on Values' (Yu, 1981), immediately distances itself from orthodox communist puritanism by distinguishing between 'enjoyment of life' and 'mere existence'. (The examples given indicate that the distance travelled from puritanism may be rather short: eating delicacies is good, smoking and nightlife are bad!.) The key question Yu poses, entirely in line with the strategy of the post-1978 reforms, is *how* (not *whether*) China should go about creating a consumer society. The second piece, written in 1984 when the small beginnings of a new prosperity visible in 1981 had unmistakably turned into a national, social trend, announced the existence of a new field of enquiry in China, namely 'life-style research' (Yu, 1985). Here Yu makes the point that lies behind the efforts of the leadership of the Communist Party to stimulate the socialist spiritual civilization. In the absence of other models legitimized by the Party and the state, the newly-rich will simply copy the capitalist life-styles of Hong Kong—a co-cultural exemplar near at hand and increasingly visible. Most of the evidence at hand, particularly from Shenzhen, suggests that this is precisely what is happening.

Most of the Chinese in Hong Kong have kin in other parts of South China and many now visit relatives in and around Shenzhen on a regular basis. There is a direct and regular train service from Kowloon to the border post adjoining the main station in Shenzhen, and the sight of Hong Kong Chinese bringing in huge boxes with televisions, videos, stereos, clothes and even washing machines is quite common. This personal import system has helped to turn Shenzhen into an Aladdin's Cave for the rest of China, until quite recently starved of modern consumer goods. This is paralleled in all the large cities by a flood of consumer imports, often of Japanese manufacture. New rich peasants on spending sprees are to be seen at railway and bus stations all over China with their 'three bigs'—television, washing machine and electric fan. This should be a cause for universal rejoicing and the Chinese people, or at least those who can afford it, are clearly enjoying their belated entrance into twentieth-century consumer society.

The official Chinese view is that while there is nothing 'capitalist' or 'exploitative' in possessing a television or a washing machine, the danger for communist values lies in the opportunities for profiteering and/or corruption that control over such scarce and valued goods permits. The core value for the transition to socialism in China is 'hard and productive' work and any rewards that can be gained in this work are, with very few exceptions, legitimate. The corrupting influence of capitalist efficiency, then, is not in the material objects that it can produce—even 'capitalist efficiency' is accorded value neutrality—but in the increased opportunities for exploitation, as is the case in capitalist societies themselves, that go with them. But how are the Chinese people to adjust to these new and potentially dangerous conditions?

One answer to this question can be found in the emulation system in China, in particular the choice of model workers. A Beijing newspaper (in JPRS–CEA–85–039: 88–9) lists three changed criteria for the selection of models in the city. Firstly, the emphasis had changed from diligent and conscientious to reform and development-seeking types; secondly, from workers to intellectuals and workers; and thirdly, from the intellectual to the physical and intellectual type. The message behind these changes is that the old reliable ox model of the past has not been entirely discarded, but that the ox should also have some of the characteristics of a winged steed! It is interesting to note that the first Hong Kong businessman to be awarded model status was the manager of a television factory in Shenzhen (*JPRS*–CEA–85–055: 76–7). Again, the message is clear, that as long as you are doing a good job and not actually organizing the overthrow of the Communist Party, your contribution can be put to good use in the planned socialist economy and you can enjoy the fruits of your labour in relative peace.

Youth presents special problems for those responsible for social control in China, as elsewhere. In the recent past, China's youth has been through the turmoil of the rustification programme and the Cultural Revolution (Bernstein, 1977). There are indications that the mood of young people in China today, at least the educated urbanites, is one of cynicism, and the dominant social attitude is opportunism. In his informative study of the Young Communist League (YCL), Rosen shows how the post-1978 reforms and their effects were instrumental in the recent decline of the influence of the YCL, only rehabilitated in 1978 after a twelve-year suspension during the Cultural Revolution. With the growing emphasis on competence and technical ability (expertness) and a concomitant devaluation of political criteria for advancement (redness), the cadres of the YCL were generally ignored by the young. These cadres themselves were unsure of the values that were to be projected to youth in the light of the rapidly changing circumstances of the early 1980s. While there are also austere models of today that match those of the past, notably the renowed Lei Feng, they command less attention amongst China's youth than those who are somewhat more prepared to enjoy life, stopping short of hedonist abandon (Rosen, 1985). Reports of contracts between Shenzhen and Hong Kong youth (Mack, 1986) further confirm the problems that the authorities are already experiencing in exercising social control over young people, at least on the level of culture.

While it is difficult to draw any very definite conclusions about the likely value-systems of the rising generation from such evidence, there are sufficient indications from all parts of the Chinese social structure to suggest that a new spirit of what can best be described as 'entrepreneurship' or 'business mind' is current in China, and especially amongst youth. The material causes of this are not hard to find. With the gradual erosion of the 'iron rice-bowl' mentality, the virtual denationalization of most Chinese enterprises and the concomitant absolute decline in the number of state employees, the responsibility systems in the rural and urban economies force people, literally, to take responsibility for their own profits and losses, for their own livelihoods. This has led to the establishment of millions of small businesses, run by one or a few people, mostly in the service sector, since 1978, serving both the free commodity market and the socialist planned economy. The small businesses have provided employment for large numbers of youth (many not so young) recently returned from temporary exile in the countryside, as well as for urban school graduates for whom jobs in the state and collective employment were not available. For the Party the problem is that many of these successful young entrepreneurs are also the youth who go around with long hair, bell-bottom trousers, and gaudy clothes—in short, those who emulate the outward trappings of the capitalist life-styles they see from over the border. Party ideologists have the difficult task of reconciling the good—the new spirit of initiative and personal enrichment for those who work hard to deserve it with the bad—the adoption of frivolous life-styles that often accompany it. In a recent article, important enough to be printed in the overseas edition of the *People's Daily* and in *Beijing Review*, Zhao Fushan, a Vice-President of the Chinese Academy of Social Sciences, presented the view that socialist ethics in China permitted the expression of individual initiative, not, of course, in opposition to collective interests, but in a manner that was consistent with collective interests (Zhao, 1985). This is what Schram, in his analysis of the post-1978 reforms, calls the 'Yan Fu argument' (Schram, 1984: 423). Exactly how this is to be achieved is not confronted by CCP ideologues, which is hardly surprising considering that this very question has taxed Western social philosophy at least since the Greeks.

The seriously complicating feature of this ideological debate is the peculiar dialectic between the after-effects of the Gang of Four and the immediate effects of foreign capitalist influence. From the very start, the campaign against spiritual pollution made the connection between the 'extreme individualism and anarchism' of the Cultural Revolution and the bourgeois habits picked up from foreign contacts, which compounded the damage done to the minds of the young (see, for example, Zhao, 1981). The identification of the ultra-left and the ultra-right was, of course, a favourite tactic during the Cultural Revolution itself. There is no doubt that there are still many 'Maoists', if not exactly followers of the Gang of Four left in China, at all levels of the state and Party apparatus, and the continuing campaign against spiritual pollution and the repeated insistence on the distance between the reforms and capitalist exploitation, indicates the ongoing political and ideological struggle.

Conclusions

The results of a recent survey, broadcast to the world by Xinhua, the official Chinese news agency, revealed that 60 per cent of a sample of young people in Shenzhen wished to become entrepreneurs, and that even more, 68 per cent, admired 'competence' over all other qualities in a person (see JPRS–CEA–85–086: 76–7). These findings further confirm the general impressions of other surveys on China's youth (in Chu, 1983–4; and in Rosen, 1985: 24–8). While it would be rash to ignore the methodological shortcomings of much of this research, there is no denying that in the 1980s the cultural and material life of China's youth began to be significantly influenced by foreign products in a qualitatively new way. Most visibly in styles of dress and consumption of popular music, urban and suburban youth (and with the rapid spread of the cassette recorder, even youth deep in the countryside) have seized with apparent enthusiasm all the West has to offer. The authorities, while cracking down hard on economic crimes to the point of summary execution, and trying to control the importation of pornography, appear to be prepared to tolerate, if not exactly encourage, the less objectionable manifestations of Western popular culture.

We may speculate that there are both pragmatic and ideological reasons for this policy, and that they exactly parallel what is happening in the economic sphere. Foreign investment is a reality, and although attracting even more of it is not the priority, it is clearly an important secondary goal. Foreign investment, it is admitted, does bring some exploitation, but this can be controlled, and it is more than compensated for by the benefits of efficiency and new technology it also brings. Likewise, the new entrepreneurial spirit among the Chinese people depends for its success on a new set of attitudes. The young, the rising generation on whom the future depends, must be allowed to express their individual initiative, and if this involves the adoption of some cultural traits that had seemed decadent to a previous generation, then so be it. Dress styles, tastes in popular music, and personal attitudes towards leisure can all, without great difficulty, be distanced from capitalist exploitation, where capitalist exploitation can more easily be identified with profiteering, currency speculation, and swindling cadres. Pragmatically, then, the authorities have much more to lose by alienating the young over matters of culture than they have to gain by keeping the trappings of Western, even capitalist culture out. What appears to be operating, at an informal and scarcely articulated level, is a sort of threefold classification of foreign, capitalist influence. Firstly, capitalist efficiency is deliberately sought, nurtured and encouraged. Secondly, capitalist culture is generally regarded as relatively neutral or, perhaps, tolerable. (Obvious exceptions here are pornography, which is outlawed, and some forms of 'high culture', such as classical music and 'great literature' which are officially legitimized as part of a global heritage, somewhat akin to the status that Shakespeare and Burns enjoy in the Soviet Union.) Thirdly, capitalist exploitation is generally abhorred, whether it is practised by wayward Chinese or by decadent foreign capitalists in China. Even where it cannot be avoided, as in the Special Economic Zones or other sites of foreign-ownership in China, it can only be tolerated if the economic benefits are seen to compensate for it, in the long run. The pragmatism of this compromise is plain for all to see, for on this view it is the state that is the guarantor of the 'socialist' nature of the mode of production through its control over the extraction and disposition of the surplus (McCarthy in Brugger, 1985: Chap. 5).

The ideological reasons for the apparent and relative conversion to cultural pluralism, despite the campaign against spiritual pollution, and attacks on 'bourgeois liberalism' in early 1987, have to do with the survivals of more traditionally Chinese cultural traits. This question has always presented a great problem to the Chinese Communists, as, indeed, it does to all so-called 'modernizing elites'. Legal reform, education, and extraordinary efforts at political socialization directed towards the creation of a 'communism with Chinese characteristics', have undoubtedly wrought great changes in China since 1949, but it is entirely unsurprising to learn that many traditional practices have not died out and that, on the contrary, they have reappeared often in an open and barely concealed fashion all over the country. Reports of renewed ancestor worship, the use of prime farmland for cemeteries, acts ...aditional male chauvinism, lavish weddings, and various forms of magic, are now common. It is likely that the growth of such practices is of even greater concern to the CPC than the long hair, sharp clothes and pop music of the young. One may go even further. Seizing on the view cited above, that it is important to supply cultural models, we can argue that a controlled license to import and permit distribution of the more palatable forms of Western popular culture may even be preferable when faced with the prospect of a wholesale renaissance of superstition and anti-rationalist behaviour. At least, there is a technological pay-off to learning how to operate and perhaps repair cassette recorders and television sets, and new fashions in clothes may stimulate useful interest in materials.

These are, admittedly, speculations, but speculations on a firm material base. China has committed itself to socialist modernization and Deng and other top leaders have insisted, repeatedly, that it cannot be achieved 'behind closed doors'. The socialist nature of China's modernization will be judged less by how many people get rich, how quickly, and by what means, than by what happens to the rest of the population, specifically the hundred million or more mainly rural Chinese who are officially said to be existing below the poverty line. A whole new apparatus of personal and enterprise taxation, production incentives and redistribution is in the process of construction. The real question may turn out to be whether 'welfare socialism' will be better at delivering the goods to those who most need them than 'welfare capitalism' has been. The economic, political and ideological struggles are crystalizing around the issue of whether all these reforms are mediations in the transition to socialism or signposts on a path that leads somewhere else.

Those in China responsible for ensuring capitalist efficiency without capitalist exploitation are adrift in largely uncharted waters, as events in late 1986 have shown.

References

Bahro, Rudolf (1978). *The Alternative in Eastern Europe*. London, New Left Books.
Bao Xinyi (1985). 'A discussion of the socialist nature of China's open door policy'. *JPRS–85–CEA–035*: 151–8.
Bernstein, Thomas (1977). *Up to the Mountains and Down to the Villages*. New Haven, Yale University Press.
Bettelheim, Charles (1975). *The Transition to Socialist Economy*. Sussex, Harvester Press.
Brugger, Bill (1977). *Contemporary China*. London, Croom Helm.
Brugger, Bill (ed.) (1985). *Chinese Marxism in Flux 1978–1984*. London, Croom Helm.
Chen, S. & Ridley, C. (1969). *Rural People's Commune in Lien-chiang*. Stanford, Hoover Institution.
Chu, David S. K. (ed). (1983–4). 'Sociology and Society in Contemporary China 1979–83'. *Chinese Sociology and Anthropology*, 16, whole issue.
Fang Jun (1985). 'On contract system of employment by election'. *JPRS–CEA–85–035*: 159–61.
Frolic, B. M. (1980). *Mao's People*. Cambridge, Mass., Harvard University Press.
Gold, Thomas (1984). '"Just in Time!" China Battles Spiritual Pollution on the Eve of 1984'. *Asian Survey*, 20: 947–74.
Hsu, Robert (1985). 'Conceptions of the Market in Post-Mao China'. *Modern China*, 11, 436–60.
Jia Chunfeng (1985). 'Develop scientific socialism in the course of new practice'. (In JPRS–CEA–85–005: 3–8).
Lardy, N. & Lieberthal, K. (eds) (1983). *Chen Yun's Strategy for China's Development: A Non-Maoist Alternative*. Armonk, M. E. Sharpe.
Lockett, M. & Littler, C. (1983). 'Trends in Chinese enterprise management, 1978–1982'. *World Development*, 11: 683–704.
Ma Hong (1985). 'Commodity economy under the socialist system'. *JPRS–CEA–85*: 1–21.
Mack, Nancy (1986). 'Today's Shenzhen—Tomorrow's China?'. Undergraduate dissertation, sociology, London School of Economics.
Meszaros, I. (1970). *Marx's Theory of Alienation*. London, Merlin Press.
Rosen, Stanley (1985). 'Prosperity, Privatization, and China's Youth'. *Problems of Communism*, 34: 1–28.
Schram, Stuart (1984). '"Economics in Command?" Ideology and Policy since the Third Plenum, 1978–1984'. *China Quarterly*, 99: 417–61.
Shen Zhongjun & Jiang Tingsheng (1985–6). 'On economic reform and the development of morality'. *Chinese studies in Philosophy*, 17: 82–94.
Sklair, L. (1985). 'Shenzhen: A Chinese "Development Zone" in Global Perspective'. *Development and Change*, 16: 571–602.
Wang Renzhong (1982). 'Communist party members should adhere to communism and overcome individualism'. SWB/FE/7072/BII/1–8, 8 July 1982.
Wang Yixuan (1985). 'An inquiry into certain problems in overseas joint venture companies'. JPRS–CEA–85–038: 129–38.
Warner, Malcolm (1985). 'Training China's Managers'. *Journal of General Management*, 11: 12–26.

Wolpe, H. (ed.) (1979). *The Articulation of Modes of Production*. London, Routledge.

Wong Kwan yiu, & Chu, David K. Y. (eds) (1985). *Modernization in China: the case of the Shenzhen Special Economic Zone*. Oxford, Oxford University Press.

Xu Jingde & Yang Zhichao (1985). 'Socialism is the highest and final phase of the commodity economy'. *JPRS*–CEA–85–016: 13–14.

Xu Jinshui (1985). 'On regulation by market mechanism practised in Special Zones under the guidance of macroeconomic planning'. JPRS–CEA–85–016: 108–15.

Yang Daonan (1985). 'The world is studying Ancient China's management ideas on establishing operations and management science with Chinese characteristics'. *JPRS*–CEA–85–054: 1–6.

Yu Guangyuan (1981). 'Socialist viewpoint on values'. *JPRS*–78640–PSM–207: 25–8.

Yu Guangyuan (1985). 'Changing life style and consumption patterns'. JPRS–CEA–85–049: 1–4.

Zhao Fushan (1985). 'Socialist culture and ethics in the making'. *Beijing Review*, **46**: 15–16.

Zhao Wande (1981). 'Is it necessary to prevent "Spiritual Pollution"?'. *JPRS*–78709–PSM–209: 24–5.

13 Managing Technology in China — Is The Development and Application of Computers The Answer?

Denis F. Simon

Introduction

In the 1950s we began to develop computers through copying; since then, there has always been a tendency to emphasize hardware over software, mainframes over peripherals and components, research and design over technology and production, applicative experiments over practical results. Thus, for a long time, computers produced in our country have been known to be unreliable, unsupported, not easy to use, and not easy to repair. Moreover, we have too many varieties of computers which are largely identical, with only a few minor differences. In addition, our computers are not produced in batches and development is rather slow. As facts have proven, this is not a good strategy for developing computers. [Remarks of a researcher from the Institute of Computer Technology, Chinese Academy of Sciences, see Wang, 1982: 3].

The computer and information revolution that has been steadily taking place in the industrialized nations has not gone unnoticed by the leadership in the People's Republic of China. Since the announcement of the 'Four Modernizations' in the mid-1970s, China has paid special attention to the development of its computer industry. In the March 1978 S&T plan, for example, computers were one of the eight priority areas singled out by the leadership. The main impetus for pushing ahead in the computer area derives from a blend of scientific, industrial, and defense-related imperatives. Computers are needed in all major facets of China's modernization; Chinese leaders hope to move China into the so-called 'age of informatics' by encouraging the widespread utilization of computers in all key sectors of the economy and society. This recognition of the need for greater computerization is best reflected in the comments made by Chen Liwei, Chief Engineer of China's computer administration:

If China is to succeed in its goal of quadrupling its gross national product by the turn of the century, and if the four modernizations are pursued with the same unrelenting vigour as they have been to date, then the need for computers and computer-related technology will grow by a factor of ten many times over in the intervening period up to the year 2000. [Chen, 1985: 2].

Overall Perspective

Chinese leaders attach great importance to the expanded development and more effective application of computers. The PRC's push in the computer area bears a number of similarities to the French effort of the early 1970s and the Brazilian and Indian efforts in the early 1980s (see Rushing & Brown, 1986). Nora and Minc, in their seminal work entitled *The Computerization of Society* (1980) highlight the features of a national plan in France designed to minimize dependence on foreign sources of technology and equipment while harnessing computers to stimulate economic and social change. Similarly, the PRC's *primary* aim is to establish a strong indigenous-based computer capability. The leadership, from Premier Zhao Ziyang on down, sees increased computerization as a necessary prerequisite to attaining desired advances in scientific research, industrial productivity, national communications, and defense capabilities, especially regarding strategic weapons programs. This high level of support is manifested in increased investment and related funding for indigenous computer R&D modernization of key manufacturing facilities, and training programs in all segments of the education system.

As of the end of 1985, China had approximately 250–300,000 computers in place. Mainframes and minicomputers accounted for about seven thousand or so of this total (*China Daily*, 6 June 1986). Between 1983 and 1985, the number of microcomputers, including single-board machines, increased by almost 600 percent, growing from about 40,000 to over 250,000 during this short span of time (*China Daily*, 7 July 1986). The dominant field of use was in computation in research and engineering, accounting for 60 percent of the user-rate. In contrast, by early 1985 there were well over five million microcomputers in use in the United States, with the dominant users (as measured by relative spending) being the banking, insurance, and business services industries.

Since the implementation of the so-called 'open door policy', the most remarkable feature of China's computerization experience has been the rapid growth of imported computers, especially microcomputers. One estimate suggests that such imports grew from 4,500 in 1983 to over 75,000 in 1984! Only about 5.0 percent of these imports, however, were acquired as final product units; the majority were brought into China via Hong Kong as assembly kits owing to the structure of China's import duties at the time and to Western controls/delays on the export of the technology embodied in many of these machines. In large part, it is the *immediate* dissatisfaction with the growing dependence on imports combined with concerns about excessive expenditures of foreign exchange that have driven the push to build up indigenous R&D and manufacturing capacity.

Current development efforts must also be seen against the backdrop of China's pre-1978 experience with computer R&D and production. The history of computer development has been characterized by uneven perform-ance, with serious problems of machine compatibility and software generalizability. The Chinese produced their first electron-tube computer (103) in 1958; the first transistorized computers (109B, 441B, 121, and X-2) appeared in the mid-1960s. The onset of the Cultural Revolution, however, dealt a severe setback to computer development at a time when the West was just starting to catapult ahead. None the less, by the early 1970s, the first series of computers with integrated circuit technology appeared (Models 111, 112, 150, and 655). These achievements were attained by a small, selected group of specialists working, in many cases, without the benefit of a strong R&D support network.

The milestone in China's computer development occurred in 1973 with the introduction of the first serialized machines, the DJS-100 series. Modelled on the NOVA computer developed in the United States, the DJS-100 series expanded to include a number of different models capable of meeting the needs of a variety of users (Tadashi, 1980). In general, these machines were much slower than their Western counterparts and lacked much of the software to support widespread use. At about the same time, the DJS-200 series also appeared, modelled on various models in the IBM-360 series (see Berney, 1981). While a number of machines were produced, they never really attained the levels of performance associated with the IBM. While some of these machines were hand-tailored to meet the needs of special end-users, such as the PRC defense sector, they never entered large-scale serial produc-tion. In essence, the most serious Chinese deficiency is that they have been able to produce many one-or-two-of-a-kind machines, most of which are of the stand-alone variety, but have never been able to move ahead into the stage of large-scale production owing to specific technical shortcomings and a host of political problems.

The objective of developing a technologically advanced computer industry is to be supported, in large part, by the concerted effort being made to improve the quality of China's domestic semiconductor and electronic com-ponents industry, including several large programs to perfect large-scale integrated circuits in both the memory and logic areas. There are seventeen major enterprises in China engaged in research and production of integrated circuits (*China Daily*, 7 April 1986). Low yields and poor reliability have been major problems plaguing China's IC industry. At present, almost all the manufacturers of *key* computers in China rely extensively on imported chips, etc. Recognizing that backwardness in microelectronics has been a major obstacle to further computer development, enhancement of existing capabilities is now a high priority element of the country's overall computer development strategy.

Structure and Organization

Organizationally, the computer industry is dominated by the Ministry of Electronics Industry, which supervises eight research institutes, 130 manufacturing facilities for computers (eight-three) and peripherals (forty-seven), and thirteen application units, with a total of 107,000 workers and staff—out of which approximately 16,300 are researchers, technicians and engineers (see Figure 13.1). The MEI has direct administrative control over seventeen of the manufacturing units (*China Daily*, 9 May 1986), while the remaining ones are under some combination of local and/or central control. Within the MEI, direct responsibility for management of computer-related matters belongs to the department of the computer industry which is the former State Administration for the Computer Industry (SACI). SACI was originally established in 1979 to unify the management of R&D, production, and the marketing of computers on a nationwide scale. It was incorporated into the MEI as part of the May 1982 bureaucratic reforms.

Along with MEI, several other ministries play a key role in computer development and application. The two most important are the Ministry of Space Industry (space and weapons programs) and the Ministry of Machine-Building Industry (industrial applications). According to one source, for example, the MSI already has over two thousand computers in place and has the capacity to produce 5,600 microcomputers (*Xinhua*, 13 June 1986). In addition, there are five specialized computer institutes within the Chinese Academy of Sciences (e.g. the Institute for Computing Technology in Beijing, the Institute of Computer Applications in Chengdu, etc.). Their major focus is on basic design, computer architecture and software development. Several of China's major universities also play an important role in computer development, including Qinghua, Beijing, Fudan, and Shanghai Jiaotong.

Sitting above these various organizations is the State Council 'special leading group for electronics', headed by Vice-Premier Li Peng, which has overall responsibility for developing and coordinating China's national computer strategy. This leading group, which was reorganized in 1984 after a somewhat inauspicious start under the direction of Vice-Premier Wan Li, relies on inputs from key ministerial representatives from the civilian and military sectors as well as an advisory group of about ten to fifteen computer specialists from leading universities and research institutes around the country (Simon & Rehn, 1986). While the leading group does not have a specific budget for project purposes, it works directly with the State Planning Commission to ensure that sufficient funds are available for key projects. Its

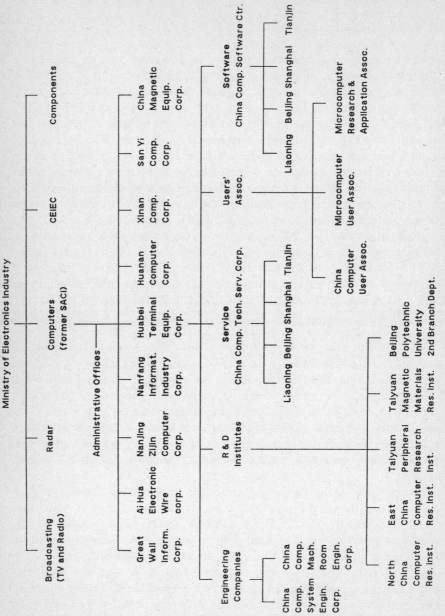

Figure 13.1 Organization of China's computer industry (within the MEI)

emergence is highly significant because of its mandate to provide overall policy guidance and cross-ministerial coordination in an industry where both have been severely lacking in the past.

Along with the State Council 'leading group', the State Science and Technology Commission, the State Education Commission, and the State Economic Commission also have substantive responsibilities for helping to formulate China's informatics policy and manage the country's computer development. These national-level organizations are complemented by a series of provincial and municipal commissions and corporations for management of local computer development and applications. Three cities stand out in this regard: Beijing, Tianjin, and Shanghai. Shanghai Municipality, for example, has its own 'local level' leading group for electronics and computers (*Jisuanji Shijie*, 5 July, 1983).

Interactions among computer users, as well as the R&D community involved with computers, have been facilitated by the creation of the Chinese Computer Federation (CCF), in March 1985. Prior to this date, the CCF was a professional society under the Chinese Institute of Electronics. The aim of the CCF is to develop computer science and technology in China, promote the application of computers, and stimulate the growth of the local computer industry. The CCF has eleven professional committees, eight professional groups, seven working committees, and an office to handle day-to-day affairs. As of January 1986, there were over fifteen thousand members. The CCF has relations with the computer societies of twenty-eight provinces, cities, and municipalities.

China's Strategy for Computer Development

China's strategy for developing its computer industry has been an evolving one, heavily influenced by a combination of domestic political as well as technological and economic factors. In addition, considerations of self-reliance and technological dependence have also played a role in the definition of an overall strategy, though it must be acknowledged that great uncertainty has existed in the past and will continue to exist in the future regarding the balance between foreign imports and indigenous efforts. In early 1982, the Chinese leadership articulated a blueprint for computer development which would catapult China by 1990 to the same technological levels achieved in the advanced developed countries in the early 1980s. This was a very ambitious target given the fact that China's computer design and manufacturing capabilities have been considered by most foreign experts to be from seven to ten years behind those of the United States and Japan. Total computer output was designed to triple by 1990, reaching an annual production capacity of 1,000 large and medium computers *and* 40,000 micro- and single-board computers. The role of foreign technology, although assigned an important place in the strategy, was clearly viewed with a large dose of caution.

In both 1983 and 1984, major nationwide conferences were held to further map out the appropriate course for computer development. At the 1983 meeting, a decision was made to give greater emphasis to micro and minicomputers, reflecting the increased appreciation of the potential role of computers in industrial management and production, engineering design, etc. The strongest imperative for progressing ahead in computers, however, began to appear in late 1983 as discussions about the 'new global technological revolution' began to sweep China. At a January 1984 symposium on the future, Huan Xiang cited computers as the key to China's ability to catch up with the West.

> Some new rising industrial countries . . . are beginning to devote attention to arming themselves with the application of computers. Brazil in South America is doing so. India is also promoting computers as a major component of its national construction planning. South Korea has also worked out a 10-year development plan for the computer. The computer is developing fast in Singapore . . . Taiwan—a part of China—has concentrated funds on developing microelectronic technology and has founded the Xinzhu Science Area. Hong Kong industrial circles have suggested the founding of a development center for computer technology. They are all devoting major efforts to developing technology-intensive industries and are engaged in rearranging their economies. This trend cannot but arouse our concern and attention. [Huan, 1984: 4].

At the February 1984 conference, the essential elements of the current computer development strategy began to take shape. Jiang Zemin, former Minister of the MEI (and currently Mayor of Shanghai), stated the following objectives:

1. . . . we will concentrate our efforts on building a technological basis for the microcomputer industry and raise our ability to produce complete equipment. We will energetically develop the production of 8-bit computers, 16-bit computers, and a general system for microcomputers to form several assembly and adjustment lines for microcomputer sets.
2. . . . we will energetically raise the percentage of China-made components and parts used for manufacturing microcomputers and focus our attention on making China-made circuit boards.
3. We will pay close attention to the construction of three computer industrial bases of north China, south China, and east China and to forming combined service bodies for computer research and production to create favourable conditions for rapidly developing the computer industry in the Seventh 5-Year Plan period.
4. To develop the electronics industry, we should centralize financial and material resources, pay special attention to key points, . . . expand foreign

economic exchanges, introduce advanced technology, and strive to raise our ability to stand on our own feet to blaze a new trail in the electronics industry. [*Zhonggno Xinwen She*, 21 February 1984].

For the rest of the decade (1986–90), China's strategy for developing its computer industry will continue to contain many, if not all, of the points spelled out in 1984. For the most part, China's primary focus is on the linking together of electronics and informatics development. The centrality of this thrust was established in January 1985 in a speech made by Vice-Premier Li Peng. According to Li, the 'emphasis of development of the electronics industry will be shifted onto the course of developing microelectronics technology as the foundation, and computer and telecommunications equipment as the main body.' (*Xinhua*, 13 January 1986). These themes were reiterated by MEI head Li Tieying in his announcement of the development goals for China's electronics industry in the Seventh Five-Year Plan.

In terms of specific types of computers, the development of microcomputers, which are regarded as the most suitable in terms of prevailing production capabilities and potential applications, will continue to be emphasized. Technologically, the Chinese have been able to develop and produce 8-bit and single-board computers, many of which have been modelled upon existing Western machines. They have also been able to develop and manufacture on a limited basis 16-bit microcomputers; here again many of these machines resemble Western equivalents, such as the IBM-PC/XT. In the area of imports, the Chinese have shifted away from the purchase of almost all 8-bit machines and many types of 16-bit computers since they are now able to produce varieties of both machines on their own. This move towards greater indigenous production was recently re-emphasized by MEI Vice-Minister Zhang Xuedong in mid-1986 (reported in *China Daily*, 7 July 1986). By 1990, officials from the MEI anticipate that about 80 per cent of China's microcomputer needs will be met by domestic suppliers—an ambitious target that will be difficult to meet.

The development of mainframe computers (and super computers), which experienced serious problems in the past, is now entering a recovery stage in terms of the overall strategic orientation of the industry. This is best exemplified by the attention being given to the 757 computer (10 mips), designed and produced by the Chinese Academy of Sciences *and* the Galaxy (100 mips), designed and produced by the National Defense S&T University in Changsha, Hunan. A decision was made in late 1985 to designate Beijing, which was chosen over several other cities, including Shanghai, as a special site for mainframe computer development. The basic orientation, dictated in large part by networking needs, will be to emulate Western models produced by such prominent firms as DEC, IBM, and Control Data Corporation. This will ensure that domestic-built machines can effectively interface with many, if not most, of the computers that have been imported over the last several years.

None the less, while mainframe development will be given additional capital investment and support, it appears likely that the stress on the development of microcomputers will continue during the rest of the 1980s, with increasing emphasis placed on domestic production of both components and complete machines. There is also some evidence of a growing interest in minicomputers because of their price-performance ratio compared to large mainframes. One driving force behind the concentration on microcomputers, and more recently minicomputers, is the shift away from stand-alone machines towards more networking both within and between organizations, as well as the growing emphasis on the application of computers in industrial, management, and office settings (Liao, 1986: 2). At a national conference on computer application in June 1986, Lu Dong, Minister-in-Charge of the State Economic Commission and Vice-Chairman of the State Council's Electronics Leading Group, stressed that *all* enterprises in the machine-building and electronics industries were required to experiment with computer-assisted management and production during the 1986–90 time frame (*China Daily*, 15 June 1986). In this regard, China hopes to gradually, though steadily, approach the current breadth of Western uses as well as quality levels and processing capabilities by the 1990s.

Tianjin is one key city where the current national strategy has been implemented successfully, albeit partially and quite gradually in some cases, and where overall computer development and application appears to have responded well to the directives coming out of Beijing. The rise of the local computer industry has been spearheaded by the R&D work of the Tianjin Institute of Applied Computer Technology, which played an important role in the development of the DJS-153 minicomputer *and* the Tianjin No. 2 Radio Factory. With its over six thousand-person work-force in the computer industry, Tianjin has been able to popularize the use of microcomputers throughout all facets of industry by responding to end-user needs. City leaders have been able to use the advances of the industry to overcome local hesitation and lack of knowledge about the use of computers. One major success in this area was the successful application of a microcomputer to the distributor system of the Tianjin No. 2 Cotton Mill.

Constraints and Progress in Computer Development

The major constraints in establishing an advanced Chinese computer industry fall into four categories:

1. manufacturing capabilities;
2. peripheral equipment;
3. technical personnel; and
4. software (*China Daily*, 10 April 1986).

Techniques for mass production of final products as well as computer components are severely lacking in China. Even though advanced components are being developed in the laboratory, many factories lack the necessary production equipment and managerial know-how to produce these items in sufficient quantities and at necessary reliability levels. A good example of how these shortcomings can affect the development of a specific machine involves the case of the DJS-186, a 16-bit minicomputer similar to DEC's PDP-11 series. The DJS-186, whose development began in 1978, experienced numerous problems because the delivery of domestic-made ICs did not materialize and imports had to be used instead, and also because of continued uncertainty over which factory was going to take over manufacture of the prototype.

Relatedly, the Chinese remain unable to meet the growing needs of computer users in most facets of peripherals, mainly because they are lacking in both technology and manufacturing capabilities. This is particularly true regarding items such as disk drives, printers and monitors. For example, while places such as Taiwan and South Korea have been able to push forward on monitor development because of their achievements in black-and-white/colour televisions, China has not been able to rely on such a technological foundation to move ahead in this area.

In terms of personnel, while the Chinese have set out to train a substantially increased number of computer scientists, engineers, and programmers, the fact remains that they still do not have a broad base pool of experts to support a fully-fledged national effort throughout the country. As of the beginning of 1985, there were 89,800 persons employed in China's computer industry, 15,300 of whom can be described as 'technical workers'; by mid-1986 that total number grew to over 107,000. Estimates are that China will need some 600,000 computer personnel by 1990, a target that will remain difficult to attain even with the on-going improvement and expansion in computer education.

Understandably, training is an important aspect of China's computer development and application drive. A good example of one of China's better computer science programs is the one at Nanjing University. Initially part of the mathematics department when it was established in 1958, it formally became a department in 1978. There are fifty-four faculty members in the department: two full professors, seven assistant professors, thirty-seven lecturers, and eight teaching assistants. As of the early 1980s, there were approximately over six-hundred undergraduates, twenty postgraduates, and eight advanced students in the department. In addition, over eight hundred students from other parts of the university were given training through courses in computer science offered by the department. All together, about thirty-five courses of instruction are offered. The department has also been steadily involved in national computer development efforts, having completed thirteen national and local-level projects, eight of which 'have filled gaps in China' and six of which have won awards. Through work on these projects, it has formed cooperative relationships with a number of key production units, including the Shanghai No. 13 Radio Factory, the Changzhou No. 2 Radio Plant, and the Nanjing No. 734 Plant. Faculty and students from Nanjing University have been sent abroad to study computer science.

Programs such as the Computer Science Department at Nanjing University have sprung up throughout China's higher education system. The US$200 million education loan given to China by the World Bank in 1982 has helped facilitate the purchase of equipment and the introduction of higher-level courses dealing with computer programming, languages, etc. These advanced programs are complemented by a broad-based effort to introduce China's younger students at the elementary and high school levels to the role of computers (see *FBIS-PRC*, 28 February 1984:1). In both respects, the Chinese have gone far beyond the Soviet Union so far in trying to spread computer literacy throughout the country (see *Science*, 10 January 1986). Yet, while education programs, including ones such as the computer education project supported by the World Bank and the Beijing Computerland Institute, are a step in the right direction. Chinese officials acknowledge that they still remain inadequate in terms of meeting current and projected future needs for a wide range of computer-literate technicians. According to one estimate by an official from the MEI's State Computer Administration, at least one hundred thousand trained specialists are needed in research and production, while an additional five hundred thousand will be needed as computer operators by the 1990s.

With respect to computer software, substantial progress does appear to have been made in the development of Chinese character input systems as well as software. In mid-1985, for example, a computerized Chinese-language information storage system was introduced by the Beijing Teachers' University. It can automatically process any Chinese language information into corresponding key word and phrase data-banks, print out lists of word usage frequency, edit, and compile word entry indexes. A national university computer software center was established in Beijing through the Ministry of education in early 1984 to offer technical services to various local- and national-level organizations. A few months later in the same year, a national software industry association was also established to share information on research projects in the software area.

Relatedly, in late 1983 China's first CAD system for exterior car body design was produced through the joint effort of the Shanghai Tractor and Automobile Research Institute and the Institute of Mathematics at Fudan University. And, in early 1986, China's first comprehensive software package, called 'The Software Package for Modern Digital Signal Processing', was introduced by the Northern Jiaotung University in Xian in conjunction with five other institutes in Beijing, Shanghai, and Xian. The package covers a total of forty-two programs ranging from measurement statistics to modern spectral analysis.

However, as in the past, the problem of 'generalizability' continues to be widespread since a significant percentage of the software being developed still tends to be machine-specific. In the past, software development was considered to be the Achilles' heel of Chinese computer development. Today, the introduction of several central government standards for software development, as well as the appearance of various organizations such as the China Software Corporation and the China Computer Users Association, will help remedy a large number of these problems. The latter organization, which was formed in March 1983, has numerous branches throughout the country (see *FBIS-PRC*, 29 March 1983).

The Application of Computers in China

In spite of the proliferation of computers, however, obstacles, and in some cases resistance, to the introduction and expanded use of computers remains. Even in Shanghai, one of the country's leaders in terms of computer development and application, a relatively small number of work units employ computers. In addition, even where computers have been acquired, under-utilization remains a serious and widespread problem. The investment made in the development of application systems is hardly proportional to that made in the development or import of basic systems. According to an *EDP China* report (17 June 1986: 242), 'users are usually only willing to pay for hardware and hand out money almost grudgingly for software. The importance of researching and designing application systems is not yet widely recognized.' The problem is particularly acute regarding domestic-made machines. In fact, many questions remain about the future of some existing lines of domestic computers, such as the DJS-100 series, because of the realization that many of these machines do not meet international standards in terms of quality, type of operation, and/or software compatibility.

According to sources in Beijing, 32,000 microcomputers were manufactured in 1985, while there were still 40,000 stocked in warehouses with no customers in sight. In addition, officials in the computer industry have suggested that, in Beijing Municipality, for example, the utilization rate of installed microcomputers is only 26 per cent, while the national average is in the range of 15–20 per cent. The problem of poor utilization has its roots in personnel shortages, although other key factors include organizational rivalry and intense bureaucratic jealousy, poor maintenance, limited software availability, and poor after-sales service. One estimate suggests that the Chinese will waste between US$20–$85 million over the next three years because of improper use and maintenance of imported computers (see *New York Times*, 5 May 1985: 85).In some cases, enterprises have been 'ordered' to have a computer, without having the personnel to operate it or any idea about how best to put the machine to use (*China Daily*, 3 April 1985). These problems hold true with both domestic-made and foreign-imported computers (see Lu, 1985: 69–70).

Political problems can also be pervasive in the computer industry. At the Hunan Provincial Computer Centre, eight persons had to be dismissed from their posts because they lacked the skills to handle their particular assignments. The Hunan Center is one of the key links in China's national computer network; its responsibilities include collecting, processing, storage, and exchange of economic information within and outside the province. Through a 'network of personal connections,' high-level cadres used their positions to secure jobs for their relatives and children. The Center became known as 'a home for the lazy.' At one point, of the thirty-nine children of leading cadres above the rank of department director, more than 60 percent (twenty-four persons) knew little or nothing about computers. After numerous problems, the situation was brought to the attention of the provincial party committee for resolution.

Although the above-mentioned utilization problems are pervasive, the fact remains that use of computers has spread throughout the economy and society. According to an official from the MEI, there were about a hundred types of uses for computers in 1980 (with most computers being used for calculations), while, as of mid-1985, there were 15,000 uses. The Chinese have even gone so far as to establish a computer-dating service! In many cases, computers have been introduced in the form of industrial control systems, such as in the Ministry of Machine-Building Industry (MMBI), where work on automation has gone rapidly forward over the last two years. There is a computer research center in the MMBI that has as its principle function the expanded introduction of CAD/CAM technologies—though some of its efforts are being held back by the lack of specialized components from MEI to support its development efforts.

Most importantly, the drive to introduce computers into industry and society has stimulated expanded interactions among computer manufacturers and potential end-users. Given the gap that has often existed between developers and users in China, this trend could be highly significant. For example, the Shaoguan Radio Factory in Guangdong, which is a leading manufacturer of 8-bit and 16-bit microcomputers in South China, has transferred a number of its engineers and skilled workers to form an outreach/sales team for the promotion of microcomputer use. In addition, the factory has instituted user-training classes, a lecture series, etc.

China also has plans to boost development efforts in robotics—which is still in its infancy in comparison with similar efforts in Japan and the United States. The Seventh Five-Year Plan contains provisions for the manufacture of industrial robots for paint spraying, point and arc welding, and cargo carrying (*China Daily*, 1 February 1986). As of the end of 1985, China had more than one hundred industrial robots and one thousand mechanical handling devices in place. Among China's twenty robot research institutes and development centers, the Institute of Automation of the CAS in Shenyang will be the site of a major robotics research and development center.

Among the successful examples of effective application of computers are the following:

(a) establishment of a computer-based flood warning system under the Ministry of Water Conservancy and Electric Power;

(b) formation of a computer center under the People's Bank to manage financial transactions;

(c) application of computer controls to boiler operation in thermal power stations in Guizhou province;

(d) safety analysis in power plants;

(e) social science data storage and analysis in the Chinese Academy of Social Sciences;

(f) establishment of a computer center at the Daqing Oilfield to handle prospecting information and research work; and

(g) computer-aided architectural design, especially concerning earthquake-proof construction.

Significantly, the Communist Party has also gotten caught up in China's computer revolution; the provincial party office in Shaanxi, with the help of the Lishan Microelectronics Company, has introduced a computer system for general management tasks. Thus, while problems abound, China has gone much further than, for example, the Soviet Union in allowing the roots of the new information society to take hold (see Graham, 1984).

One area where some rather interesting work has already been done deals with the attempt to establish several nationwide economic and S&T information networks. According to comments made by Vice-Premier Li Peng, the Chinese intend to establish eleven national computerized information systems for such fields as telecommunications and weather forecasting during the Seventh Five-Year Plan. There is also a program under way to establish an information network linked through the China National Science and Technology Center in Beijing. A number of the key coastal cities (ten), along with the Institute for Scientific and Technical Information (ISTIC) under the SSTC, are the key organizations involved. The Chinese are attempting to draw upon Western data-bases as well as create their own data-retrieval systems. Progress, however, has been impeded by China's poor communications infrastructure, which has added a large element of insecurity and unreliability into the process of data-transfer and computer communication. By early 1985, for example, there were only 0.5 telephones per hundred people in China. Recent improvements in communications, obtained primarily through technology and equipment imports, may help alleviate some of these problems in the near future. For the present, however, the existence of local area networks as well as distributed processing remains the exception rather than the rule.

The Role of Foreign Computer Imports and Technology

Since importing was emphasized in the 1980s, China's computer industry has suffered a great blow. Importing is a correct policy, but how to organize imports properly has not been resolved very well. Any unit can now arrange for its own imports, but what is being imported is mostly equipment, not technology. This is not only wasteful, it also hits domestic industrial production and scientific research work hard. Computer plants are now worried about their own production, since the more they produce the more they lose money . . . In contrast, they make a lot of money by selling imported machines either with a changed outside appearance or by selling them as soon as they are imported . . . There is a policy problem here. [*Guangming Ribao*, 2 April 1984].

In the attempt to modernize their computer industry as rapidly as possible, the Chinese have continued to emphasize the import of technology and computers from abroad. Reliance on foreign ideas and know-how is nothing new as far as China's computer development is concerned. Beginning with the initial start-up of the industry in the 1950s, China relied on Soviet technical specification to launch its own domestic development program and, as indicated earlier, utilized IBM designs to initiate the DJS-200 series in the 1970s. In addition, foreign technical literature and data regarding computers and electronics has continued to flow into China throughout the last two decades—continuing even during the Cultural Revolution. Moreover, during visits to any number of Chinese universities and research institutes, it quickly becomes apparent that there is no dearth of information or journals regarding computer development in the West. Were it not for the availability of these published materials, as well as China's increased access to Western hardware since 1978, it is likely that computer development would have been even further delayed and even distorted.

According to comments by Chinese officials in the MEI, foreign computer companies that introduce sophisticated technology and management skills will be allowed a share of China's domestic market. This policy was introduced, in all likelihood, because, proportional to overall equipment imports, very little *computer-related technology* in disembodied form has flowed into the PRC over the last several years. Within China, in some cases, a tension has arisen between those who are potential end-users and want access to a computer immediately and those who believe that excessive imports should be controlled so that domestic technological capabilities can be allowed to develop. This debate, which is reflected in the above comments by a computer engineer at the Tianjin Computer Factory, has been particularly acute with respect to microcomputers. Between 1981 and 1985, excessive imports of foreign microcomputers basically undermined the effort to create a viable domestic base. More specifically, so-called 'development efforts' were actually limited to assembly of imported SKD (semi-knocked down) and CKD (completely knocked down) kits. This brought in large amounts of revenue to those doing the assembly operations because of the great demand for foreign-made personal computers, but did little to stimulate indigenous technological progress.

As a result, computers are on the list of forty-five items requiring an import license issued by the Ministry of Foreign Economic Relations and Trade. In some respects, Chinese officials in the computer industry see China's development alternatives as lying somewhere between the 'self-reliance-oriented' approaches of Brazil and India and the import and imitation-oriented strategy of South Korea and Taiwan (see Rushing & Brown, 1986). In the case of the former, strong protectionist policies were imposed as a means to moderate foreign competition and to pressure foreign firms to provide technology in return for greater market access. In the case of the latter, foreign models have been used for imitation and copying; firms in these two sites have seen linkages with foreign firms as a way to get into the computer industry rather than as a threat to indigenous development. Based on discussions in China and a number of recent articles in the Chinese press, there appears to be a growing trend towards greater 'selectivity' and elements of 'protectionism' in terms of computer imports, especially in the microcomputer area. This tightening-up over imports, however, while addressing fundamental concerns among the leadership about technological dependency, still takes place in an environment where people tend to denigrate the quality of Chinese-made machines.

China's computer specialists hope that the appearance of the 'Great Wall' 0520 microcomputer can represent the first step in building a more credible domestic computer industry. Basically an IBM-PC/XT clone using American, Japanese, and South Korean components, the 'Great Wall' is produced at three factories in China, the premier one being the Beijing Wire Communications Factory (along with factories in Sichuan and Shandong Provinces), which accounted for half of total production and has a capacity to manufacture 10,000 a year. The 0520 series includes three models, in order to respond to specialized user-needs in engineering design, scientific research, and factory management. The 'Great Wall' 0520A uses the Intel 8088 16-bit microprocessor, has a storage of 512 kilobytes and a high resolution colour display of 640×200. It also features a Chinese character disk operating system and is readily supported by a wide variety of Chinese characters and IBM software, a factor which makes it more attractive than previous machines. Moreover, to encourage its acceptance in China, the SACI of MEI established an 0520 computer software development consortium; it has signed contracts with over twenty units for over fifty software-related tasks (*Jisuanji Shijie*, 8 May 1984).

The concern about the slow progress in indigenous computer development has meant that the PRC has no real alternative in the short term but to rely on technology transfer as a means to stimulate more rapid and sustained domestic progress. China's key focus, however, is on the acquisition of foreign computer design and manufacturing know-how rather than on the purchase of a large number of foreign-produced machines. Technology acquisition—as opposed to equipment acquisition—is being strongly encouraged because it is viewed as an intermediate step on the way to avoiding long-term dependence on external sources for foreign computers and eventually foreign technology. A good example of a project consistent with Chinese objectives involves the import of a disk drive production line from France in mid-1984 by the Jiannan Electronic Equipment Factory in Hunan (*Jisuanji Shijie*, 8 June 1984). (The line, which was the first peripheral production line imported into China, has the capacity to produce 500 Model ZPC-204 hard disk-drives and 3000 ZPC-3 floppy disk-drives.)

This perspective is quite consistent with Chinese practice since the 1970s, when the IBM 360 series was used as a model for the Chinese DJS-200 series—though, as indicated, the performance of these machines never attained IBM levels, owing to architecture and software problems. In order to gain access to technology, the Chinese have signed a number of joint venture-type agreements with firms such as IBM, Burroughs, and Hewlett Packard. China's expectation is that its relationship with these foreign firms will evolve away from just sales and distribution, and eventually include provisions to manufacture computers and related components (see Wang, 1982: 3–5).

Sending students, scholars, and technical experts abroad for formal training is a major part of China's strategy for building a modern computer industry. People are being sent to American universities such as MIT, Carnegie-Mellon, Cal. Tech., Stanford, etc. to learn the latest thinking in the West about computer design and architecture. In addition, groups of Chinese engineers are being sent overseas for training as part of the equipment purchase agreement. Unlike Taiwan, most of these visitors have returned or will return to China. In some cases, individuals have come with very specific objectives in mind, for example computer memory development, specific applications or software enhancement—making it highly likely that when they return to China they will be able to easily apply their newly garnered information—a situation that stands in sharp contrast to the cases of other students/scholars who come to the United States with somewhat more vague goals. Over the long term, it is this group of visiting scholars in the computer field that will form the technological backbone of the industry.

Conclusions

Summarizing, the problems of computer development and use in China are being attacked from a multitude of directions. Component manufacture is being given highest priority as the Chinese seek to minimize their dependence on foreign sources for both components and final products, especially in the microcomputer area. None the less, the emphasis on acquisition of computer manufacturing technology will persist, with a growing emphasis on minicomputers. Greater centralized control seems to be emerging as the need for standardization and quality control has been recognized. Application problems remain and there is an insufficient number of qualified personnel on both the development and applications side. Thus, while progress has been substantial, it remains unlikely, with some exceptions, that China will meet its goal of attaining overall, by 1990, Western technological and utilization levels of the 1980s in the field of computers.

China's problem is that, even as it gains expanded access to more sophisticated equipment and higher levels of technology, it continues to be plagued by inefficiency and ineffectiveness when it comes to the application of computers and related equipment. Introducing computers is a difficult process, especially if a country lacks the technical and managerial expertise to ensure effective utilization on a consistent and continuous basis. And, even if these experts can secure needed training and assistance from abroad, there is little evidence heretofore, except perhaps for the defense sector, that they have been able to take that critical step into the world of the informatics revolution. As one Chinese colleague recently stated in addressing China's penchant for buying equipment and ignoring applications, 'despite the efficacy of this new [computer] technology, it is management that must make the technology work and not the other way around.' For China, developing this cadre of managers will be more easily said than done until the mid-1990s.

Out of the multiple possibilities, China's banking system and financial institutions appear to be one of the largest potential clients for both domestic and imported foreign computers. The five key banks in China, the People's Bank, the Bank of China, the Industrial and Commercial Bank of China, the Agricultural Bank of China, and the People's Construction Bank of China all plan to greatly expand the use of computers to conduct their business and link their offices throughout the country. Along with banking, other major uses in the immediate future will be in the tourist/travel industry and the education system as well as in general overall industrial management and national defense.

References

Berney, Karen (1981). 'China's Computer Revolution'. *China Business Review*, November–December.

Chen Liwei (1985). 'China's Computer Hunt'. *Intertrade* (Spectrum Supplement), March: 2–5.

Graham, Loren (1984). 'Science and Computers in Soviet Society', in Erik Hoffman (ed.), *The Soviet Union in the 1980s*. New York, Academy of Political Sciences, pp. 124–34.

Huan Xiang (1984). 'Catch up with the Industrially Advanced Countries'. *Guangming Ribao*, 2 March, 4, (trans. in JPRS–CST–85–013, 1 May 1985: 10–12).

Liao Youming (1986). 'Challenges Facing the Computer Industry in China'. *China Computerworld*, 23 June: 2.

Lu, Cary (1985). 'China's Emerging Micro Industry'. *High Technology*, March: 69–70.

Nora, Simon & Minc, Alain (1980). *The Computerization of Society*. Cambridge, Mass., MIT Press.

Rushing, Francis & Brown, Carol G. (eds) (1986). *National Policies for Developing High Technology Industries: International Comparisons*. Boulder, Westview Press.

Simon, Denis, & Rehn, Detlef (1986). 'Understanding China's Electronics Industry'. *China Business Review*, March/April.

Tadashi Yoshioka (1980). 'China's Computer Industry'. *Japan External Trade Organization (JETRO) China Newsletter*, October.

Wang Xinggang (1982). 'Ideas on Developing Computers in Our Country'. *Ziran Biauzhengfa Tongxun*, No. 6: 3–5 (trans. in *JPRS* 83064, 14 March, 1983: 1–5).

14 Industrial Feudalism and Enterprise Reform — Could the Chinese Use Some More Bureaucracy?

Max H. Boisot

Introduction

'Socialism with Chinese Characteristics' is a difficult expression for foreigners to grasp. It is a label that describes in a summary form one country's attempt to overcome the well-known rigidities of a centrally planned economy built according to the Soviet model (Nove, 1977; Kornai, 1982; Barnett, 1981) through a limited application of the market mechanism. Although the conceptual basis for such an attempt remains elusive to Western minds trained to thinking of planning and markets as institutional alternatives, the presence within our own hemisphere of a sizeable industrial public sector, often under direct public control, should put us on our guard against dismissing the Chinese experiment out of hand as inherently unworkable.

To be sure, both the Yugoslav and the Hungarian experiments with some forms of market socialism in Eastern Europe, and the current efforts in the Soviet Union itself to inject some vitality into its industrial enterprises, have highlighted the many problems that one encounters in trying to occupy the middle ground between economic philosophies that appear opposed if not downright antagonistic to each other. Yet the very complexity of these experiments prevents them from being conclusive, and, as the 1985 World Bank Report on China aptly puts it, 'The lessons of international experience are often ambiguous and controversial. In any event they are hard to apply to a country that in important respects differs from all others, and is not easy for an outsider to understand.' (World Bank Report, 1985).

Implicit in this view is the idea that the laws of development, whether rooted in liberal or Marxist ideology, must be subordinated to the cultural imperative. Even in the most doctrinaire applications of ideology, culture interposes itself between theory and practice to produce unique non-generalizable outcomes (Sahlins, 1976; Douglas, 1970). Is culture, therefore, the shock absorber that China intends to rely on to soften the impact of irresistible market forces upon immovable socialist plans? A brief look at the encounter between existing cultural practices in the Chinese industrial enterprise and the objectives of the current reforms will address this issue. We shall first briefly describe the reforms themselves and what they are aiming for. Next we shall examine some of the problems they pose for industrial enterprises given their current way of doing things. Then we shall present a conceptual model designed to help us understand to what extent culture might play a role either in creating the problem or in solving it. Finally, we shall assess how far 'socialism with Chinese characteristics' in effect expresses a culture-specific development strategy rather than a more universal, ideologically motivated one.

The Current Reforms

System reform in the PRC has been at the same time a bold and a cautious affair. Bold in the extent to which the leadership has been willing to discard cherished doctrine when this has proved to be unworkable in practice. Cautious in the pace at which alternative approaches have been tried out in the field. Experiments in reform were first tried out in the rural sector in Sichuan Province in 1979, and gradually extended to other parts of the country. By the early 1980s it had become apparent that the rural sector could not be reformed in isolation and that the more industrialized urban sector would also have to be tackled if the rate of the progress was to be maintained (Yu, 1984). Accordingly, in October 1984, the Central Committee of the Communist Party published an extensive set of measures designed to introduce some sweeping reforms in the industrial sector. These were followed in 1985 by fiscal reforms designed to change the nature of the relationship between state bodies and industrial enterprises, and later by price reforms that would allow resource allocation to reflect 'the law of value'.

The reforms, for convenience, can be placed into two categories:

1. *Administrative delegation*—An attempt to decongest the planning mechanism gives more power to the provinces and, in particular, to the cities. Under a certain budget these are now given more freedom to make their own investment decision, providing that these are consistent with centrally determined planning guidelines. In many cases, now, either local investment proposals no longer have to wind their way through the labyrinths of the central bureaucracy in Beijing, or, where they still do, the path has been made shorter. More importantly perhaps, the creation of a central bank in 1984—the People's Bank of China—and of an embryonic banking network, will allow the central authorities to regulate economic activity through indirect controls—i.e. market processes—rather than through the central plan as hitherto. Thus, with the exception of certain key commodities that will remain subject to the old planning system, the rest of the Chinese economy will gradually be moved over to a system of 'guidance' planning not unlike the kind of indicative planning developed in France during the 1960s.

2. *Economic decentralization*: Enterprises are to be given a freer hand in their day-to-day management. The new 'Enterprise responsibility system' makes individual firms, whether state-owned or collective, responsible for their own profits and losses. A bankruptcy law, currently under discussion by policy-makers, is further designed to concentrate minds on enterprise performance. Enterprise managers will gradually cease to be the mere executors of party committee decisions inside their organizations and will be allowed to design their organizations to suit their requirements, to dispose of their above-quota production in ways and at prices that, within a certain range, they are free to set for themselves, and to distribute bonuses in non-egalitarian ways that reflect individual performance and break the 'iron rice-bowl' as it is called. Relationships with the state will be mediated through a corporation tax rather than through a profit remittance so that firms that make a profit are allowed to hold on to it, and finally, subsidies given to enterprises by the state to cover investment needs will gradually be phased out and replaced by bank loans, for which a market rate of interest will have to be paid.

A number of China watchers have argued that the trendline running through the current reforms foreshadows a return to a capitalist order, albeit one shrouded in socialist rhetoric. Yet the Chinese leadership has been emphatic that it has absolutely no intention of reintroducing capitalism through the back-door, and that market transactions taking place within an institutional framework created by the central plan are of a different nature to those embedded in a free-market liberal order. The replacement of Hu Yaobang as Party Secretary in early 1987 can only underline this point further, whatever the political motives for this move.

Recent developments in the Chinese economy are certainly putting these assertions to the test and have led even the most cautious ouside observers to ask whether the current mix of market and hierarchical co-ordination is sustainable, and whether the leadership, faced with the growing prospects of runaway inflation, corruption, and unequal development will not soon be confronted with the difficult choice of retrenching towards more politically tractable socialist nostrums or of moving ever further down the capitalist road.

One of the problems that the leadership faces in managing a rapidly changing economy is a lack of tested macroeconomic controls that can be inserted into the existing institutional fabric to steer the behaviour of economic agents in the desired direction. In the past, when the going got tough, the tendency was to revert to 'administrative methods' to re-establish order. But if these methods proved serviceable in an economy at an earlier level of development, as a response they no longer match the complexity of current requirements. Furthermore, to Westerners, the term 'administrative methods' conjures up images of faceless bureaucrats hiding behind ramparts of paper in the inaccessible realms of a massive and impersonal hierarchy; in China the image is quite misleading. The celestial bureaucracy remains what it has always been, a local, face-to-face affair, much dependent on the exercise of personal power—often arbitrarily—and on the diffuse quality of personal relationships and reciprocal obligations (*guanxi*). Chinese bureaucracy is feudal rather than rational-legal in the Weberian sense: relations are built up around a personalized trade in loyalty and protection rather than the impersonalized application of rationality to tasks (Balazs, 1968). Three examples will illustrate the point:

Example 1

The absence of a viable price system makes it hard for supervising bureaux to come up with an objective evaluation of enterprise performance. Inefficient enterprises can make fat profits just as easily as efficient ones can incur heavy losses. Much will depend on whether they are in industries or regions that the central or provincial governments have decided to smile on. But since a worker's bonus—now up to four months of his salary—welfare payments, and future investments are now all in theory paid out of enterprise profits, much unfairness can result which cannot be tolerated in a deeply egalitarian country. The remedy? A regulation or adjustment tax negotiated on a case-by-case basis with each enterprise's supervising bureau. The tax is designed to equalize the profits earned by different firms under the bureau's supervision, and hence the amount of money available for worker bonuses, welfare, and future investment. Thus, until the price reforms begin to bite and until higher enterprise earnings are generally acknowledged to reflect superior performance (this is only happening in isolated cases in the case of state enterprises) much of the freedom granted to enterprises with one hand is clawed back with the other, and that by the very industrial bureau that the enterprise was supposed to be getting away from. With many enterprises retaining little more than 10–15 per cent of their pre-tax profits to cover bonuses and welfare payments and to invest in growth, the quality of the enterprise manager's personal relationship with relevant bureau personnel becomes the supremely important determinant of the enterprise's future prospects, not the firm's financial performance.

Example 2

In March 1985, the English-language newspaper, the *China Daily* ran a puzzling headline: 'Money supply out of control in Hubei Province'. To get the full meaning of this news, picture an article in the *Wall Street Journal* under the heading 'Money supply out of control in Oklahoma!' Until the creation of a central bank in 1984, credit creation in the PRC seems to have been directly linked to the workings of the central plan and managed by the ministry of finance. The economic reforms have created a need for an independant management of the money supply since the plan is destined to cover an ever-diminishing proportion—down to some fixed ratio—of economic transactions. Yet the devolution of power down to the regions was not compensated for by a free flow of financial information that would allow self-regulatory market mechanisms to function properly. Enterprises were increasingly free to borrow from banks at rates of interest that were well below the cost of capital and were able to apply 'informal pressure' on local branches of the state banks to increase their lending well beyond what was specified by their production quota. This 'investment hunger', as it came to be known, could not be controlled from Beijing. In the absence of reliable central controls, local branch managers are much more responsive to the local network of peers and superiors and the immediate web of reciprocal obligations that they participate in, than to the distant pressures inadequately applied by their own organizations. Undeniably, such parochial pressures also exist in geographically dispersed Western organizations. The difference is that in the Western case the existence of tried and tested administrative control systems, impersonally applied, acts as an effective counterweight to the dysfunctional effects of over-personalized relationships and reciprocal obligations.

Example 3
In order to even out the regional disparities that are being exacerbated by the faster rate of growth of the eastern seaboard provinces, the latter are being encouraged to develop commercial links with the more backward central and western provinces. Yet, in many if not most cases so far, the linking process has been an administrative rather than a market phenomenon. Cities and provinces designate a firm that will be asked to collaborate with a firm chosen by another province. The current debate in China at present is over whether these links should be voluntarily entered into by the firms themselves, the point being that, given the current institutional structure, such horizontal relationships do not come naturally to firms and may never even get started, let alone developed, without an administrative push. Enterprises are subordinated to state, provincial and city or county authorities, with by far the greatest number falling into the last two categories. Cities and provinces in China have a tradition of self-sufficiency that discourages interregional trade and that is greatly reinforced by the weakness of the communications infrastructure. Purchasing from another province is a costly, time-consuming hassle to be avoided as far as possible. In a seller's market in which everything that a firm is capable of producing can be disposed of locally without difficulty there is no need to go and seek customers in far-away places. It is those involved in purchasing who do the travelling: at any one time anything up to a million people are travelling uncomfortably on slow trains, scouring the country for supplies. Why? In the PRC, mailing in an order or phoning it through is a waste of time. What counts is the *personal* relationship that can be built up with a given supplier, that has to be nursed and fed with time-consuming care if a buyer is to secure even a minimal allocation. How much easier if the seller lives just down the road, speaks the same dialect, and possibly shares common acquaintances. If 'favours' have to be traded between buyer and seller, how much more enforceable do these become in regularly recurring face-to-face

encounters occasioned by geographical proximity than in the more impersonal market exchanges that, despite a very fragile legal framework, seem to be the target of the current modernization drive?

Inside the Chinese Industrial Enterprise

If particularistic 'feudal' relations rather than universalistic 'market' relations still characterize the Chinese industrial enterprise's relations with its industrial and political environment, does this show up in a firm's internal management processes and, if so, how will the current reforms change things? By unshackling industrial enterprises from the state's administrative apparatus, the reforms aim to foster their sense of initiative and responsibility and to establish more direct links between enterprise reward and performance. Nevertheless, I list below four characteristics of current managerial practice which in my view ultimately serve to reinforce a feudal management style and thus tend to work against a speedy implementation of the reform at the level of the firm.

1. Enterprise performance is hard to define and measure

As we saw earlier, the existing price system nullifies the use of profits as a useful guide to performance. Internal measures of performance might be gleaned from the accounts, but Chinese accounting systems, with their emphasis on physical quantities and their poor integration of financial figures, do not yield a coherent view of the firm. Yet, even with a coherent picture of enterprise performance, not much of it could be attributed to the firm's own action. The external dependencies are too great. To illustrate: the sheer irregularity and scarcity of supplies frequently leads to stockouts and overstocking in many sectors. Inventory management is opportunistic rather than analytical. In one Beijing electronics firm that I have worked with, several years' worth of stock of one scarce component was lying in the stockroom. As the enterprise director explained it, 'This is what the supplier is offering in a single batch. Given current supply conditions, we either take the lot or we spend the next several years looking for alternative sources. Naturally, we take it'. And, with the cost of capital so low, who is to blame him? Maintaining a good relationship with the supplier is far more important under conditions of scarcity than optimizing on stocks. That relation must be reckoned as an asset that will never show up on the firm's balance sheet—certainly not as goodwill since firms are not bought or sold—but that remains crucial to the firms' future prospects.

2. The definition of responsibility is vague

Formal procedures are at least as extensive in Chinese industrial enterprises as they are in Western ones. But most of them have been imposed on the enterprise from above and reflect the uniform administrative practices of the supervising bureaucracy rather than the managerial and technical needs of the enterprise itself. For example, wage grades have been developed outside the enterprise and are applied with little exception to all industrial firms. The same applies to the enterprise's organization structure—although, with the new director responsibility system, this is beginning to change. The organization chart is not derived from the enterprise's own analysis of its operation's requirement and no job description that would link individuals to particular clusters of responsibility exists as such. Thus, the formal procedures that exist encourage a ritual obedience and a constant search for informal pro-cedures—'going through the back door'—that will actually solve the real task-related problems that the enterprise is called upon to solve. To be sure, formal and informal organizations co-exist in Western enterprises. However, in the Chinese enterprise not only are they much further apart, but the hierarchical nature of the face-to-face relationship that predominates creates a compartmentalization and fragmentation of the organization that makes horizontal co-ordination extremely difficult and the use of the 'back door' both imperative and inefficient.

3. Rewards for good performance are still low

An enterprise worker earns a basic wage of ¥60–70 a month (US\$1 = ¥3.15), to which will be added various subsidies for transport, housing, food, etc., amounting to, perhaps, another ¥30. A factory director will earn between ¥140 and ¥200 and a slightly higher level of subsidy. Both will receive bonuses which are paid for with what is left of profits after corporation tax (55 per cent) and the adjustment tax (5–35 per cent) have been paid. In state-owned firms, the bonus fund cannot exceed 15 per cent of the enterprise's payroll and usually does not exceed four months of any one worker's salary. The department heads and managers of a firm receive as a bonus payment the *average* of what is paid to their department. Thus, many workers end up with higher pay than their supervisors. The very low pay differentials between managers and workers reflect the view still widely prevalent that enterprise performance is essentially the result of worker rather than managerial contributions. And since, for reasons cited above, individual performance is so hard to identify and measure, whatever differen-tials exist in theory are further flattered in practice by workers putting pressures on management for an egalitarian distribution of bonuses. The enterprise manager, his authority and room for manoeuvre already limited by the presence of the party secretary—and more recently by the prospects of being elected by his labour-force—finds it hard to resist such pressures. If he cannot reward good performance, can he at least penalize bad performance? The labour bureaux, anxious to avoid unemployment, regularly assign unqualified manpower to enterprises in excess of their needs. Poor perfor-mers can only be dismissed in the light of circumstance, and then only after protracted negotiations with the supervising authorities. In such circums-tances an enterprise managers' ability to act does not reside in his constitu-tional powers, which by Western standards are almost non-existent, but rather in his natural 'charismatic' authority, in his ability to secure a personal following among his colleagues that works independently of what the system has to offer in the way of rewards and punishments.

4. A cost centre mentality prevails

The economic reforms aim to transform enterprises into profit centres responsible for their own profits and losses. In Western industrialized countries, profit centres achieve their objectives by striking a balance between inputs and outputs, over both of which they have some measure of control. Thus, for example, by judicious purchasing and technical redesign they can reduce the cost or volume of their inputs and by adjusting their sales and pricing strategies to market conditions they can affect the volume and profitability of their outputs. In the absence of efficient factor markets, Chinese enterprises have little control over their inputs, and, with very limited discretion over price and production volume, even less control over their outputs. Municipal bureaux still largely set the sales price and the difficulties, already discussed, of trading ouside the region have led many state-owned enterprises to concentrate on local sales for the part of their ouput that is above their quota and that is not simply handed on to state distributors. In fact, given the limitations of bonus payments, enterprises have neither the incentive to maximize profits, nor even—given the low level of managerial salaries—to maximize sales. It is in the maximization of *assets*, in the technical improvements that ease the burden of work, that the state-owned firm finds its salvation. In effect, much conspires to keep the enterprise working as a cost centre responsible for inputs alone, in which a production-oriented mentality will prevail. There is a strong tendency to leave the problem of dealing with the broader external environment of market changes and competitors to the supervising bureaux. These are, of course, only too happy to oblige. Things are changing—particularly in the consumer goods sector where the wind of competition between firms and regions is now blowing—but it will be some time before the market orientation required by a fully-fledged profit centre can be said to exist in the typical state-owned industrial enterprise in China.

To summarize: the organizational culture that currently prevails within Chinese enterprises is inward-looking, diffuse, and non-performance oriented. There are signs that the reforms are bringing about some changes in the way that these enterprises define themselves; but progress would be much faster if enterprises were not so strongly shackled to a particular set of bureaux and a given locality. In fact, unlike firms in market economies, Chinese enterprises are essentially territorial entities that are expected to serve their local authorities with the provision of housing, schooling, health care facilities, and other welfare services, to the detriment of both their internal development—new funds left for reinvestment—and their geographical expansion—no firm can serve two masters. In return for loyal service, the local authority will protect its brood of enterprises from outside competition, much as fifteenth-century Italian city states used to do for their guilds and corporations. The non-tariff barriers erected by one province against another's exports create a further obstacle to interregional trade that results in a highly fragmented industrial structure. State-owned enterprises, in spite of their sub-optimal size, end up enjoying monopoly positions in local markets; and high transport costs, the lack of market integration, and an inability to finance an expansion in sales all conspire to make their goods uncompetitive in export markets.

Ironically, there is a sense in which the reforms themselves have exacerbated the problem. The absence of administrative controls at the centre has turned what was meant to be a controlled delegation of power to the provinces into a *de facto* decentralization in which each locality frequently pursues its own parochial aims, oblivious of the centre's wishes. This has allowed local authorities in many instances to consolidate their hierarchical grip on the enterprises under them at the very moment when the centre was trying to achieve a greater measure of decentralization of economic decisions. It could plausibly be argued that industrial feudalism has been reinforced rather than weakened by the system reforms. Is this necessarily a bad thing? We shall discuss the issue in the next section with the help of a conceptual model.

Interpreting The Reforms: a Conceptual Framework

China's future development and competitiveness will turn on her ability to move from a system of vertical, 'feudal' relationships, still largely based on the exercise of personal power, to one of horizontal 'market' relationships, based on impersonal power. To ideological opponents of the reforms, and to others, this might be seen as the move from feudalism to capitalism, identified by Marx as a law of development. I shall argue in what follows that the shift from one ism to another fails to capture the essence of the process and I shall briefly present a conceptual model described in more detail in Boisot (1983a, b; 1986). The model approaches economic development as a cultural process embodied in a configuration of institutional structures.

Kroeber and Kluckhohn, after examining several hundred definitions of culture (1952), came to the conclusion that the term described the ways that people structure and share information. For example, several studies of Japanese culture (Boisot, 1983a; Lebra, 1976) indicate that it shows a marked preference for ambiguous and implicit communications and imposes a considerable load on prior interpersonal understanding. American culture, by contrast, tends towards the impersonal and the explicit. One could thus say that Japanese culture is relationship-minded and that American culture is contract-minded. The anthropologist Edward Hall (1976) has distinguished between cultures that resist the structuring of knowledge and experience and

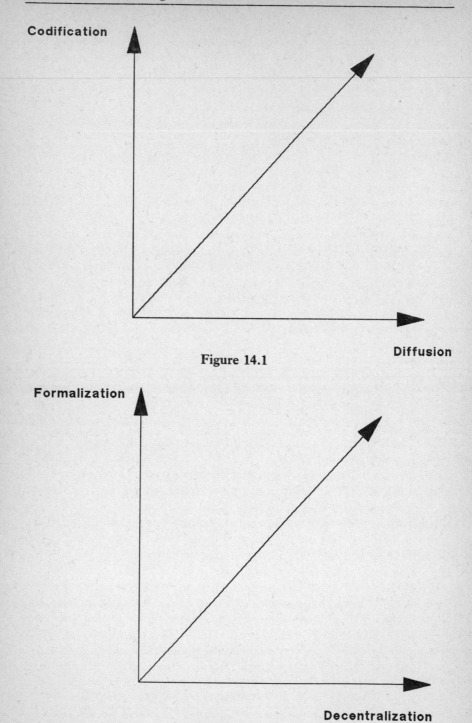

Codification

Diffusion

Figure 14.1

Formalization

Decentralization

Figure 14.2

those that, on the contrary, push for it. He calls the first 'high context' cultures, and the second 'low context' cultures.

Less studied by anthropologists, however, is the unremarkable fact that the structuring and sharing of information are closely related. The more information can be structured or *codified* the more easily and quickly it can be shared and *diffused* (Figure 14.1). Thus, it comes as no surprise to find that American culture, with its preference for well-codified information, is also an information-sharing culture in which free access to information—both political and economic—is constitutionally guaranteed, whereas Japanese culture with its preference for the uncodified tends to be more of an information-hoarding culture. To be sure, much information is published in Japan in the form of statistical summaries, but the most important material is only given on a 'need to know' basis, and that within closed groups bound by ties of personal loyalty.

The relationship between the codification and diffusion of information may appear pretty obvious until one comes to examine how it works out in practice, at which point some very unobvious features of the relationship begin to appear. Before we look at these more closely, let us give Figure 14.1 a more organizational orientation. We can do this by equating the codification dimension—following a number of adaptations which will not be discussed here—with the degree of *formalization* of any transaction involving the exchange of information, and the diffusion dimension with the degree of *decentralization* which can be achieved in a transaction. Thus, cultural strategies concerning the codification and diffusion of information translate into organizational strategies concerning the formalization and decentralization of transactions (Figure 14.2). Both diagrams describe a *culture space* (which we abreviate to *C-space*) in which transactions occur in forms that are shaped by their information environment. If, for example, the dimensions of Figure 14.2 are dichotomized to keep the exposition simple, we end up with the transactional typology shown in Figure 14.3.

What does the diagram tell us? It tells us that, in quadrant 1, the diffusion of information is limited by the fact that it cannot be codified and that communication can therefore only take place in face-to-face situations. Yet, in such a situation, one person, possessing information that the other does not, is in a position to impose a personalized hierarchical relationship. Furthermore, given the diffuse and ambiguous nature of the information conveyed, some trust and sharing of values between the parties will be required for effective performance of any transaction, and prior acquaintance between them will often be necessary. The personal exercise of hierarchical power associated with such a transaction is characteristic of a *fief*.

As one moves up the C-space towards quadrant 2, information gets codified and diffusible, but barriers are set up to keep control on who gains access to it. The ease with which codified information can be transmitted allows it to be communicated impersonally and in circumstances which do not call for interpersonal trust and value sharing, the control system itself

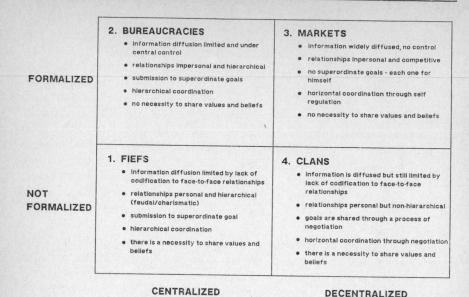

Figure 14.3 Transactional styles

taking care of the effectiveness of the transaction. *Bureaucracies* typify this kind of transaction and, despite their impersonal setting, they frequently require the sharing of superordinate (i.e. organizational) goals between the parties.

In quadrant 3, information is also well codified, but this time it is widely available to all transacting parties. Here again, relationships can be quite impersonal and everyone is free to use the information he possesses in pursuit of his own goals. The transactional style of this quadrant is competitive and does not call for any trust or sharing of values beyond the minimum necessary for completing the transaction. We are in the world of *markets*.

Finally, as we move back down the C-space into quadrant 4, we move back into an environment in which information being uncodified is hard to diffuse. When it is shared—as is the case in this quadrant—it becomes the exclusive property of small groups whose size is related to the number of face-to-face relationships that can be sustained. These are non-hierarchical, but again, the diffuse and ambiguous nature of the information involved makes them open to abuse, so that interpersonal trust and a sharing of values is necessary. Superordinate goals may be involved but these are established through a process of negotiation. In quadrant 4 we transact through *clans*.

These transactional forms may, over time, articulate themselves into stable structures—organizational functions at the level of an individual enterprise (Figure 14.4), or institutions at the societal level (Figure 14.5)—providing that the volume of transactions is large enough and their location in the C-space is stable enough to justify infrastructural investments that will

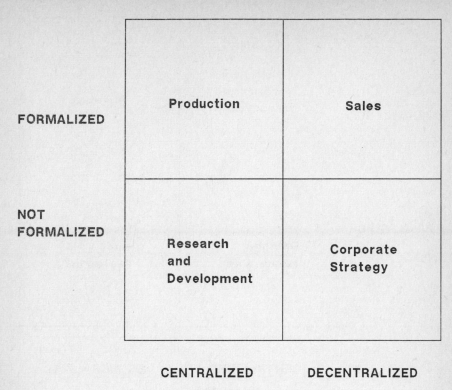

FORMALIZED

Production	Sales

NOT
FORMALIZED

| Research and Development | Corporate Strategy |

CENTRALIZED   DECENTRALIZED

Figure 14.4

ultimately lower the cost of transacting in that region. Transaction cost economics (Williamson, 1975; Francis *et al.*, 1983) tells us that the uncommitted transaction will then be drawn to that region of the C-space that enjoys the largest prior infrastructural investment and hence can offer the lowest marginal cost.

Where infrastructural investments are widely distributed throughout the C-space, a culture's transactional style will be diversified, flexible and changeable. The belief and value system will display a degree of pluralism that matches the complexity of the social order. Where, on the other hand, infrastructural investments are highly concentrated in one of the quadrants, the transactions will all be pressed into the same mould, irrespective of specific requirements, and the belief and value system will display a single-mindedness that we may term ideological. One can imagine situations intermediate between those just described in which a culture exhibits some preference for transacting in one part of the C-space but not necessarily to the exclusion of other regions where circumstances warrant it.

How does the conceptual framework just presented help us to understand the enterprise reforms currently under way in the PRC? The analysis presented in the first two sections argues for the existence of a strong cultural

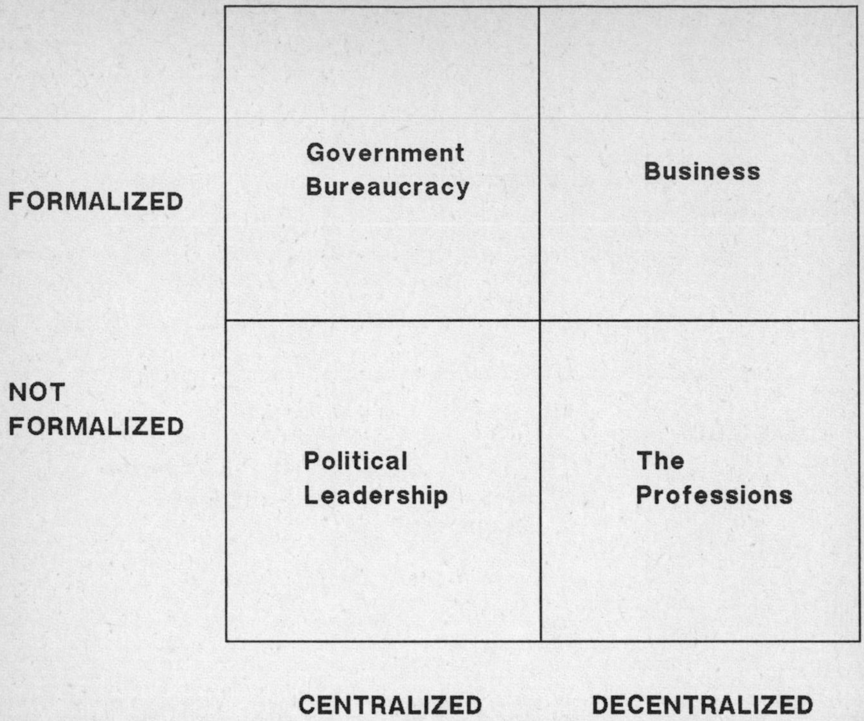

	CENTRALIZED	DECENTRALIZED
FORMALIZED	Government Bureaucracy	Business
NOT FORMALIZED	Political Leadership	The Professions

CENTRALIZED   **DECENTRALIZED**

Figure 14.5

preference for transacting in quadrant one. In other words, Confucian feudalism provides a better guide to managerial behaviour and value in Chinese industry than Leninist bureaucracy. This may come as a surprise to those who have learnt to view the PRC as the bureaucratic state *par excellence*. Yet, the system functions in spite of its bureaucracy—a Soviet transplant of the 1950s—and not because of it. Indeed, the bureaucracy itself was designed to help the country escape from the feudal quadrant and Marxist-Leninism was the ideology that would legitimate a massive shift of transactions from quadrant 1 to quadrant 2. The development strategy is described in Figure 14.6.

By branding pre-communist China as feudal, however, the reader might ask: are we not performing a sleight of hand in which China's ancient bureaucratic tradition is simply being done away with? Such a tradition was an essential component of China's imperial past, as well as a source of inspiration to Western political thinkers such as Montesquieu and Voltaire. Yet it should be placed in context. The imperial bureaucracy figures prominently in a Western traveller's experience of China—this was particularly true of the Jesuits—since to a large extent it mediated his access to the rest of the culture. But it was of a very modest size and limited in its administrative scope.

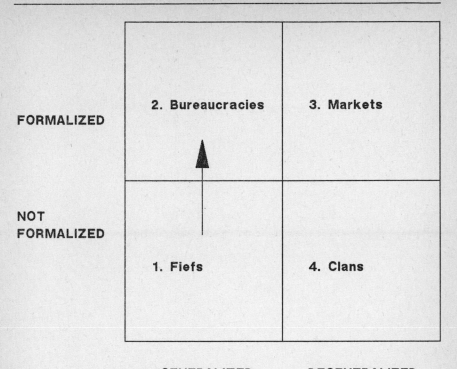

CENTRALIZED   DECENTRALIZED

Figure 14.6 China's development strategy in the late 1950s

China's unification following the period of the Warring States was built upon a bureaucratic order that was open to all and in which promotion was granted according to merit or favour. Bureaucratic merit, however, was not defined by rational-legal requirements, but by benevolence, a knowledge of the rites and literary accomplishments. Over time the imperial bureaucracy became the fief of a small group of literati whose administrative style was patrimonial and whose ideology was Confucian. Yet, a far-flung patrimonial state with underdeveloped means of communication limits the scope for administrative centralization. As Max Weber summed it up in *The Religion of China* (1951): 'Considering the all-encompassing duties of Chinese officials one must conclude that a district the size of a Prussian county, administered by one official, could not be efficiently administered even by hundreds. The Empire resembled a confederation of satrapies under a pontifical head' (Weber, 1951: 48). Thus, the distinction that Weber first made between a patrimonial bureaucracy on the one hand, which is both compatible with and implies a feudal order, and a rational-legal bureaucracy, which is in direct contradiction to such an order, is the one that we have in mind.

China's enduring feudal order was not the only obstacle to building a Soviet-inspired bureaucracy. Mao Zedong, a highly charismatic leader and a natural product of quadrant 1—was also threatened by a move to quadrant 2.

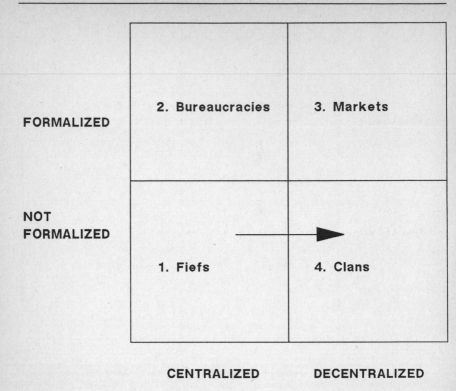

Figure 14.7 China's development strategy in the Cultural Revolution

He clearly saw how the 'routinization' of his charisma into bureaucratic rule would entail a serious loss of personal power. In launching the Great Proletarian Cultural Revolution, Mao tried to counter the move up the C-space into the bureaucratic quadrant. By appealing directly to the idealistic youth of his country, by trying to establish a direct and intangible relationship between himself and his followers based on his personal charismatic authority, Mao was trying to exploit a culture still anchored in quadrant 1. Yet the task proved too daunting even for Mao and by 1967 he had lost control of the process. As the factionalism that ensued suggests (Karnow, 1972), he had landed in the clan quadrant (see Figure 14.7); but without the broadly-based sharing of values that can compensate for a lack of structure, the social fabric was torn apart. A charismatic leadership strategy that proved effective in keeping a smaller band of supporters together under conditions of adversity in pre-liberation days could not be extended to a whole population without inflicting intolerable strains on people's ability to live as neighbours.

In sum, if China's development strategy in the 1950s could be described as a move from quadrant 1 to quadrant 2, its strategy in the 1960s—if strategy it can be called—aimed at a shift from quadrant 1 to quadrant 4. Today's leadership is promoting a cautious move towards quadrant 3, the market

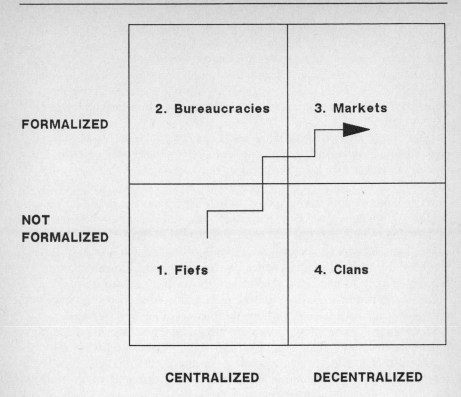

CENTRALIZED   DECENTRALIZED

Figure 14.8 China's current modernization strategy

quadrant. Clearly, however, this is very far from constituting a wholesale commitment to quadrant 3, which would indeed amount to a move towards capitalism. Pragmatism rather than ideology is in the driving seat, so that one may be witnessing a diversification of transactional strategies and a more dispersed configuration in the culture space.

Yet, as our earlier discussion and examples make clear, the cultural pull of quadrant 1 remains a strong one in the PRC—the past thirty-six years notwithstanding. The current concerns of the leadership to develop a workable and impartial legal system—a move towards formalization—and simultaneously to increase the autonomy of industrial enterprises—a move towards decentralization—suggest that it has an intuitive grasp of the problem.

If, in effect, the possibilities for decentralization are linked to the progress of formalization, then the two will have to progress in tandem, as shown in Figure 14.8. The development of a legal system will not by itself meet the demands for more formalization of transactions. A properly functioning administrative apparatus that can give it effect will also be required. The need for it shows up daily through the autonomous actions of innumerable local fiefdoms that act according to their own lights in ways that central government finds increasingly hard to control. The Hainan Island import scandal at the end of 1985 in which over two hundred industrial enterprises on the island were found to be working in cahoots with the local administration and party cadres for the illegal importation of nearly two billion dollars' worth of cars and other consumer goods, is but one example among many of how ill-adapted current administrative controls are to the decentralization of the economy.

Our conceptual framework, then, leads us to an unexpected—and to some, possibly offensive—conclusion. To succeed in its modernization drive, China needs *more* rather than less bureaucracy, but of the rational-legal kind that is rooted in task requirements rather than either of the patrimonial or Marxist-Leninist kind that is rooted in ideology. Only the first kind represents a genuine move up the formalization scale; the second and third sooner or later degenerate into ritual. In other words, the country is not called upon to make an exclusive choice between bureaucracies and markets, as observers on both sides of the ideological fault line seem to think: China needs both. To be sure, markets operating outside the administrative framework provided by a professional bureaucracy are indeed blind. But then so is a bureaucracy arrogantly making decisions without the benefit of market feedback.

Developing a Weberian type of rational-legal bureaucracy will take time. It involves much more than promulgating well thought-out laws, rules and regulations. The shift from quadrant 1 to any other quadrant involves a profound change in the cultural values and beliefs that underpin a transaction. New transactional infrastructures tend to develop well ahead of the mentalities required to operate within them. Marx called this the gap between the forces of production and the relations of production. We shall call it the problem of cultural adaptation. How does this problem appear at the enterprise level?

Cultural Adaptation at The Enterprise Level

The Chinese manager who today successfully 'makes out' in the existing industrial system, who has mastered the informal requirements of 'backdoor' operations, and who has learnt to play his cards very close to his chest would find the purest application of a market transactional style very hardgoing. Firstly, with typically only a high school education behind him, he would lack the codification skills that would allow him to analyse and structure management problems in such a way that rules and procedures for addressing them could be efficiently specified. Secondly, he would lack the communication skills that would enable him to share his analysis with relevant decisionmakers—customers, suppliers, employees, administrators, etc.

Such skills can be provided by training and, indeed, a massive effort is currently under way, spearheaded by the China Enterprise Management

Association (CEMA) to build up the competence of industrial managers in these two areas. But on their own, however, the mere possession of these skills will not bring about the required changes. If a mentality adapted to the objectives of the reforms is to emerge, then opportunities favourable to the exercise of these skills must be available to these newly-trained managers when they return to their enterprises. Otherwise the cultural imperative of the feudal quadrant will reassert itself and the skills will atrophy, thereby sapping the credibility of the training effort.

In fact, the Chinese industrial enterprise as described in this paper still affords precious few opportunities for the exercise and development of management skills. The institutional confusion that arises from having a feudal cultural order hiding inside an artificially constructed bureaucratic structure makes the development of a coherent transactional style problematic. Little guidance is offered by official pronouncements since policy, in the absence of a reliable administrative apparatus acting as a transmission belt, translates into practice in unpredictable and sometimes capricious ways. As the old Chinese saying puts it, 'Heaven is high and the Emperor is far away'.

To be sure, things are changing. China is a country on the move and is showing a dynamism that few would have suspected possible only ten years ago. It is also showing a boldness in its willingness to experiment with new methods and ways of organizing that makes for optimism. The snapshot we have presented of the Chinese industrial enterprise in its existing institutional environment can hardly do justice to the considerable transformation and achievements it has brought to the economic landscape. Clearly, by simply keeping up the momentum, China will be a very different place in ten years' time to what it is today.

But *can* it keep up the momentum? Moving mentalities out of quadrants will be a much more challenging business than moving transactions. A pure materialist would argue that if one takes care of the transactions, the mentalities will take care of themselves—i.e., sooner or later they will follow. A pure idealist, conversely, would say that, until the mentalities shift out of quadrants, they will continue to draw transactions in there. Under the first view, the momentum will be maintained and a modernization of the economic structure will drag the culture along in its wake. Under the second view, the modernization drive is doomed to run itself into the sand unless managers and workers can be socialized to the new, more complex institutional order.

A more organic view of the modernization issue would see cultural values and beliefs, and transactional strategies as exerting a reciprocal influence on each other, simultaneously motivating and constraining shifts into different regions of the C-space. Thus considered, the institutional and transactional confusion mentioned above emerges as a natural outcome of this interplay between changing mentalities and evolving transactional infrastructures. Modernization is a vast and complex process that may draw inspiration from the blueprints of policy-makers but rarely follows them mechanically.

Conclusion

To conclude, 'socialism with Chinese characteristics' expresses both the care and the boldness with which the current leadership intends to move key transactions out of quadrant 1 and into different regions of the culture space: the care, because many of the core values of the culture reside in quadrant 1 and will require to be fed with transactions if they are not to perish; the boldness, because socialism as a value system is ultimately compatible with a large number of transactional configurations in the C-space and does not require a country to live in monastic seclusion in the bureaucratic quadrant. Transactions can—within limits—be left free to find their own niches inside the C-space. Thus, while the reconciliation of central planning and market processes remains problematic for economic theory that sees them as alternatives, considered from a more general cultural perspective, the obstacles seem less insurmountable. Ironically, it is China's position in quadrant 1, where things remain fluid and as yet unstructured, that gives it the cognitive and institutional flexibility to achieve the necessary integration. Such are the advantages that accrue to late developers.

In this paper, we have presented a conceptual framework that seeks to capture the cultural dimension of the development process. The People's Republic of China today offers a potentially fruitful site for the framework's application since discussions of the country's future have so often polarized around either purely ideological or purely economic issues. Both are important to development, but they have tended to mask the slower, more discreet and possibly more fundamental movements of cultural transformation, the gradual accretions of Braudel's *longue durée* (Braudel, 1979) that underpin all fundamental change. This paper may be claiming a larger role for culture than many of those concerned with economic development may be willing to grant it, and indeed there may not be that many situations in which it should be placed centre stage. One can suffer from over-exposure as much as from the opposite condition. But until now culture has only been given a walk-on part on the development stage. It deserves better.

References

Balazs, E. (1968). *La Bureaucratie Céleste*. Paris, Gallimard.

Barnett, D. (1981). *China's Economy in Global Perspective*. Washington, The Brookings Institute.

Boisot, M. (1983a). 'Convergence Revisited: The Codification and Diffusion of Knowledge in a British and a Japanese Firm'. *Journal of Management Studies*, 20, 2.

Boisot, M. (1983b). 'The shaping of Technological Strategy: European Chemical firms in South East Asia'. *Management International Review*, 2, 3.

Boisot, M. (1986). 'Markets and Hierarchies in Cultural Perspective'. *Organization Studies*, 7, 2.

Braudel, F. (1979). *Civilisation Matérielle, Économique et Capitalisme XVe-XVIIIe Siècle*. Paris, Armand Colin.

Douglas, M. (1970). *Natural Symbols*. Middlesex, Penguin.

Francis, A., Turk, J., Willman, P. (eds) (1983) *Power Efficiency and Institutions*. London, Heinemann Educational.

Hall, E. (1976). *Beyond Culture*. New York, Doubleday.

Karnow, S. (1972). *Mao and China*. Harmondsworth, Penguin.

Kornai, J. (1982). *Growth, Shortage and Efficiency*. Oxford, Blackwell.

Kroeber, A., & Kluckhohn, C. (1952). 'Culture: a Critical Review of Concepts and Definitions', *Papers of the Peabody Museum of American Archeology and Ethnology*. Harvard University, **47**, 1.

Lebra, T. S. (1976). *Japanese Patterns of Behaviour*. Honolulu, The University Press of Hawaii.

Nove, A. (1977). *The Soviet Economic System*. London, Allen & Unwin.

Sahlins, M. (1976). *Culture and Practical Reason*. Chicago, Chicago University Press.

Weber, M. (1951). *The Religion of China*. New York, The Free Press.

Williamson, O. (1975). *Markets and Hierarchies: Analysis and Antitrust Implications* New York, The Free Press.

World Bank (1985) *Report: China—Long-term Issues and Options*. Washington, DC, 22 May, No. 5206–CHA.

Yu, G. (1984). *China's Socialist Modernization*. Beijing, Foreign Languages Press.

Index

DATE DUE
